ROU
JUSTICE

About the author

Dick Kirby joined the Metropolitan Police in 1967 and in the following 26 years spent over half of his service as a Detective Sergeant with the Serious Crime Squad and the elite Flying Squad. He was involved in many notorious cases of the 1970s and 80s, cases which sometimes required him to travel overseas in pursuit of international crime gangs. His forthright testimony as a key witness in trials at the Old Bailey won him respect and condemnation in equal part from the lawyers and judges he came up against. But, as one Old Bailey judge remarked, 'He is one of the best detectives at Scotland Yard' and a senior detective in Belfast described him as 'a good man to have in an explosive situation.'

He was commended by Commissioners, judges and magistrates on 40 occasions for catching criminals and in so doing, made more visits to hospitals and Divisional Surgeons than he cares to remember.

He is married with four children and lives in Suffolk.

ROUGH JUSTICE

Memoirs of a Flying Squad detective

DICK KIRBY

SERIOUS CRIME SQUAD & FLYING SQUAD, METROPOLITAN POLICE, LONDON

MERLIN UNWIN BOOKS

First published in Great Britain by Merlin Unwin Books, 2001

Published by

Merlin Unwin Books
Palmers House
7 Corve Street
Ludlow
Shropshire SY8 1DB
U. K.

A CIP catalogue record for this book is available from the British Library

ISBN 1–873674–47-3

Designed and produced by Merlin Unwin Books, Ludlow
Jacket design: Mary Hayter
Printed in Great Britain by Bell & Bain Ltd, Glasgow

Contents

Introduction

Answer me this. Are you politically correct? Do you anxiously search for political correctness in others? If your answer to either of these questions is 'Yes', chuck this book away. You will not like it. Reading these pages will make your face pucker up with genuine social worker-like concern. In fact, you would have a good case for demanding your money back, were it not for the fact that to deny a contribution to a worthy charity, such as the Police Pensioners' Housing Association might, in itself, be regarded as politically incorrect.

The stories that follow describe some of the adventures and misadventures that happened to me and my fellow police officers. It is not intended to be either an autobiography, nor a chronicle of the Metropolitan Police and if appears to be either, it is, I assure you, entirely coincidental. It is a series of reminiscences and anecdotes, spanning over a quarter of a century in the Metropolitan Police, where I spent many happy, rewarding and often exciting times. On other occasions, it was frustrating and sometimes sad. It was seldom boring.

I wish I could tell you that ever since I read the 1948 edition of *The Boys' Book of Scotland Yard*, there ignited in my breast a burning desire to become a Scotland Yard detective, but it would not be true. I had never had any dealings with the police until I was almost 24 years of age, and had I been required to express an opinion of them, I imagine that I would have said that I thought that they did a difficult job well.

No, my attraction to the Metropolitan Police was the result of a simple case of economics, due purely to my domestic circumstances and nothing else. I was married with two very young children, living in a rented flat and working in a dead-end job, which I hated. I answered the advertisement in the *Sunday Express*, because I was assured that by joining the Metropolitan Police, I would become assimilated into the ranks of what was then known as 'the thousand-pounds-a-year Copper'. I was also informed that I would have a secure job for life and rent-free accommodation and that was enough for me. Had anyone asked me (and nobody did) I would probably have admitted a desire for a little more adventure and excitement than the printing industry could provide. Well, although I certainly got plenty of exhilaration, it took a little while for me to begin my love affair with the Metropolitan Police. When it did start, like most affairs, it captivated, overtook and consumed me.

It was my fault that the start to my career was less than meteoric. When my supervising officers recklessly decided that I might be sent out unescorted to walk my beat, it was a commitment that I took very seriously. This was my beat and I felt it was my responsibility to maintain a high level of peace and tranquillity amongst its inhabitants. Certainly, I tried very hard, and, in so doing, I made some awful, gasp-producing errors of judgment. Because of my mistakes or even in spite of them, I learnt from them, but it did take a long time. Sadly, a number of the other officers at the Station, both of Constable and Sergeant rank, were the laziest, most stunningly bone-idle bunch of uniform carriers that God ever blew breath into and I received little assistance and no encouragement whatsoever from them. I do not blame them for my lack of achievement because with hindsight, I should have slowed down and reassessed my situation. But that wisdom had not been imparted to me in the 1960s and as I blundered through my beat, so eager to become a success it took me three months before I carried out my first proper arrest for Drunk and Disorderly. Time after time, I was hauled up in front of the Chief Inspector to have my lack of progress witheringly pointed out to me. I would leave his office, smarting with embarrassment and furious that the bone-idle brigade got off scot-free. During the two years of a Constable's probation, his services could be dispensed with at any time if it was considered that he would not become a good and efficient Constable. How my services were retained still remains a mystery to this day. I must have been hanging on by my eyelids.

If the Uniform Branch did little to inspire me, the CID did even less. As far as I was concerned they were an arrogant bunch, who'd stagger back from the pub after drinking their lunch, bawling insults to the uniform staff. Mind you, with the opinion that I had of many of the uniform branch, I thought that the CID's behaviour was, to some extent, justified.

And then, this happened.

I was posted night-duty communications officer, which for me, being shut up inside the Police Station, was a hateful duty. It was, however, just as bad for the column-dodging Police Constables, who had to go out and patrol the streets. So when two of them spotted a couple of young lads at 4 o'clock in the morning, who ran off at the sight of a uniform, it was clear to the officers that firstly they should be brought in, because they were up to no good and secondly, and far more importantly, it afforded an excellent opportunity to get back to the sanctuary of the Police Station, where the delights of a game of cribbage awaited them.

Having dragged in the two scowling little bullet-headed miscreants who volunteered their names only after getting a clump round the ear, one of the arresting officers was eventually cajoled into going back out into the cold, in order to search the Panda Car in which they'd conveyed their prisoners to the Station. He then discovered that a screwdriver had been thrust down the back of the seat where the lads had been sitting. Returning to the charge room, he spent the next five minutes screaming into the faces of the two sullen boys, without the slightest admission of guilt or cooperation from either of them.

At the end of this furious tirade, the officer, whose face had started to resemble both the colour and the texture of a rotting strawberry, gasped out his only sensible contribution to the evening's work.

'Get hold of the night-duty CID, if you can find 'em,' he wheezed to me. 'They're probably in the pub,' he added bitterly, as an afterthought. As I pushed an outgoing plug into the switchboard, I admitted to myself that he might well be right.

But within fifteen minutes, I looked up as a stranger walked into the Station. He was short, slim, sober and neatly but casually dressed in a sports jacket and slacks. 'Good evening, night-duty CID,' he said courteously, which was astonishing, considering the other CID officers that I'd met. 'I understand that you've a couple of young suspects in the cells.'

''ang on, 'ang on,' grunted the overweight arresting officer, who was involved in some very tricky calculations. 'Fifteen two, fifteen four, fifteen six and a pair's eight. Gotcha, you bastard!' he triumphantly crowed to his cribbage-playing chum. 'Wot?' he said irritably, turning to the CID officer. 'Oh, yeah, them little fuckers. You won't get nothing out of them,' he added to the detective's back, as he walked off towards the cells. I went back to my newspaper.

I was suddenly aware that the detective had re-entered the charge room and I looked up with a start because not much more than five minutes had lapsed since his departure. 'The names they gave you are bollocks,' said the detective, quietly. 'These are their real ones,' and handed the cribbage-players a piece of paper, on which he'd made some notes. 'Both of them went over the wall from Approved School last night, and they've broken into two houses, one at Woodford, the other at Chadwell Heath. They'd just done the quarterlight of a car using that screwdriver, when you saw 'em. Leave them for the day-duty CID and they'll make statements to them. Right, well, I'm off. There's an arson at Leyton for me to deal with.' And with that, he was gone. I have no idea who he was or where he was from. I never saw him again.

The arresting officer blinked once or twice. 'Huh!' he finally grunted. 'I knew them little bastards were well at it. Good arrest, that,' he mused. And then, with a flash of self-righteousness, he added, 'I ought to get a commendation out of it!'

'No chance of that, John,' sourly commented his partner. 'The fucking CID grab all the glory!'

No-one asked my opinion and they wouldn't have wanted it, if I'd offered it. But if there was any glory going, I thought, that detective should have got it. The mottle-faced Uniform Officer had spent five minutes screaming at the two kids and had been rewarded with their open contempt and two bogus names. In the same amount of time, that quiet anonymous man had acquired every bit of worthwhile information, simply by talking quietly and firmly to them. Then and there, I decided that I wanted to be just like that detective. And in the end, if I got close to it, it was because I was helped by some of the finest men and women, in all the branches of the Metropolitan Police. Because you mustn't think that laziness was endemic and institutionalised in those days of the Police Force, because it was not. I just thought it was, due to the shiftless work-shy lot I'd fallen in with.

I hold strong opinions on what constitutes professionalism in the police with regard to combating crime and inspiring leadership. I also happen to possess intractable views on violent criminals, the lawyers who consistently invent defences for them and the Criminal Justice system in general. These, and all of the other opinions I express in this book are mine but I do not possess a copyright on them. I happen to know that they are shared by several thousand other retired and serving Police Officers.

I have done my best to record these stories in an accurate manner, but sometimes, alas, I have fallen by the wayside. A fondness in the past for Scotch whisky has probably eroded my brain-cells and middle-age has compounded my forgetfulness. I also ask you to remember that nearly all stories improve with the telling.

But to excuse my short-comings, Hillaire Belloc unwittingly comes to my assistance in his *Cautionary Tales for Children*, when a small child demands to know whether the stories in his book are true. In reply, he wrote,

> And is it true? It is not true.
> And if it were, it wouldn't do,
> For people such as me and you
> Who pretty nearly all day long
> Are doing something rather wrong.

I do hope you enjoy the book. It is dedicated to all those right-minded men and women in the Metropolitan Police who performed a difficult, dangerous job for little reward or thanks; it is also dedicated to their families who, like mine, supported them when few others did.

Dick Kirby
May, 2001

Acknowledgments

First of all, my thanks go to Joseph Wambaugh, long-time chum, drinking partner and inspiration. Next, my thanks to all of the correctly-named people in these pages, without whom the book would not be quite the same.

In addition, my appreciation goes out to Robin Gillies who first mentioned that he thought 'I might have a book in me' and also to Steve Earl of the Metropolitan Police Museum for his kindness and imagination regarding the photographs.

The Special Forces Club is represented by Dr Steve Weiss MA, PhD, American Bronze Star, Legion d'honneur, Croix de Guerre, Medaille de la Resistance, who gave some much-needed suggestions and encouragement; as did the late Lt. Col. Terry Message and Peri Morton (now Mrs Giles Chapman).

Merlin Unwin and his wife, Karen McCall who undertook the daunting task of publishing the book and gave enormous help and encouragement.

My wife Ann, our children Suzanne, Mark, Robert and Barbara, John and Sue Woodhouse, Anna Giacon and Diana Lightwing, who critically reviewed the odd chapter or two and were gracious enough to laugh in all the right places.

Royalties from this book

All the royalties from this book will be donated to two thoroughly worthwhile police charities.

The first of these is the Police Pensioners' Housing Association. For many years, an enormous effort from a variety of sources has been made to raise funds for sheltered accommodation for those of our number and their spouses who require this form of assistance.

The second beneficiary is the Metropolitan Police Combined Benevolence Trust which dispenses funds to the neadiest of the Metropolitan Police charities.

Donations to police charities from the public have diminished during the past few years; I have no doubt that this is due to a lack of confidence on their part just as I feel that this undesirable state of affairs has been brought about due to the chronically weak leadership from senior police officers in recent years.

With a new Commissioner and a new Millennium, I sincerely hope that this particular tide will turn and at the same time, that this book will make a lot of much-needed money for these charities.

Cover illustrations

Front cover A collage of photos of Metropolitan Police detectives and forensic experts going about their daily tasks, including the notorious David Martin (bottom right) whose story begins this book.
These photographs are reproduced courtesy of the Metropolitan Police Service.

Back cover Arches, loops, whorls and composites: the four basic patterns of the human fingerprint (*Reproduced courtesy of the Metropolitan Police Service*).
Inset: the author, Dick Kirby. This photograph was taken as he stepped out of the Old Bailey on 16 September 1985, after giving expert evidence before a judge. A hostile crowd outside the court mistook him for the leader of a ring of paedophiles who were currently on trial at the Bailey. This may explain the look of mild bafflement as he walks calmly away from the fray!

No Hiding Place

If I mention the name David Martin, it would mean nothing to most readers of this book. However, if I were to mention a yellow Mini and the name of Stephen Waldorf, who was inside the Mini when he was shot by police, it might make matters a little clearer because, even though it's over 15 years since it happened, many people remember the case which was to rock the Metropolitan Police to its very core. As a member of the Flying Squad team tasked to trace and arrest Martin, I suppose I can give an account of what happened as well as anybody because I was there for the 11 days it took from start to finish. There were some matters about which I was (and still am) profoundly unhappy but because it means identifying certain police officers and also runs the risk of libel action from a number of people who featured to a lesser or greater extent during this and other parallel investigations, I shall for once, hold my tongue. But to get the flavour of my involvement in the story, we have to go back a further 10 years before the manhunt even began...

It was the early 1970s in East London, and Forest Gate was held to be the busiest sub-divisional Station in the Metropolitan Police District. It appeared to me that the telephones never stopped ringing and the one that I picked up at random on that spring morning was a call from a nearby jewellers in Green Street. The manager informed me that a man was in the shop, trying to purchase property by means of a stolen credit card.

I ran down the stairs to the yard, where my car was parked, shouting out to another Detective Constable to accompany me.

As I raced along Green Street, my companion sighed. 'You'll break our necks, the way you're driving,' he complained. 'He won't be there, you know - as soon as the manager went to phone, he'll have been long gone.'

Privately, I thought he could well be right, but nonetheless, I concentrated all my efforts in reaching the shop in record time. Pulling up outside the premises, I ran from the car and as I reached the door, an extremely smartly dressed young man was leaving the shop. He courteously stepped to one side to let me in and having done so, he stopped and peered at the selection of wares in the window, the way that any customer might, who had not yet fully made up his mind.

I walked straight up to the manager. 'Right, where is he?' I abruptly asked him. Upon reflection, bearing in mind what was to occur, I concede that a clearer, more courteous introduction might have been called for.

He raised his eyebrows. 'To whom are you referring?' he asked.

'The bloke with the stolen credit card,' I replied.

'And you are?' he inquired.

'Police from Forest Gate,' I said testily, because it was obvious that he knew who I was.

He nodded thoughtfully. 'Have you any - er, identification?' he asked.

I pulled out my warrant card, which he examined carefully and finally pursed his lips and nodded again, thereby accepting verification of my profession. 'Right,' I said, and by now I was quite satisfied that the fraudster had long since vanished. 'Now, was it you that I spoke to on the phone at Forest Gate about five minutes ago?'

He conceded that he was indeed the telephone caller.

'And did you tell me that there was someone in the shop trying to buy goods with a stolen credit card?' I asked, wearily, because this was turning into a watching-paint-dry scenario.

Again, he nodded, acknowledging that this was so.

'So how long ago was it that he left?' I asked.

The manager waved casually in the direction of the door. 'He went out,' he replied, 'just as you came in.'

'You wanker!' I roared and dashed out of the shop. I looked left, then right, just in time to see a pair of well-tailored legs vanish round the corner into Plashet Grove.

I panted up to the junction and I heard the roar of a powerful car engine starting up. As I turned the corner, there was the fraudster behind the wheel of a Jaguar XJ-12. I ran towards the car, noticing that the window on the front seat passenger side of the car was wound down. I reached in, to try and somehow pull the keys out of the ignition and with that, the driver slammed the car into gear and drove off fast. Clinging on with one hand, I managed one punch to the side of his head before I was thrown from the car.

As I got to my feet, the car swerved crazily into Green Street and amidst the sound of furious car horns, it swung left into Plashet Road. I chased it on foot to the junction but I was far too late.

I limped back to the Police Station where not for the first time and certainly not the last, I was examined by the Divisional Surgeon, Dr. Sid Lazarus. Sid tut-tutted and diagnosed strained chest muscles from trying to hang on to the car and various lumps and bumps from being chucked off it. Almost 20 years later, he would still click his tongue disapprovingly as he tended my freshly bashed-up body; and in those later years he would always say, 'Dick, don't you think you're getting a bit old for this sort of thing?' When Sid was appointed MBE in the Honours List a couple of years ago, I was delighted and I wrote to him telling him so, mentioning that I did harbour a suspicion that I had been his best customer.

The Jaguar, which had been stolen from the Paddington area, was later found abandoned in Lucas Avenue, a few streets away and it was thought that the fraudster had escaped by running into nearby Upton Park Tube Station. Disregarding the enormous wave of concern for my well-being from the CID office ('Couldn't catch a bleedin' cold,' scoffed the First Class Sergeant) I circulated the fraudster's description and the details of the card that he'd been using and since there were no other clues worth following up, I got on with the next case.

A few months later, I received notification that the fraudster had been arrested by the Regional Crime Squad. The attempted deception for which I'd circulated him was one of many offences which he'd asked the court to take into consideration when he'd been sentenced to a term of imprisonment. He had not been charged with the assault with intent to resist arrest on me which, I reasoned, was probably a bargaining point between him and the RCS when they caught him. What was his name? Martin. David Ralph Martin. Aged 25 and born in Paddington. Never heard of him. Still, I couldn't get out of my mind the slick way he'd got out of that shop. That, I thought, took a lot of nerve. Then I shrugged my shoulders and forgot about him.

Some 10 years later, as my Flying Squad team and I were returning to London one Saturday morning, having successfully obtained a confession to a robbery from a suspect who had been detained out in the sticks, I called up the Yard on the radio, to inform them that we were back in the Metropolitan Police District. Immediately, the unforgettable voice of the Squad's radio operator, the late Jim Moon, told us to get over to Paddington Green Police Station, as soon as possible. 'There's a bit of a flap on,' added Jim. The Squad driver, Tony Freeman, slammed the big Squad Rover 3500 through a series of short-cuts, guaranteed to get us to Paddington Green in double-quick time.

The 'flap' referred to was the shooting of a young man named Stephen Waldorf by police the previous evening. Waldorf had been mistaken for one David Ralph Martin, who by now had established a reputation as a highly dangerous, very intelligent and elusive criminal. In August 1982, police had been called to a premises where Martin had been discovered, posing as a security man, complete with bogus documentation. He had coolly bluffed his way through the questioning until the Police Constable decided to search him.

At this point, Martin drew a gun from his pocket and shot the police officer, seriously wounding him, and escaped. Following some very efficient detective work, the Divisional CID officers discovered that Martin was responsible and found out where he was living. They kept observation on the address and then saw a smartly dressed blonde woman approaching the front door. Thinking that the woman might be Martin's girl-friend, or be someone who knew his whereabouts, they decided to have a word with her. They were shocked when they suddenly realised that the blonde woman was, in fact, Martin who turned and drew a 9mm pistol from his handbag. They flung themselves at Martin and grabbing hold of his gun-wrist, wrestled him to the ground. After a ferocious struggle, the gun was pulled from Martin's grasp. 'Alright, alright!' gasped Martin. 'That's it!'

Relieved to have confiscated the pistol, the officers relaxed; it was just the moment that Martin had been waiting for. As quick as a flash, he drew a Smith and Wesson .38 revolver from his waistband but before he could use it, an armed police officer shot him, fracturing his collar bone. Not withstanding this, Martin continued to fight like a tiger until he was eventually overpowered by sheer weight of numbers.

Now that he had been identified as the Constable's attacker, Martin was charged and remanded into custody. The investigators discovered that Martin had two safety deposit boxes. Inside were jewellery, a considerable sum of money and a total of eleven handguns, the part-proceeds of a burglary at a gunsmiths; the two guns found on Martin at the time of his arrest were part of the same haul. A car, used by Martin, was traced to Calais and after searching it, the Police Judiciare discovered five more handguns, one of which had been used to shoot a security guard during the course of a robbery, where £25,000 had been stolen.

The evidence was now mounting up against Martin but on 24 December 1982, whilst making a remand appearance at Marlborough Street Magistrates' Court, the blond, slim Martin coolly managed to slip out of his cell and disappear amongst the late Christmas shoppers in Oxford Street.

Just over two weeks later, the officers who were investigating both the various offences committed by Martin and his escape from custody, acting on information received, followed a yellow Mini in Earls Court. As the car stopped in traffic, the officers (including some who had taken part in the original arrest of Martin) approached the car. Due to movements inside the car, knowing how dangerous Martin was from personal experience and, most importantly, believing that the front seat passenger was Martin, they opened fire. The passenger, Stephen Waldorf, who bore a strong resemblance to Martin, was hit by the police bullets and severely wounded. In fact, Waldorf was *not* an associate of Martin, unlike the other occupants of the car, one of whom was the driver who fled from the scene, the other being Martin's blonde girl-friend.

So the following day, the Flying Squad were called in to take over the investigation and I headed one of the arrest teams. Detective Sergeant Johnny Redgrave and Detective Constable Steve Holloway were more or less permanently armed and we responded to the majority of the large number of calls which reported sightings of Martin. You will by now realise that this whole episode was eminently newsworthy. Firstly, an innocent man had been shot by police; next, the real villain of the piece was a gun-toting desperado who dressed convincingly as a woman. Thirdly, he was a veritable Houdini who had escaped from his police cell. The newspapers and the television were full of it.

As a result of Martin's cross-dressing habit, we received a number of telephone calls from apprehensive Hotel Managers, who were convinced that Martin was abusing their hospitality. Several be-wigged transvestites were astonished when, to the accompaniment of the sound of splintering wood, their bedroom doors burst open and they found themselves flung to the floor, with the business-end of a Model 64 Smith & Wesson caressing their nostrils. 'Gracious!' one of them gasped. 'What a fright you gave me!' Another had to be recompensed for a new pair of tights since the ones he was wearing were badly laddered en route to the carpet where he landed, face-first. 'O-h-h!' he squealed under the combined weight of approximately 30 stone. 'I hope that's a gun you're poking in my ear!'

Because of Martin's audacity - I've already mentioned a couple of examples - he was certainly not beyond booking into a hotel in his real name and then, the following day, telephoning the newspapers and bragging that the police were *still* unable to catch him, even after he had offered himself on a plate to them. So when a blond, slim pop singer by the name of David Martin booked into the Rembrandt Hotel in Kensington with his blonde girl-friend, and was just about to step into the bath, he was annoyed to hear the sound of his telephone ringing. He picked up the phone and suddenly froze. 'David Martin, this is the Flying Squad,' said the voice that the *Daily Mail* described as 'chilling'. (It was mine, I'm afraid.)

'Your room is surrounded. Get on your hands and knees and open the door - NOW!' Fearfully, Martin did as he was bid and opened the door to discover that some of the most frightening-looking men in the entire universe were pointing revolvers directly at the centre of his forehead.

Martin's girl-friend who had, of course, heard nothing of the content of the telephone call, was understandably alarmed to see her near-naked boy-friend attempting to drag a towel around his midriff while padding on his hands and knees towards the bedroom door. Seeing, to her absolute horror the group of large, armed strangers, she suddenly caught on and screamed, 'It's not him!'

Soothed by a number of large drinks afterwards, the innocent Martin told reporters, 'They were so tough and professional. There was no way I was going to try anything on.' Suddenly thinking we might return, he added hastily, 'They were only doing their job and they behaved perfectly.' As an afterthought, he added, 'I might change my name if this goes on much longer!'

We stormed a house in Belsize Park, Kilburn, armed to the teeth and wearing bullet-proof vests, following a tip-off that Martin was there. He wasn't. And so it was on to the next sighting of Martin, and the next...

During the course of the investigation, a number of people, including Martin's girl-friend and the driver of the Mini were arrested and charged with dishonestly assisting in the disposal of the proceeds of burglaries which had been carried out by Martin.

Since Martin had still not been arrested at that time, the media seized upon this as being newsworthy, which resulted in my getting a fair share of publicity. At the committal proceedings of the receivers, I walked out of Marylebone Magistrates' Court and stood a little way from the entrance, keeping back from the press photographers, who were waiting for the defendants to emerge from court. All of a sudden, I noticed a Woman Police Constable looking in my direction. I was transfixed. She was blonde, with the most perfectly beautiful face I had ever seen. She smiled and started to walk towards me. She looked and moved like a model - no, not a model, a princess! Yes, that was it, a real fairy-tale princess, stepping right out of the pages of the brothers Grimm. And here she was, walking straight towards me, smiling that radiant smile. I resisted the very strong temptation to look behind me, and see who she was really smiling at, but no, she walked straight up to me and stopped.

'Hello,' she said. It really was a dazzling smile.

'Hello,' I replied.

'You're from the Flying Squad, aren't you?' she asked.

Calm down, Richard, I thought. Just be cool about this whole business. I gave her a lazy smile. 'That's right,' I replied.

'You're - don't tell me, you're Detective Sergeant Dick Kirby - you are, aren't you?' she asked, hesitantly.

My chest swelled and my stomach automatically flattened. I preened. This, without doubt, was my finest hour. 'Quite right, I am,' I replied and added nonchalantly, 'I guess you've seen me on the television?'

'Oh, no,' she replied. 'I saw you in court, the other week, when the Magistrate, Sir Ivor Rigby gave you the biggest bollocking of all time! It was so funny! I just wanted to make sure it was you! I can't wait to tell them back at the nick!'

But the funniest thing of all happened some time later at the trial of the three receivers of stolen goods. I had interviewed two of the prisoners, and one of these interviews had been conducted in the presence of Detective Constable Steve Farley, an excellent detective, with whom I got on very well. I want to mention straightaway that Steve was the possessor of a very sharp tongue, and it is necessary for you to be aware of this fact right now, so that you can savour all the better what was later to occur.

I gave my evidence concerning the interview of the prisoner which I had conducted with Steve and it was very fiercely put to me, in no uncertain terms that we had ill-treated the prisoner in order to obtain his confession. This was blatantly untrue and I strongly denied it. Having given my evidence, I sat down in court and watched Steve do his bit.

'When you took my client to the interview room,' intoned the defence Counsel to Steve, 'I suggest that you pulled my clients jacket down from his shoulders, thereby effectively trapping his arms, and Kirby slapped my client round the face, saying, "We're not the local nancy-pansy boys, we're the Squad and we want some fucking answers." '

'We did not,' replied Steve, firmly.

'And then,' continued the Counsel, as though Steve had never denied the allegation, 'you generally abused him, taking turns to slap him.'

'No Sir,' replied Steve.

'I suggest you did more,' said the Counsel, in a robust fashion. 'I suggest it was you - it may have been Kirby, but I suggest it was you - who made my client drop his trousers.'

'No Sir,' said Steve, boredom beginning to creep into his voice.

'And having done so,' went on the Counsel, 'you took a ruler and you humiliated my client, by pretending to measure his member, this causing considerable amusement to you and Kirby.'

'Quite untrue,' replied Steve.

'Having humiliated him in that fashion,' continued the Counsel, 'you made him bend over, and you prodded - yes, prodded him with the ruler in the area of his buttocks, and you pretended to peer up his anus.'

'No Sir,' replied Steve, and I could see from the glint in Steve's eyes that he was getting very fed-up indeed, with these wild allegations.

'David Ralph Martin had not been caught at that time, had he?' asked Counsel.

'No, Sir,' replied Steve.

'Detective Sergeant Kirby has told the court that he regarded Martin as being the most dangerous man in London,' said the Counsel. 'I take it that you would agree with Sergeant Kirby's opinion?'

'I certainly would, Sir,' replied Steve.

'You were desperate to get hold of Martin, WEREN'T YOU?' bellowed the Counsel.

'Well,' said Steve, scornfully, 'I didn't think I'd find him hiding up your client's arsehole!'

The learned Judge laughed so loud that his wig started to slip. All of the barristers were laughing, including the one who had asked Steve the question. The dock officers, solicitors and the public gallery were giggling helplessly and Detective Sergeant Nicky Benwell, who was the exhibits officer, had to be helped out of court, supported between two ushers. His whoops of laughter could be heard streets away. And me? I never thought I'd be able to stop laughing.

But all that was in the future and you'll remember that before you were side-tracked with this little anecdote, Martin was still at large and still as dangerous as ever.

Eleven days after the Flying Squad took up this assignment, an observation was set up at The Milk Churn Restaurant, in Hampstead. Reliable information had been received that during the evening, Martin was going to arrive there. As a result of some excellent detective work, Detective Sergeant Cam Burnell had discovered that Martin was in possession of a red Ford Sierra saloon, stolen from London's Heathrow Airport. We were briefed and were told our observation points, so that when Martin went to enter the restaurant, there would be no escape.

'Guv'nor,' I said to the senior officer. 'There's no-one covering the route to Hampstead Underground Station. If he gets through, he can go straight down the unders and we'll have lost him.' The Guv'nor sighed, as if to say, 'there's always got to be one, hasn't there?' and replied, wearily, 'Dick, once he's outside the restaurant, he's bollocksed. He's had it. There's enough of us to eat him. You follow?' I shrugged my shoulders and sat down. One or two sycophantic officers, desperately trying to ingratiate themselves, sighed loudly and rolled their eyes. Someone muttered, 'Mr Thicko!'

Martin dutifully arrived in the stolen Red Sierra and just as dutifully sensed a trap. Sprinting down to Hampstead Underground Station, his flight uninterrupted by anybody and followed by a large group of Squadmen, he raced down the stairs to the platform, jumped on to the electrified track and ran off in the direction of Belsize Park. Having reached the bottom of the stairs, gasping for breath and with my heart jumping around inside my chest, I was ordered to re-climb the steps and get down to Belsize Park station in order to cut off his escape.

In the meantime, shouting for the current to be switched off, and not knowing whether it was or not, Detective Chief Superintendent Don Brown (who by then was very close to retirement) led his men along the darkened tunnel in pursuit, unable to see Martin who they knew might well be armed. With the lights of Belsize Park station coming closer, Brown and Detective Sergeant Nicky Benwell suddenly saw Martin pressed into an alcove and grabbed hold of him. 'Take it easy, guys,' said

Martin. 'You've got me.' And he gave up without a struggle.

Martin did not have a gun in his possession when he was arrested. He did, it is true, have a bottle of ammonia, a knife and a set of picklocks. And at Paddington Police Station, when Detective Constable Davy Walker noticed something odd and asked him, 'What's the matter with your speech?' and Martin sullenly made no reply, Walker prised his jaws apart, and removed the miniature multi-purpose penknife that Martin had stuck to the roof of his mouth with chewing gum.

The newspapers were jubilant. 'Martin arrested!' were the headlines in the *Daily Mail*. 'Martin caught in tube tunnel,' cried *The Sun*. 'Captured!' shouted the *Daily Express*. The popular television detective series, *The Gentle Touch,* was interrupted with a news flash, to reveal that Martin had been caught. The Commissioner sighed with relief. Martin had finally been caught without a shot being fired. It was fortunate that the detectives were alright as well, of course.

By the time I'd struggled back up the steps at Hampstead Underground, got hold of a car, driven to Belsize Park and made my way down to the platform, I was completely surplus to requirements because Martin had been arrested. Wearily, I made my way to Paddington Green Police Station. There, in the charge room, I saw for the second and last time the man that I'd hunted 10 years earlier. We had never spoken to each other and now we never would. He was sitting on a bench, looking rather dishevelled but relaxed. Martin sensed my gaze and looked up at me. I wanted to see if I could detect even a flicker of recognition in his eyes, but there was nothing; just disinterest. 'Ten bloody years,' I thought, 'and still I didn't catch you!'

But what did it matter? One dangerous young man was out of circulation and that was all that mattered; that, and the desire for a large drink, my first in eleven days.

Nine months later, after a two-week trial at the Old Bailey, during which Martin displayed complete contempt for the proceedings, Mr Justice Kilner-Brown told him :

'Those who carry loaded guns to shoot their way out of impending arrest, must expect very severe sentences indeed and that is what you're going to get.' He then sentenced Martin to 25 years imprisonment.

Apparently, Martin had formed a friendship with Dennis Nilsen, the mass murderer whilst they were on remand in Brixton Prison but after sentence, Martin was sent to Parkhurst on the Isle of Wight, the maximum security prison. He lasted 5 months before he was found hanged in his cell.

And the rest of the story?

The two police officers who had mistaken Waldorf for Martin were tried at the Old Bailey and acquitted. Quite a lot of police officers who were authorised to carry firearms, furious at what they saw as a lack of support, handed in their firearms authorisation cards. The whole system of firearms training was hastily reviewed and overhauled. Waldorf who was never charged with any offence, recovered from his injuries and sued the police, receiving £120,000 in compensation. Martin's cronies were convicted of handling Martin's stolen property and received prison sentences.

Many officers - and I was one of them - thought that Don Brown, Nicky Benwell and the others would receive gallantry awards for their cold-blooded courage in chasing Martin through that unlit tunnel, not knowing if Martin was armed nor if the track's electric current had been switched off. It takes a special brand of courage to do that and it's not a particular category of pluck that I possess. However, it was decided that because members of the Metropolitan Police had shot the wrong man in the first place, it would not have been politically correct for these officers (who were not, of course, connected in any way with the shooting of Waldorf) to be seen to benefit. And they didn't. Not only were no medals forthcoming, they did not receive any kind of recognition whatsoever. It was that sort of gutlessness on the part of senior officers that should have made the Metropolitan Police hang its head in shame.

So that was the end of David Martin. I met men who were tougher than him and those who were cleverer when it came to multi-million pound swindles. But pound for pound, he was, as I said in court, 'the most dangerous man in London.' Who else, whilst serving a sentence, would be made a prison trustee, become genuinely liked by the prison officials, in order that (almost at the end of his sentence) he could get close enough to attack the prison Governor whom he disliked, thereby forfeiting all of his remission? And as for cool behaviour under pressure, well... you know about that.

Martin's father shared his son's loathing and contempt for authority and in a series of almost raving newspaper quotes, urged his son to keep running. In the end, he seemed almost jubilant at his son's demise. To the reporters, he boasted, 'To me, he has done them in the eye. He is better off where he is, now. It is the police and the system that killed him. In the finish, he beat them, anyway.'

Did he? Well, whichever way you view things, he won't be shooting any more policemen.

The Aids System

Since the formation of the Criminal Investigation Department of the Metropolitan Police in 1878 until fairly recent times, I should think there were always 'Aids' - those police officers who were neither Uniform, nor CID, but were in an in-betwixt state - uniformed police officers who aspired to be fully-fledged members of the CID. In the latter part of the nineteenth century and for at least the first quarter of the twentieth, these officers were known as 'Winter Patrols'. Donning shabby old caps and mufflers, they would patrol the back streets of London, with a view to identifying and catching the thieves who infested these areas, who were perpetually breaking into vulnerable premises. Later, these aspiring detectives became known as 'Aids to CID' and this label of 'Aid' lasted for over 30 years.

Following the demise of Detective Sergeant Harold Gordon Challenor M.M. and the imprisoning of three of his Aids for planting evidence on suspects, a public enquiry's findings were submitted to the then-Home-Secretary, Sir Frank Soskice Q.C. in 1965, and later the system of 'Temporary Detective Constables' (T.D.Cs) was implemented. The death of the T.D.Cs came far quicker than that of the Aids, because they were abolished during the early 1970s and Crime Squads, under the direction of the local uniform Chief Superintendents took their place. Although the hopeful young P.Cs who made up the Crime Squads were dressed in plain clothes, they still retained their Divisional number and would continue to do so until such time as they were accepted into the Criminal Investigation Department. This, too, has gone by the board and it was followed by a system of Trainee Investigators (T.Is) and later, Accredited Investigators (A.Is). The system became so complicated that now it is almost impossible for an outsider to understand, which was not helped by the fact that if the uniform Chief Superintendents thought that their Division didn't require a Crime Squad, they didn't have one. Matters were made far worse during the late 1990s by the introduction of the ludicrous system of 'tenure' which resulted in officers being swapped from one specialised department to another, so what with that and Chief Superintendents insisting on 'doing their own thing' everyone appeared to be in imminent danger of vanishing up their own arseholes.

The rot can be pin-pointed to the time when Sir Robert Mark was Commissioner. Mark was, in many ways a fine Commissioner but he had a mistrust of the CID and he was determined to break their power. Certainly, something had to be done because corruption in the CID was rife. But in my opinion, Mark went about the business of rooting out corruption like an exterminating angel, wielding a flaming sword. Yes, the senior CID officers who were crooked or in any other way unsuitable needed to be kicked out of office, but I believe that they could have been replaced by skilful investigators from the CID who were completely straight - believe me, there were plenty of them - who had the admiration and loyalty of their subordinates. In what I still believe was an almost hysterical action, Mark replaced the senior CID officers with senior uniformed officers; men who, at best had very limited knowledge of detective work and at worst, none at all. In addition, he introduced 'Interchange' - the swapping of personnel between uniform and CID. It was the beginning of a disaster which has lasted up until the present time. The present Commissioner, Sir John Stevens (himself a former detective) has stated that he wants career CID officers in the Metropolitan Police, once again. I hope that his desire is implemented sooner, rather than later; but even if it is, I fear it will take a generation before the CID is staffed with officers who are really well suited to the job.

I was part of the T.D.C. system, which, like most good formulas, was basically quite simple. You were given another T.D.C. as a partner, you were told to go out on the streets in plain clothes and nick as many thieves and suspects as you could, and in this fashion, providing you didn't upset the First-class Detective Sergeant (who traditionally was in overall charge of the Aids), successfully passed a ten-week CID course, two stiff selection boards and, ideally the Sergeant's Promotion examination, you might possibly, one day, reach the heady ranks of the CID. The title of Temporary Detective Constable was regarded as a bit of a mouthful, so we were always referred to as 'Aids', 'Scalys' or 'Scaly Aids'.

Being but lowly Aids, we were at the beck and call of the CID proper and it really was worth our while, once we'd booked on duty, to get out of the CID office or else it was highly likely we'd get lumbered by the

Second-class Detective Sergeant, who had immediate charge of us. With hindsight, perhaps being inconvenienced wasn't such a bad thing, because having to go and collect exhibits or files showed us the workings of the laboratory or Criminal Records Office. Not that that would have occurred to us, then. All we wanted to do, was get out on the streets and cover ourselves with glory and George Medals.

I remember that one Detective Chief Superintendent thought it would be a good idea to have Detective Constables in charge of pairs of Aids. One such loathsome character (destined never to grow old in the service of the Metropolitan Police and who later hurriedly tendered his resignation, as a result of a major internal enquiry) was put in charge of me and my partner.

'Oi, you,' he said to me, rejoicing in his new-found power. 'You and your mate - on top of Barkers hardware shop, all night. I've had a tip the place is gonna get screwed.' (Of course, he hadn't heard anything of the kind - the manager of Barkers was too stingy to afford a proper alarm system, and he'd complained to the Detective Constable that he'd got a lot of stock in overnight, on the run-up to Christmas - hence us being offered up as Barkers' private night security, for a sizable consideration to the detective. It must have been sizable, too - if it hadn't, I've no doubt that this little bastard would have set up a break-in with a local team of villains, for an even bigger cut!)

'Do me a favour, Harry,' I said, wearily. 'Steve and I have been on the go since five this morning. Can't you get someone off late-turn to do it?'

'Look,' he replied, poking me in the chest. 'You're just a fucking Aid' - (prod) - 'see?' - (prod) - 'and I'm in charge of you,' - (prod) - 'so just do as you're fucking told,' - (prod) - 'see?'

I blinked once or twice, quite rapidly. 'You prick,' I said, quietly. 'I'm going to smash your lights in!'

As I was prised away from this unpleasant exchange, word of our encounter reached the ears of the Detective Chief Superintendent, who not long after concluded that his revolutionary concept might best be discontinued there and then.

Every Wednesday morning, our week's work was written up in a diary, together with details of our expenses and a summary of our arrests, which were shown in the back of the diary under the heading, 'Summary of Apprehensions'. We would fill in this column, working backwards towards the main body of the diary. I cannot begin the explain to you the joy we experienced when, due to the sheer number of arrests, this title at the top of the page ran out, and we had to put a neat line through the title at the top of the page, which read, 'Details of duties and time employed', and write in pen, 'Summary of Apprehensions' in order to continue with the details of the arrests.

But it was really a hard slog. There was no paid overtime in those days, and instead, we were paid a Detective Duty Allowance, which, in September 1975, when we were eventually paid overtime, amounted to £38 per month. Transport was very limited indeed, and what vehicles there were always went to the CID proper first - even if we, the Aids, wanted a car to arrest and convey a prisoner, and the CID wanted the car to convey themselves to the pub, which, I'm sorry to say, was often the case. We were often forced to use our own private vehicles and this was a disciplinary offence, for which we could be reported and disciplined, if we were caught. I remember one night, several of us Aids were in one of our private cars, when we received a call over the personal radio, that a man had been brutally attacked and robbed by three tearaways wielding a hammer, and was now in a very serious condition. As we rounded a corner, we spotted three youths, who, as soon as they saw us, threw a blood-stained hammer into a shop doorway, and tried to make a run for it. There was a terrific fight, (I remember that my prisoner was so violent, that it was the first time that I'd seen handcuffs used to restrain someone) and they were all arrested, all confessed to the offence and were later jailed at the Old Bailey. There was some talk of a commendation for us. 'Commendation?' gasped the horrified Second-class Sergeant, who would have had to have written the short report. 'Using your own motor, weren't you?' And that was that.

Speaking of commendations, I remember my partner, Steve Gardner and I stopping and arresting ten juveniles in the street, who were armed with the worst collection of offensive weapons I'd ever seen. Apart from knives, coshes and broken chair legs, one of the youths had constructed a home-made mace, such as a mediaeval knight would have used at the lists - a chain, attached to a metal handle at one end, and at the other end of the chain, a collection of huge nuts and bolts. Even the lightest of glancing blows on the thickest of skulls would have caused, quite liter- ally, the most shattering injuries.

The youths confirmed that at the time of their arrest, they were en route to a nearby park, to have a confrontation with a rival gang of youths. It was just as well we stopped them when we did.

All of these lads appeared at the Juvenile Court and with the sort of light penalties reserved for delinquents, walked right out again. But the Chairman of the Magistrates called me and Steve in front of the bench, and commended us, for our diligence and prompt action. Back we went to the CID office. 'Here, Sarge,' I said to our Detective Sergeant. 'I think Steve and I have just been given a commendation,' and I explained the circumstances.

'Uh-huh!' said the Sergeant, and nodded sagely. After a pause, he added, 'Was the Court Inspector in court at the time, by any chance?'

I thought for a moment. 'No, Sarge, I don't think he was,' I replied.

'Ah yes, well, that's it,' he said, obviously relieved at my reply. 'To get a Commissioners Commendation, the Court Inspector's got to be present.'

'Oh, O.K., then,' I said, obviously disappointed, but not knowing any better. It was all bollocks, of course. With five or six courts to run, the Court Inspector couldn't possibly be in them all at the same time. Naturally, he didn't have to be present. It was this lazy bastard's way of getting out of doing a half-hour report. When I discovered the truth some considerable time later, it was, of course, too late for me and Steve.

A few weeks later, I was one half of the night-duty CID, covering from Barking in the west, to Upminster in the east. This enormous area could get quite busy and the Detective Sergeant had been called away to Dagenham, to deal with an allegation of rape. I was at Harold Hill Police Station, dealing with a local tearaway, who had an enormous amount of form. He had been stopped in a stolen car and I interviewed him. Not only did he admit a string of offences, including car thefts and house burglaries, he also admitted a conspiracy to rob, and having thus committed himself, also named his companions on this venture. They had all decided to rob the manager of an all-night garage of his takings, and had acquired a fearsome iron bar with which to encourage his compliance. Whilst they were consolidating their plans in the stolen car in a car park, they were spotted by a police patrol car and, in making their escape, had got rid of the incriminating iron bar. The car park was within the boundaries of the nearby Essex Constabulary so I sent a message to the local Police Station, giving them explicit instructions as to the description and the exact whereabouts in the car park of the piece of metal, and requesting that they retrieve it. I then pulled in the amateur robbers' accomplices, and because the Sergeant was still busy, I set about single-handedly questioning them. All of them made complete confessions to the whole range of the offences alleged, and they were duly committed to stand their trial at the Central Criminal Court.

All of them pleaded guilty to this catalogue of offences and sadly, the most cogent of their barristers' pleas for clemency fell on deaf ears. 'Isn't it a fact that my client was but 16 years of age, when these offences were committed?' desperately entreated one of the barristers to me. I sighed. 'Young in years, indeed,' I replied, sorrowfully shaking my head, and adding, 'but old and well-versed in the ways of criminality.' The late Judge Michael Argyle MC, QC, who was a much admired hard-line Judge at the Bailey, took up this point and tartly declared that any chance of leniency was out of the question. To reinforce his argument, he read aloud the passage in the 16 year-old's confession, in which he stated that the others had easily persuaded him to be the one to bash the Garage manager over the head, 'cos I like 'urting people', and dished out substantial terms of porridge.

But going back to the morning after that busy night-duty, the Detective Constable who was deputed to deal with the case, and who had very little to do except pen a covering report to the Director of Public Prosecutions, promptly nicked two of the prisoners off me. This was an infuriating trick, used by CID officers who were too lazy and too incompetent to arrest prisoners of their own, and who wanted to mendaciously show in their weekly returns of work that they'd been busy. But I simply couldn't understand it in this case, because this officer had already tendered his resignation, and in two weeks time was emigrating to Canada! Old habits die hard, I suppose.

Whilst I was explaining the case to him, in came two Constables from the Essex Constabulary, triumphantly bearing the iron bar. Although I was very pleased to have it because it provided corroboration for the confessions, to be fair, they would have had to have been blind to have missed it, because my directions to them were so precise. Still, it was nice to see the expressions of pleasure creep across their simple faces, after the Detective Constable informed them that it would be highly likely that they'd be receiving a Commendation for their sterling work. I don't suppose for one minute they did. I certainly didn't. I shouldn't complain, I suppose, because I've had my fair share of Commendations over the years, but I can't help sometimes thinking about the ones I didn't get! It was about this time that I made up my mind, that if I ever reached a responsible position in the CID, and an officer's good work was brought to my attention, I would be only too pleased to recommend them for official commendation. I'm delighted to say that over the years, literally dozens of officers have received commendations on my say-so, and two were decorated by the Queen.

I have always thought that by having pairs of Aids out on the street, it is not only a terrific weapon in the fight against crime, it is moulding the embryo detective's character and crime-fighting abilities. Although I wouldn't say Aiding was the happiest time of my career - the Flying Squad was that - none the less, they were good times, where friendships were formed which still exist to this day. Later, I ran Crime Squads of my own - on 'J' Division, covering Barkingside and the surrounding area and later, 'N' Division, covering Holloway, Kings Cross and Islington. I impressed on all of my hopefuls, that the only reason that they were there was to serve an apprenticeship, with a view to permanently joining the CID, and for no other reason. One or two people tried it on, thinking that being out of uniform would give them unlimited freedom to do whatever they wanted, quite apart from police work. I was quite draconian with those who didn't measure up and the ones who were sent back to a 'big hat' had their papers minuted by me that they should not be employed on plain-clothes duty, again. A bit despotic? Well, again with hindsight, perhaps. But I considered it essential in those far-off days that only the very best of the young men and women in my charge should join the permanent ranks of the CID; and they did.

Whilst I may have been fairly hard on my officers, I did encourage (and, indeed, insist upon) positive policing and stopping, searching and arresting villains was top of my agenda.

I certainly would not have written, in the back of any of my Aid's diaries, what Detective Chief Inspector John Hacker wrote in the back of mine, when, following a tiring 76 hour week in 1970, (and having had only the briefest of birthday celebrations) I had arrested 12 persons, including three burglars, three people in possession of loaded firearms, four handlers of stolen property and a car thief. His comments were, 'Numerically speaking, a good week's work!'

The Home Counties Cock-up

A gang of highly organised criminals was touring the Home Counties and the outer Divisions of the Metropolitan Police District in 1970, committing burglaries, stealing cars and impersonating police officers. Their style was so daring and the number of offences that they were committing was so prolific that a special edition of *Police Gazette* devoted purely to them was published. Not surprisingly, they were known as 'The Home Counties Gang.'

One night, Dick Miles, who then, like me, was an Aid to CID (and who now is Assistant Chief Constable in the Ministry of Defence Police) was working on a 'Q' Car, with a uniformed Sergeant. During the night, they had found an abandoned car, and had run a series of checks on it, which revealed that something about it was not quite right. They came to the conclusion that this car was connected with the Home Counties Gang, and they were right. That's how I got a knock on the door at 4am (I hadn't a phone in those days) and I blearily opened my front door, to see a grinning Dick Miles shout 'April Fool!' After my initial bellow of rage, Dick told me what had happened, and told me to be at Romford Police Station at 6am that morning. There, a large number of officers received a briefing and I was one of several young detectives who got into the back of a nondescript van, which was then driven to the vicinity of the abandoned car and parked nearby. Other officers were in unmarked police cars in the adjacent streets, others were in the front gardens of nearby houses and still others positioned themselves behind hedges.

We waited no longer than 15 minutes, before a shifty looking chap walked up to the car, completely oblivious, of course, to us in the observation van, took a key from his pocket and inserted it in the car door. That was the signal for about twenty rabid officers to erupt with a mighty roar upon this unfortunate, and literally bury him under an avalanche of bodies. The suspect, who had never seen so many police officers concentrated in such a small area in his life before, was so frightened that he immediately admitted that, yes, he was indeed one of the Home Counties gang, and that, in fact, the remainder of the team could be found residing at 14 Acacia Avenue, not a quarter of a mile away.

So far, then, so good. It was at this stage that disaster struck. Detective Chief Inspector John Hacker (he of the grudging remarks in the back of my diary) and the most incompetent buffoon that God ever blew breath into, took control of the operation. Another senior police officer once told me that he had solved 14 out of 15 murders that he had investigated, and would have solved all 15, if only Hacker hadn't got to the murder scene first, and so hopelessly contaminated the area that any further investigation was useless. I think the murderer got ticked off, and told not to do it again.

Having been appraised that the rest of the gang were at 14 Acacia Avenue, Hacker went straight round to No. 41, and arrested the wrong people. It took him a little while to realise that the family of chartered accountants whom he had arrested were not a band of roving brigands and eventually, Hacker lost interest, wandering off to find some other investigation that he could thoroughly compromise.

A more competent team of detectives went to the correct address and found the real miscreants still there. They had been rather apprehensive when their driver had failed to return with the stolen car and when they witnessed Hacker roaring up the front path of No. 41, pointedly ignoring the cries for prudence from the rest of his team, they believed this to be some sort of cunning police trick so, surrounded by incriminating evidence, they decided to stay put and see what happened next. All of the prisoners were skilfully interrogated, were later committed to the Central Criminal Court and, after admitting an enormous number of offences, were each sentenced to five years imprisonment and Dick Miles and some other officers were rightly commended.

So all was well that ended well. Wasn't it?

Ten years later, Hacker, by now a Detective Chief Superintendent, and I, a Detective Sergeant, were both involved in a murder enquiry. We met for a drink in a local pub, which was no hardship, because when he wasn't compromising investigations, writing prattish comments in the back of my diary and otherwise being a pain, he could be quite a decent sort of chap and convivial company.

We chatted about the progress on the murder enquiry and then, right out of the blue he said, 'Dick, do you remember the Home Counties case, all those years ago?'

'I do indeed, Sir,' I replied.

'Yes...' he said thoughtfully and took a sip of his beer. After a short pause, he continued, 'You know, that was a right cock-up.'

Immediately, I felt for the man. It takes a lot to put your hands up to that sort of mistake, and paradoxically I felt obliged to jump to his defence.

'Well, it wasn't as bad as all that,' I protested.

Hacker gave a short, bitter laugh. 'Come on, who are you kidding?' he asked. 'Admit it, Dick, it was an embarrassing balls-up.'

'Look, Sir,' I said, soothingly. 'What does it matter? Everything came alright in the end.'

'But that's not the point,' said Hacker firmly. 'It was a fuck-up, pure and simple. Be fair, Dick, it was, wasn't it? Come on, wasn't it?'

It had been a long day, I was tired and I felt I had finally run out of excuses for him. I shrugged my shoulders. 'Yeah, alright,' I said. 'It was.'

'That's right,' said Hacker, smugly. 'Just as well I was on hand to sort it all out for you!'

Big Brother is Watching You!

There'd been one of those sudden explosions of violence, inside a pub in Barking, East London, on that Friday night. The place had been wrecked, a great deal of blood had been spilled and only one of the combatants had been arrested. The names of the other trouble-makers had been extracted from him, and on the following morning, all of the local Aids to CID and the 'Q' Car crews (of which I was one), were summoned to the CID office at Barking Police Station, by the First-class Detective Sergeant there. He had nine names and addresses, which he distributed amongst us. 'Just tell 'em I want to see 'em,' he drawled. 'They won't be any trouble.'

'Oh, yeah?' I thought, looking at the name I'd drawn. Although I personally didn't know Mark Higgins, his terrifying reputation for violence was legendary.

There are places all over the world where the hatred of police or indeed any form of authority is so intense that it is almost a physical thing - walk down the street and even if no-one's about, the hostility seems to radiate off the buildings! If you've ever been in the Republican areas of Belfast or Londonderry, you'll know exactly what I mean. This was the resentment that I experienced as the 'Q' Car drove into a very tough housing estate in Barking. I felt that suspicious eyes were following the passage of the unmarked vehicle which, in reality, was just as easily identifiable as a police car to the inhabitants as if it had had a revolving blue light on its roof. Getting out of the car, I walked, as nonchalantly as possible, to one of the prefabricated buildings and tapped on the door.

My knock was answered by a man of about fifty, completely bald and wearing only a pair of shorts. He was about my height, 5' 9", but his physique displayed a fit, muscular body. He looked like a light-heavyweight who was still paying considerable attention to detail in the ring. He looked at me quite calmly, instinctively identifying my profession. 'Yeah?' he inquired.

'Er - from the local Police Station,' I said nervously, offering my warrant card for inspection.

'I can fucking see that,' he replied scornfully, ignoring the card. 'What do you want?'

'Is Mark in?' I asked casually, because by now, I was hoping against hope that he wasn't.

The big man's eyes narrowed. 'Yeah, why?' he replied. 'Is he nicked?'

In a particularly craven manner, I replied, 'Well, it's just that the First-class down at Barking wants a word with him.'

At that moment, the bald man was joined by another man. He, too, was wearing only shorts. He, too, had an enormously impressive physique. There, the similarity ended. The newcomer had a full head of hair, was at least five inches taller than the other man and was some thirty years younger. Between them, they effectively blocked out the light in the doorway.

The older man turned to the younger one, and said the worst words I had ever heard in my life.

'John,' he said. 'Go and get your big brother.'

As I waited, trembling, for this modern-day Tyrannosaurus Rex to appear, I rapidly debated what would be the most humiliating course of action for me to take - flight, fainting or incontinence; mercifully, it was not a choice that I had to make.

Mark Higgins, a charming young man when not in his cups, accompanied me to the Police Station as gentle as a lamb. In the fullness of time, he was arraigned at the Central Criminal Court for causing an affray, where he gracefully accepted 9 months imprisonment as a proper rebuke for his violent Friday evening.

Terry's Surprise

'Just two weeks,' I thought, 'and I'll have made it.' I had been posted to two weeks night-duty CID, and at the end of it, I was going to be appointed a fully fledged Detective Constable. Being an Aid to CID was all very well, but as an old 'Q' Car driver, Johnny Gray had told me, 'Once you've been accepted into the CID, it's like having full membership of an exclusive club, instead of just having honorary membership, and you'll be entitled to all the privileges and facilities of that club.' Quite a verbose old chap, he was, but he was right. My partner on this night-duty tour was Terry Johnson, who was a very affable sort of fellow. Terry had sat the Constable to Sergeant examination for many years past, and this annual attendance had been regarded as quite a social gathering for him and his chums. Nobody was more astonished than Terry when he actually passed the exam, and at the end of the night-duty tour, he too was going to be posted, on promotion, to a new Station.

'Look here, Dick,' he said, on the first night. 'There's something I want to get straight with you. I've been waiting a long time to get this promotion to Sergeant.'

'I expect you have, Terry,' I said, politely.

'And I'm looking forward to being posted,' he said.

'Yes, so am I,' I replied.

'And I don't want anything to go wrong,' continued Terry, grimly.

'I don't suppose you do,' I said, getting more and more mystified.

Terry took a deep breath. 'So if we are obliged to arrest anyone in the next two weeks,' he said, 'I don't want to see you bashing them, if you come to the conclusion that on the flimsiest of evidence, they're going to offer the slightest bit of resistance.' (By way of explanation, during my time as a Uniformed Police Constable, I had been involved in a couple of near-riots, and in consequence, I had obtained a quite unjustified reputation as a brawler.)

'Cheek!' I replied, and I don't mind telling you, I was quite shocked. 'Certainly not!'

'I'll make sure of it,' said Terry, very firmly.

And he did. It was a very quiet night-duty and Terry took the opportunity of visiting all of his old Uniform chums on the Division, and bidding them farewell. And when we weren't doing that, we were having two-hour meal breaks, playing darts, cribbage and anything else to pass the time.

To start off with, I was a bit annoyed, not at being so grossly slandered, but because I loved getting out and about during night-duty, with a chance, perhaps, of catching a night-time burglar. But as the fortnight drew on, I thought, 'Well, what's it matter?' Terry was happy, and, as I've said, he was a very affable companion.

And then, on the very last night, as we were admiring the boats in Lewis Marines' window at three o'clock in the morning, Upminster received its once a year call to its wireless car.

'Kilo Six, Kilo Six, from M.P. The tobacconists at the junction of St. Mary's Lane and Argyle Gardens – a suspect at the rear.'

This was about three-quarters of a mile from where we were standing. Terry was as excited as I was. We jumped into the clapped-out old Hillman Hunter that served as the CID car, and tore off down the road. As we reached our destination, I jumped out of the car, just in time to see a shadowy figure emerge from the rear of the tobacconists.

I grabbed hold of him, and rammed him up against the wall. 'Quick, Terry, get round the back,' I said. 'See if he's got any mates round there.'

Off went Terry, leaving the two of us there. I suddenly realised that I was having to expend considerable energy in keeping my prisoner up against the wall, because he was sagging badly. At the same moment, I also realised that he stank like a distillery. My suspected burglar was nothing more than a confirmed drunk.

'Come on, pal, try to stand up straight,' I said.

'Get your fuckin' hands off me,' slurred the drunk, and then suddenly, he stood upright, under his own steam. Relieved of the burden of his weight, I let go of him, and stepped back, and with that, he suddenly and unexpectedly punched me in the ear. I just stood there with my mouth hanging open, a sight which prompted the young man to firstly howl with laughter and secondly, to punch me in the ear again, same place, only harder. I let out a roar of rage and pain, and blocking his third excursion towards my ear with my left, flattened him with a right hook.

This was the sight that confronted Terry as he emerged from the rear of the tobacconists. He looked absolutely aghast, his worse fears confirmed and he cried, 'You lied! You lied!'

The whole story later emerged. This young man, whose name was Cyril Burton, lived in Brentwood, which is about 5 miles from Upminster. He had been taken by a friend to a party in Upminster and during the course of the evening, Cyril had had a monumental amount to drink. The friend had secured the attention of a delicious young lady and had wandered off with her into the night, there to pledge his love to her until the stars grew cold. Cyril, who was so smashed, was incapable of rhetoric anything like that of his friend and remained slumped in an armchair until the party finished and he was chucked out into the street. Knowing none of the other guests and having no knowledge of his where-abouts, Cyril wandered off through the darkened streets of Upminster. Suddenly realising that he would have to answer an urgent call of nature, Cyril decided to observe a modicum of decency and rather than spray the contents of his bursting bladder over the neat frontages of Argyle Gardens, he modestly retired to the rear of the tobacconist's premises. As the result of ten pints of bitter plus an unwise concoction of Babysham and sherry were voided, the tobacconist who lived in the flat above the shop awoke with a start as he heard Cyril's groans of pleasure. Pulling the net curtain carefully to one side, he saw the bulky form of Cyril in his back yard, and believing him to be about to break into the premises, he dialled 999. The result, of course, you know.

Cyril was charged with assaulting a police officer and at Havering Magistrates' Court, I saw him with his father who apologised profusely for his sons' unacceptable behaviour. Cyril had no previous convictions, but Mr Burton Senior was very concerned. 'I know that what he did was wrong, Mr Kirby,' he said, 'but do you think they'll put him in prison?'

'Don't worry,' I said, and winked. 'I'll put in a good word for him.' And I did. Cyril pleaded 'guilty' to the charge of assaulting me in front of the Chairman of the Magistrates. Gwilym Jones JP, had been a very useful Welsh rugby forward and was a stern magistrate who was also the possessor of a very nice twinkle in his eye. In addition, he was a staunch friend to the police.

'This was totally out of character, Your Worship,' I said. 'For my part, I don't think there's an ounce of malice in the lad. Drink got the better of him, which resulted in him lashing out in a couple of drunken blows.'

The Magistrates went into a quick huddle, and then Mr Jones addressed the prisoner. 'Now, look you,' he said. 'I don't approve of our policemen getting bashed about, see? And if Mr Kirby, here, hadn't spoken up for you, I'd have sent you to prison. Anyhow, taking every-thing into account, fined five pounds. Next case.'

As the defendant left the dock, one of the other lay Magistrates seemed to quietly express surprise to Mr Jones at the paucity of the fine which had been imposed. Probably due to his negligence in failing to wear a scrummage cap during his rugby days, Mr Jones' ears had received an unnecessary mauling which had resulted in him becoming slightly deaf. In the manner of many deaf people, he was therefore prone to speak a bit louder than necessary. I quite clearly heard him say, (as did the rest of the court) 'Ah, well, I know this officer, look you? And if the prisoner hadn't been well and truly sorted out before he got here, I'd be most surprised!'

Must have been speaking to Terry Johnson!

Rough Justice

I'd like to introduce you to Sheepface. I don't know his name. I call him that because he has a look of perpetual panic on his face, rather like a sheep that believes that an abattoir is awaiting it, right round the next corner. He's a Uniformed police officer whom I met at a party. His claim to fame is not that he's just vapid and gutless; it's that he's so politically correct, it oozes out of every pore. He hangs about, listening to other people's conversations, waiting for them to make a politically incorrect gaffe, no matter how small, so that he can take them to task about it and, if at all possible, grass the offender to a senior officer, in order that his own political correctness would never be in any doubt.

On the occasion that I met him, a group of us were chatting about the enormous technological advances that had been achieved in the last few years. 'It makes you wonder,' I was saying, 'how far we've all come. When I think about my Mum and Dad, they had the same old black and white television for years and years.' I was suddenly aware of flabby fingers tugging at my sleeve. It was Sheepface, his face all screwed-up with worried, genuine Social Worker-like concern. 'That last remark of yours,' he simpered softly, his eyes darting restlessly about the room to detect anybody else who might have overheard my racist slur. 'What I think you meant to say was 'monochrome T.V.' I took him to one side and told him terrible things, things so frightful that he backed away, his eyes wide with shock, desperately searching for someone of at least Chief Inspector rank, to whom I could be reported. Poor Sheepface. I didn't confide my views about criminals and their victims to him. If I had, he would truly have thought it was abattoir time.

You see, in practically all of the cases that I dealt with during my career, my sympathies went to the victim of the crime. But not always. If, for example a gang of yobs who were standing aimlessly on a street corner decided to abuse a married couple walking by; if they used all sorts of filthy language to the wife and jeered at the husband, because they thought that they were strong enough in numbers to get away with it; and if the husband took exception to this sort of anti-social behaviour and gave the ringleader a dig in the face, I would take a pretty dim view of things if the yob made a whining complaint to me. I would take exception because here was someone who had chosen to live outside the law, yet wanted to make use of it once he'd received no more than his just come-uppance. I would normally have a word with this type of whining bully and seldom did a prosecution follow. The story that follows depicts that sort of unfair situation where for once, I failed to achieve my initial object; but then again, there's is always more than one way to skin a cat...

I was called to the station's charge room where I saw Mrs Ward. She was there because she had been caught red-handed, stealing a small joint of meat from a supermarket. She was in a complete state of shock and in floods of tears - it was the first time in her life that she'd had any sort of contact with the police, let alone being in a charge room - and she was immeasurably distressed. Standing nearby with a disagreeable smirk on his face was Mr Purvis, the supermarket manager who had been responsible for Mrs Ward's detention. I sat down with Mrs Ward, brought her a soothing cup of tea and had a long chat with her, during which I found out all about her family circumstances and the events leading up to her arrest. I gently suggested that taking the joint might have been some sort of unfortunate mix-up but Mrs Ward was having none of it. No, she had deliberately taken the joint, she told me, because her money had run out and she didn't see how she'd be able to have anything to eat on Sunday. Mrs Ward had never told a lie in her life and wasn't going to start now. I left Mrs Ward with another cup of well-sugared tea and went over to have a quiet word with the store manager. Purvis was an unattractive being. Short, stout and bombastic with a ruddy complexion, he had one of those little turned-up moustaches which cry out to be pulled. I suggested that taking Mrs Ward to court might not be the best way of dealing with matters and I tried to explain to him Mrs Ward's plight which had driven her to this course of action but this self-righteous little pratt was adamant. Theft was theft, he informed me and his store took a very strong line on shoplifters. Didn't I know how much shoplifters cost the retail industry per annum? he demanded. Well... no, I didn't. I knew about receivers and rapists and murderers - but this lady who, until now, had lived a blameless life and was too ignorant or too proud to ask for any sort of supplementary benefit from a Government who paid her the pittance of a pension did not fall into any sort of category in my world of criminality - unless it was that of victim.

And the more I tried to delicately manoeuvre Purvis into forgetting the charge, the more this obstinate little beast dug his heels in. Eventually, I gave up and told Purvis to sign the charge sheet and to be at court the following morning to prosecute the case, to which he grudgingly agreed. I had already half-worked out the blueprint of revenge against Purvis and by the following morning, my plan was fully consolidated and up and running.

The next day, the still-shaken Mrs Ward appeared at the local Magistrates' Court and insisted on pleading guilty. Purvis turned up as well and pompously informed me that an adjournment would have to be sought, since head office had insisted upon legal representation for the company. A lady once told me that in moments of great cunning, I displayed the smile of an Alsatian. This was the toothy, wolfish and totally insincere smile that I now turned on Purvis. 'Please don't concern yourself,' I smiled. 'The old lady's pleading guilty. Just leave it to me. I'll outline all of the facts to the Magistrate and we'll be out of here in no time. Just take a seat in court.' I patted him reassuringly on the shoulder and walked into court. As Purvis sat down, I registered the same sort of grim satisfaction that a famished lion must have felt as it stepped from its cage into a Roman Amphitheatre to observe that the *plat du jour* was a gaggle of tubby Christians. Watch out, Purvis, I thought. The bench of Lay Magistrates were a friendly bunch, all known to me. I stepped into the witness box and respectfully asked for summary trial and that the charge be put to the defendant. In a voice quivering with emotion, poor Mrs Ward pleaded guilty. 'The facts, please, officer,' said the Clerk of the Court, in a bored voice. After all, this was only a nuisance shoplifter.

I smoothed down the front of my lucky pin-stripe suit, well-known for it's non-threatening qualities and bowed slightly at the chairman. Mrs Travis-Jones was a Magistrate known for her unequivocal backing of the police and one who could be quite ruthless in any criticism of them. 'Madam,' I said, 'in giving you the facts of this case, I should like to preface my remarks by telling you that this case represents a tragic milestone in this court's quest for justice and it is quite the saddest case that it has ever been my misfortune to deal with.'

At that, there was a rustling of paper from the Press bench as the local reporters perked up, their notebooks at a fresh page, their pencils standing to attention. Mrs Travis-Jones gave me a searching look. 'Do go on, Sergeant Kirby,' she said, quietly. Don't you worry, Dear Lady, I thought. That's just what I'm going to do.

'The defendant, Mrs Ward, has pleaded guilty to an offence of shoplifting,' I said, 'an offence, which I know is usually dealt with by these courts, by means of condign punishment. But as your Worships are aware,' I continued, 'not everything is depicted in black and white and if ever an eventuality existed where that was so, it is surely the case with this defendant.'

I stopped to take a sip of water because a pause is always beneficial at such a juncture to a story. 'Mrs Ward is 73 years of age, Your Worship.' I continued. 'She is therefore in receipt of a state pension which, as you will be aware is not unduly generous and she also receives a considerably smaller pension from the Ford Motor Company, since Mrs Ward's late husband was employed by that company, until his unfortunate death, some 12 years ago. Since then she has scrimped and saved, to make ends meet - and of her two children, since one predeceased her husband in a tragic road accident and the other lives in Canada, Your Worships will understand that she is quite alone in this world.'

Time for another pause, a slight clearing of the throat and a quick look round the court. The Court Reporters were scribbling furiously into their notebooks. Jolly good.

'Yesterday, Madam,' I went on, 'Mrs Ward went to Boggins Supermarket in the High Street. In fact, she should not have gone out at all - Your Worships will readily recall what a bitterly cold day it was - and added to which, Mrs Ward had barely recovered from an attack of shingles, an affliction which, I am reliably informed, is an extremely painful condition.' Out of the corner of my eye, I could see the third Magistrate nod knowingly. Obviously, a fellow sufferer. 'Mrs Ward chose her groceries for an entire week, which cost her £17.39. I know that, Madam,' I added, 'because I checked the till roll - just as I know that upon her arrest, Mrs Ward had just eight pence left in her purse - not even enough for the bus ride home - home, nearly two miles walk away in conditions that the BBC's weatherman described last night as being atrocious.' 'Oh, but excuse me, Sergeant Kirby,' interrupted Mrs Travis-Jones. 'It is only a small point, but because of her age, the defendant would not have had to pay her bus fare; she would have used her bus pass.' 'She certainly would have done so, had she possessed a bus pass, Madam,' I explained. 'Mrs Ward was aware of the existence of bus passes for the elderly but was unaware that they have to be applied for. She was under the misapprehension that bus passes were distributed at the same time as the state pension. When she did not receive one, she was under the impression that, for some reason, she was ineligible.' 'I see,' said Mrs Travis-Jones, nodding thoughtfully. She made a small note on a pad in front of her. 'Do go on.'

Time for another little sip of water. 'In a moment of foolishness, of panic and, you may think, Madam, of desperation,' I said, 'Mrs Ward realised that she did not have enough money for a meal on Sunday and, in an act that she will regret to her dying day, committed the only dishonest action of her long and blameless life - for I have already mentioned, I believe Madam, that Mrs Ward is a lady of unblemished character - and took a small joint of beef, valued at £1.37 from the counter and slipped it under her coat.'

Now that I'd mentioned the dirty deed, it was time for another little pause. 'This act of desperation did not go unnoticed,' I continued, 'because she came under the vigilant eye of the Store manager, Mr Purvis. He followed her around the store for another 20 minutes, whilst Mrs Ward struggled between her conscience and hunger and before she went through the check-out, she scrupulously paid for all of the other goods. It was then that Mr Purvis pounced.' I underlined my usage of the word 'pounced' by firmly smacking the flat of my hand down on the edge of the witness box - a bit theatrical, perhaps, but it had the desired effect, by causing the Magistrates to start. 'At the Police Station, Mrs Ward immediately confessed her guilt, as indeed she has done today,' I continued, 'but having ascertained the full facts of the case, the same facts that I have presented to Your Worships, I sought, rightly or wrongly to suggest to Mr Purvis that there might be an alternative way to deal with this matter, other than prosecution.'

At this point, I paused to take my third and last sip of water and also to take a covert look at the Bench. To my delight, all three of them were nodding in agreement. 'For there are alternatives to prosecution, as you are well aware, Madam,' I said, speaking directly to Mrs Travis-Jones. 'A police caution under the auspices of the Attorney-General's Guidelines, perhaps.' Again, the nod of assent. 'A stern telling-off would certainly have done the trick,' I continued, 'but perhaps, in a case like this, given Mrs Ward's circumstances, which I endeavoured unsuccessfully to explain to Mr Purvis, perhaps justice could best have been served with the help of a little Christian charity?' At this, the Clerk of the Court gave a snort of derision, thinking that I was trowelling it on a bit thick, but nobody heard him, since Mrs Ward was sobbing loudly and I saw the third Magistrate surreptitiously wipe her eye.

'Unfortunately for Mrs Ward,' I continued, 'Mr Purvis was quite adamant that she should be prosecuted and he reminded me, quite properly of the significant amount that shoplifters cost the retail industry which, I know, is considerable. He feels that the law is the law and it must be upheld.' It was coming up to *coup de grace* time. 'As it was 6 months ago,' I added, 'when the Environmental Health successfully prosecuted Boggins Supermarket after an inordinate amount of mice droppings were found in the kitchen area.' Mrs Travis-Jones nodded slowly. She had not personally dealt with the case, but she certainly recalled it. I now looked directly at Mrs Travis-Jones and continued hesitantly, 'It's just that... well, I...' and I stopped and averted my gaze from her eyes. 'What is it, Sergeant Kirby?' she said, softly.

I raised my eyes to hers again and spoke as though the words were being dragged from me. 'It's just that I felt a sense of disappointment that Mr Purvis appeared to be taking such a malevolent delight from the situation,' I said. I heard an angry gasp from my left and I did not have to turn my head to know that it had come from Purvis. Mrs Travis-Jones' lips compressed into a thin line. 'I see,' she said, grimly.

'In fact, Madam,' I said, 'Mr Purvis has turned up at court, this morning,' and I waved a negligent arm in his direction. 'He may wish to apply for compensation,' I added carelessly. 'What!' gasped Mrs Travis-Jones. I shrugged my shoulders, as if to say, 'but what can I do?'

Purvis cut a wretched figure as he struggled to his feet. 'I - I didn't... I wouldn't...' he stammered. 'Sit down!' snapped Mrs Travis-Jones, furiously.

Discharging Mrs Ward absolutely for the offence, the Bench warmly congratulated me for the humane way in which I had presented the facts. 'All rise!' shouted the Clerk of the Court, giving me a knowing, resentful look and as the bench got to their feet and turned to leave the court, I could hear Mrs Travis-Jones muttering angrily to one of the other Magistrates about 'that filthy little shopkeeper.'

I said goodbye to Mrs Ward and left her in the care of a sympathetic neighbour and a representative from Social Services whom I had telephoned and who agreed with me that there were several more benefits that Mrs Ward was fully entitled to. As I walked across the court, one of the reporters clapped me on the back. 'Best human interest story I've had in weeks!' he chortled. 'I'll be in the King's Head at lunchtime - cheerio!' A passing Probation Officer, blinking mistily, patted my hand.

And as I walked into the foyer of the Court, there was Purvis, his normally ruddy complexion chalk-white with fury. 'You haven't heard the last of this!' he shouted.

'Nor have you, Pal,' I replied cheerfully, as I put a comforting arm around his chubby shoulders. 'Just think of all the free publicity I've given to you and your lovely store!'

Rock Bottom

'It's the three Ps you want to watch out for,' portentously stated the old Sergeant Instructor at Peel House, the Metropolitan Police Training School, to me and the other recruits. 'Prisoners, property and prostitutes,' he gloomily added, by way of explanation. 'More coppers get into trouble over the three bleedin' Ps, than anything else.'

Leaving aside the unnecessary pun about a pint usually ending with a 'P' rather than starting with one, the old instructor could certainly have included *that* pit-fall in his homily. So many Coppers have come a tumble due to having taken of a glass too many, as in the case of Steve Williams, who, besides being a Detective Sergeant at Stoke Newington Police Station, was also the proud possessor of an enormous drink problem.

Following a ferocious drinking session, Steve unsteadily weaved his way home, arriving there at 3am. Spilling out of his car, he crawled into his house, surprising his estranged wife's wire-haired Dachshund, who was named Harold. The dog was a disagreeable creature, due, in part to its slipped discs, to which this breed is predisposed, but also because

Harold possessed a thoroughly tiresome disposition. Alarmed at the stumbling intruder, Harold smartly bit Steve in the calf. Slumping on to the stairs, Steve slept there solidly for the next two hours. Dehydration forced him into a state of semi-consciousness at 5am and Steve crawled up the stairs to his bedroom, sporting a large damp patch on his back, courtesy of Harold, who had contemptuously and copiously urinated on him in a fit of pique.

Falling face down, fully clothed, into bed, Steve had accomplished his objective and had finally reached rock-bottom.

At 8 o'clock, he was awakened by a repeated knocking at his front door. Getting out of bed and blearily feeling his way down the stairs, Steve hoped that he would open his door to the Grim Reaper, who would lay a seductive hand on his shoulder and lead him away to oblivion.

Instead, he found himself confronted by Albert Dale, his next-door neighbour. 'Good morning, Mr Williams,' said his neighbour, and coming straight to the point, continued, 'were you by any chance drinking, last night?'

In common with many others who are similarly afflicted, Steve was just a tad sensitive about his problem. 'How dare you!' he snapped, and swiftly rallying his thoughts, repeated in more strident tones, 'How dare you!' He then proceeded to give Mr Dale a terrific dressing down, the subject matter of which included incivility, abruptness, rudeness and insensitivity. For five minutes, this furious, one-side tirade raged. It was a pretty impressive performance. For a man, seemingly so close to death, Steve's style was brilliant. 'And anyway,' he concluded to his, by now, thoroughly abashed neighbour, 'how on earth did you reach this ridiculous assumption that I was drinking last night?'

'I'm sorry,' humbly replied Mr Dale. 'It's just that your car's parked in the middle of my front lawn!'

The Turkey that Flew

Serious crime seemed to have taken a vacation during the run-up to Christmas 1975, so the Squad of which I was a member, which was tasked with battling the providers of serious crime, decided that we could do with a break, ourselves.

Informing a friendly wholesaler that he would shortly be receiving both a visit and a substantial order, one of our members was dispatched with a large van and we settled down for a glass or two of Christmas cheer.

Later that afternoon, the officer returned, the van bulging with the slaughtered remains of erstwhile inhabitants of the farmyard and claiming our Christmas dinners, we went our respective ways.

Detective Constable Trevor Bayliss had celebrated rather too well, and picking up his turkey, he commenced his unsteady journey home.

Upon the third attempt, Trevor actually managed to insert the key into his front-door lock and let himself into the house. Staggering slightly, he made for the kitchen, clutching his prize. Pleased with himself for reaching the kitchen area without mishap, he paused, still with the turkey clasped to his breast, and leant against the door frame and closed his eyes.

This was how his wife discovered him a few minutes later, with a dressed turkey staining the front of his crumpled raincoat. She also noticed that Trevor was dishevelled, very drunk and fast asleep, in an upright position.

'Trevor!' she shouted, furiously.

'What?' gasped Trevor, coming instantly awake but quite confused as to how he could have been asleep standing up and holding a large, wet football against his chest. This unlikely combination so unnerved him that he tightened his grip and the turkey plopped out of his arms. Making a graceful arc through the air, the bird hit the kitchen floor with such force that the giblets burst out of the turkey's neck, rather like a shot from a cannon, and skidded across the floor.

Mrs Bayliss looked with horror and disgust at the gruesome mess glistening on her once spotless, tiled floor. Trevor also looked down, by now totally bemused.

'Have I just been sick?' he muttered, nervously.

'No!' snapped his fuming wife.

'Oh, well, ' said Trevor, feeling quite relieved, 'better freeze it, then!'

Ah, Sweet Mystery

The pitfalls of the three Ps, the injudicious drink too many, the Police Discipline Code that covers every eventuality between being born and dying, the armies of 'civvies' who decide the destiny of so many police officers, the omnipresent danger on the streets... Dear God, what other perils are there, in which cavalier police officers can ensnare themselves? Well, the answer is, plenty. Apart from Piss-ups, add Poking.

I read an article some years ago, which stated that the most prolific band of adulterers, after dentists, were police officers. It wasn't so long ago that 'consorting with a woman, not your wife,' was an absolute sacking offence, but did this curtail the goatish activities of so many police officers? Not a bit of it. It only made them more cunning.

Detective Constable Peter Newall secretly dreamed of the day when he would captain the Metropolitan Police Shagging Team. Until such a worthwhile organisation was actually formed, however, he resolved to put in as much training as possible. His practice was, to a certain extent, restricted because Peter (no fool he) thought it a prudent move to keep his aspirations secret from his wife.

Spending an exhausting evening cavorting with the accommodating wife of a much-hated night-duty Traffic Patrol Officer, Peter had suddenly realised the lateness of the hour, and pledging affection to his inamorata until the stars grew cold, he beat a hasty retreat towards Maison Newell. Creeping into the house at 3.30am, he silently padded upstairs and into the connubial bedroom, with the dexterity of a Commando on a night training exercise. The next move was to slip out of his clothes, and with a skill perfected over years of training, slide noise-lessly into bed, beside his slumbering wife. But with the cunning sixth-sense of many a wife who possesses a faithless husband, and before Peter could even start to unbutton his jacket, his wife snapped the bedside tablelamp on, and looking quite terrible in curlers and cold-cream, sat bolt upright in bed. Guessing, quite correctly, that her husband had returned home, fresh from the loins of another, Mrs Newell launched a blistering broadside. 'Bastard!' she shrieked. 'You've been out with some little tart, haven't you! Bloody well answer me, you dirty pig!'

Now, Peter knew that great cunning would be needed here. Several options of dealing with this distressing matter lay open to him and, in a split-second, he decided to go for the all-out riposte, a daring gambit much admired by the most seasoned of fornicators.

'Right, you bitch, you can shut your trap double-quick,' he snapped, and as this had the desired effect, he continued sternly, 'because I've had a hell of a tour of duty and the last thing I want to come home to at half-past three in the morning is you, screaming like some bloody fishwife!'

He unbuttoned his jacket and shrugged his shoulders out of it, throwing it more or less tidily on to the bedroom's reproduction Queen Anne chair. 'Been out with some little tart, have I?' He shook his head slowly. 'Well, thanks a bloody bundle! Want to know what I've really been doing?' he inquired, as he started to loosen his tie.

'Well?' demanded his simmering wife.

'We were called to a house, after a neighbour had seen some masked intruders break into this old age pensioners home,' Peter coolly explained, pulling his tie off and laying it on top of his discarded jacket. 'Just as we got round there, the gang was coming out, holding all the old lady's prized possessions,' he continued, unbuttoning his shirt. 'I don't mind telling you, the thought of those slags terrorising some old lady made my blood boil,' he said, quietly, as he undid his cuffs, 'and I just got stuck into one of them. We had a terrific tussle and we fell into a rose-bush, and that... ' stripping off his shirt, and half-turning, 'is how I got these scratches on my back.'

Had a band of fellow adulterers been present, they would have gasped with admiration at Peter's daring strategy. It was the sort of stuff that Military Crosses are made of, only to be attempted by the most skilled of philanderers with complete disregard for their own safety. But Peter knew that this was no time for half-measures. Fully aware of his wife's propensity for violence, he knew that acceptance of this alibi would mean the difference between waking up to breakfast in bed or discovering that a boning knife had been thrust into his eye. Nonchalantly turning his head, Peter glanced in the bedroom mirror to see if disbelief was displayed under his wife's cold-cream but the fact that this audacious disclosure had passed without change of expression or comment from his wife, emboldened him even more. 'So there was the team all nicked,' he explained, casually, 'and I went straight into the house, and found the old lady. Tied her up, those slags had,' he added, as he unzipped his trousers. 'Nice old girl, she was. A bit like your mum.'

His wife frowned. 'Was she alright?' she inquired. Many an amateur would have breathed an audible sigh of relief at this point, but not Peter, who was made of sterner stuff. Weakness at this point would be catastrophic. 'Well, she was after I found her heart pills and made her a cup of tea,' he replied, as he stepped out of his trousers. 'Anyway, don't expect to see it in the papers,' he added, as an afterthought. 'The old lady was most insistent that there should be no publicity. Mind you,' he added, as he put his thumbs inside his underpants and pulled them down, 'she did say that she'd like to show her appreciation in some way.'

'Really,' replied his wife coldly, as she regarded his naked body. Pointing to the used contraceptive that still adorned his manhood, she added icily, 'perhaps she could make a start by taking *that* off you.'

The Complaining Complainer

Having nothing better to do whilst I was waiting for my case to be called at the Bailey, I fell into conversation with a very junior female barrister. Very pretty she looked, too, in her pristine wig and gown. My enthusiasm started to wane a little, when I saw her feet were encased in black ankle socks and plimsolls. It was churlish of me to immediately categorise her as being a gobby, self-opinionated lefty, because this is a failing of mine. Mind you, on this occasion, I wasn't far wrong. She saw this offer of social intercourse as a heaven-sent opportunity to deliver her rock-solid conviction that all of the complaints levelled against the police (which are investigated by the police themselves) are white-washed.

Speaking from bitter personal experience, I was able, very patiently, to explain to her that every complaint alleging police misconduct is looked at, not only at face value, but also very seriously indeed. Therefore, if, for the sake of example, allegations of blackmail, attempting to pervert the course of public justice and buggering badgers were made against a police officer, every facet of the complaint would be scrupulously investigated, until months (and on many occasions, years) later, the investigating officer would be able to inform the officer concerned, that which the officer himself knew from the outset - that there was not one scrap of evidence, credible or otherwise, to support these allegations.

I recall a classic investigation where an allegation of rape had been made against a fellow-officer, by a wretched inhabitant of a 'half-way house' - a refuge for women, usually complete with their ghastly offspring who, either intentionally or through sheer bad luck, had been made homeless. I, and everybody else, knew that she had been put up to this scurrilous trick by a local villain who was on bail to this officer and by discrediting him, hoped to walk free from court. This allegation was meticulously investigated over a period of weeks by the complaints team.

Eventually, this abominable slut was brought in to see the investigators who told her that there was no substance whatsoever in her complaint because at the time of the alleged offence, it had been established by a large number of independent witnesses that the officer had been engaged in an enquiry in Nottingham. Her stunned silence lasted only a few seconds before a look of pure cunning crossed her face and she stated, 'Orl right. The week before, 'e done me gas meter!' And this allegation was then investigated with the same meticulous care, as had the previous pack of lies. However... if it had been established from the investigation that the officer had been responsible for neglect of duty, in that on the day in question, he had overlooked putting an entry in the Book 66, when booking out the CID car, to race to the scene of an armed hold-up - then for that offence, he would be reported to see if a disciplinary board should be convened... it is something, I'm sorry to say, that happens all too often.

'Oh!' exclaimed the black-socked Counsel. 'Well, that's alright, then!'

I won't bother you with my reply. I should think that you've correctly guessed that it was both profane and dismissive.

What follows is a tiresome little story and I wasn't going to weary you with it, but I do so because, it's been my experience, that if you do someone a wrong'un, they'll thank you from the bottom of their hearts, and pour Scotch down your throat, as though there's no tomorrow. Try to do them a good turn, and before you know it, they're up your arse.

I was the solitary CID officer in the office at Forest Gate Police Station. It was 6.30pm, and I was supposed to have finished my tour of duty at 5pm, but I had discovered that I could profitably use the hours between 5pm and 7pm to try to whittle down the huge pile of paperwork that I had amassed. Should any work come in during that time, I could convincingly argue that this should be dealt with by the late-turn CID. It was something that some of us did on a regular basis and it was certainly not discouraged by the senior management - well, not until we started getting paid for overtime, when, all of a sudden, our health and well-being became a matter of grave importance to them.

The tips of my fingers were starting to throb from my efforts at typing as I tried to try to get on top of my paperwork, in order that I could get out and arrest more thieves when suddenly the telephone rang. It was the Uniform Duty Officer. 'Can you come down, Dick?' he asked.

'Jesus Christ. What for?' was my dismayed reply, staring at the mountain of paperwork in front of me.

'There's a fella down here, wants some advice from a CID officer. Could be interesting...' said the Duty Officer.

I went downstairs, and spoke to the plump, non-descript middle-aged man who stood at the counter of the front office. Worry was etched into every line of Robert Worricker's face. He came straight to the point. His son, Kevin, he stated, he felt sure, was using drugs.

When I asked Mr Worricker how he had come to this conclusion, he gave all the answers which made me feel that he could be quite right in his assumption.

'But what do you want me to do about it?' I asked. 'If I come round to your house, search his bedroom and find drugs, I'm bound to arrest him, you must know that. Is that what you want?'

'Oh, no,' replied the anxious Mr Worricker. What he wanted to do, was to bring the boy to the Police Station and have me talk to him. Nowadays, the thought of counselling someone about their drug-related problems, would bring cries of delight from many members of our loving, caring Police Service, but not me, not then.

'Look,' I said, 'if you bring him round here, and he says, "Yes, I smoked a pound of cannabis yesterday" there's not much I can do about it. Equally, if he doesn't admit it, he could tell me to "Fuck off". And that's not a course of action to be encouraged. So...' I shrugged my shoulders.

'Oh, please!' begged the distraught Dad, and went on to tell me all about his invalid wife and how worried she was about her son's activities, and how upset the rest of the family was, and how he was losing sleep, and... In the end, just to shut him up and get rid of him, and also, because I was beginning to feel compassion for this put-upon family with their cannabis-puffing son, I agreed.

'Bring him in on Friday at 7pm,' I said. 'But listen! You've got to leave this to me. It may get a little rough, but if I can straighten out your boy, I will.'

'Yes, yes,' gabbled Mr Worricker, all but kissing my hand. 'Anything you say, officer. Friday, 7 o'clock, and thank you, officer, thank you, my wife, she'll be so pleased!' And off he went, nearly beside himself with glee.

Just before 7pm on Friday, I sat by myself, smoking a cigarette and considering this family dilemma. This little shit, I thought, with his anti-social habits, is destroying a family. I thought of the invalid Mrs Worricker in her wheelchair, the other children trying to understand the changes in their brother's behaviour, the desperate father trying to keep a family together that was fast coming apart at the seams. 'You rotten, selfish little bugger,' I thought.

And just then, in came father and son. 'This is my son, officer,' said Mr Worricker, quite unnecessarily. The acned, gaunt, long-haired 17-year-old, Kevin, stared defiantly at me.

'Right, let's get this straight!' I shouted, pointing a rigid forefinger in the direction of the pimply lad's left nostril, and making father and son jump 18 inches backwards. 'You've been smoking cannabis, no, don't fucking deny it! What do you think you're doing to your Mum, her in her wheelchair, you little shit!' and much more of the same, very forcibly put, over the next ten minutes.

At the end of my tirade, a suitably chastened son left with his father. And that, I thought, was that. The CID, being full of coincidences, proved me wrong.

Months later, my pal, Detective Constable Peter Connor who had nicked Kevin for a series of cheque frauds, had successfully turned him into an informant and, miles off our manor, the three of us sat down in a safe pub and had a quiet drink.

'Do you know, Mr Kirby,' said this erstwhile junkie, 'that first time I met you, and you had a go at me - remember? I thought, 'What a bastard'. But you were right, Mr Kirby. I was smoking cannabis, but what you said made sense, and I kicked the habit. It was all down to you,' he added.

I raised my glass and saluted him. 'Good for you,' I replied, 'and give my best to your Dad.'

'No, he was the trouble,' he continued. 'He was going to make an official complaint against you, after the way you spoke to me!'

'He What!' I gasped. 'You're joking!'

'No, honestly, Mr Kirby,' earnestly replied Kevin. 'First of all he was going to make a complaint, then he wasn't, then he was - and in the end he didn't, but things were so shaky by then, that I gave my stash to my Mum to get rid of and she smoked the bloody lot!'

Take Your Pick!

After the Second World War, there existed a breed of detective who lasted right up until I was a detective myself. On the plus side, they were rough and tough, knew how to make the villains toe the line and knew police work inside out. The reason why this desirable state of affairs existed was two-fold. Firstly, during their careers, legislation had altered very little. Judges Rules had been formed in 1912 and 1918 and these were the rules of evidence that police officers adhered to. It was clear to all working police officers what was right and what was wrong in dealing with suspects. The Larceny Act had existed since 1916 and the Vagrancy Act of 1824 showed how to deal (albeit in somewhat archaic language) with 'suspected persons, loitering with intent to commit a felony.' The Firearms Act had been updated in 1937 but that, and the Criminal Justice Acts of 1948 & 1961 had not altered the detectives workload by any considerable degree.

Compare that to recent years where legislation and police policies have been altered, updated, revised or abandoned as often as most folk change their socks, in an almost indecent haste to pacify whining minority groups who object to just about everything that the police do. Secondly, when a police officer was admitted to the Criminal Investigation Department, he was in it for life. If he took promotion, his promotion was within the CID. His whole world was that of crime and although some diversified and became adept at investigating fraud, drugs, robberies etc., they were still detectives committed to combating crime. The only time that they were returned to uniform duties was if their supervising officers felt that they no longer retained their trust or if the person concerned felt that he wished to pursue his or her career in uniform and volunteered to go back.

It was only when Sir Robert Mark started the contentious policy of 'interchange' that things began to go badly wrong - this was exacerbated in the 80s & 90s when people of all ranks were encouraged to flit backwards and forwards in and out of uniform; and when in the past few years the 'tenure' policy was brought in to allow officers to stay in a specialised department for only a certain period of time, the CID collapsed and I believe it will be years before fully trained detectives police the capital again. So these old-time tecs knew the villains of their manor, they knew the law, were difficult to fool and could hear a fiver being dropped onto a blanket at a distance of five miles or detect a bottle of scotch being opened at a distance of ten. Mind you, on the debit side, some of them were pretty crooked. Detective Sergeant Joe 'The Duke' Collins (so called, because of his immaculate attire and manners) used to take a 'pension' every week from the stallholders in Rathbone Street market, East London. Of course, in those austere times, money was somewhat tight, which prompted Hymie Goldblum, one of the afflicted stallholders, to rebel against The Duke's unofficial excise. Hymie issued terse instructions to his spouse. 'Listen!' said Hymie. 'When Mr Collins comes for his pension, tell him I've fucked off with some shiksa, you don't know where I've gone, and above all, you ain't got no dough!' And having delivered this steely adieu to his nearest and dearest, Hymie made a speedy departure.

There was little to disturb the tranquillity of that autumn afternoon. The drowsy hum of the bluebottles, hovering over the wares displayed on the nearby fishmonger's stall, the soft hiss of the No. 565 trollybus as it trundled past, towards the East India Docks, en route to its final destination at Holborn Circus. Until, that is, a little later, when a shadow fell across Rose Goldblum as she worked industriously at the stall. She looked up, and saw, with considerable trepidation, the swarthy face of 'Duke' Collins, his fedora at a jaunty angle, his vicuna overcoat slung negligently over his shoulders. Immediately, Rose went into her rehearsed monologue.

'Oh, Mr Collins,' she cried. 'Hymie's fucked off with some shiksa! Oy! Who can say where he's gone? And what's more, *there ain't no dough!*'

The Duke stood there, slowly taking in the interior of the stall, seeing everything, missing nothing. And then, his very sharp eyes settled on Rose Goldblum and, stroking his small Ronald Colman moustache, he uttered one of the classic remarks of all time.

'Madam,' he said politely. 'I perceive that you have rings upon your fingers!'

Ah, naughty Duke! And there were others like him. I'm not trying to excuse The Duke or his kind, and it's a very good thing that we're rid of people like that in the police. But the tearaways did know exactly where they stood with the old-time detectives. Just let me give you an example.

Detective Constable Jim West was a real tough character from the East-End. He resolved to do something fairly dramatic in respect of a gang of toughs who were running wild, frightening shopkeepers and terrifying the old-age pensioners of the area with their despicable behaviour.

Jim pulled a dozen of these prime examples of pond life into Dalston

Police Station, on the pretext of them taking part in an identity parade. 'Just wait there, boys,' he called, genially, as he walked out of the charge room, leaving them standing there. Jim returned a few moments later, carrying a large, obviously heavy box, which he dumped on the charge room desk.

The box contained the most frightful selection of offensive weapons in the entire universe.

'O.K. lads,' said Jim, breathing a little heavily from his exertions, and waving a generous hand in the direction of the box. 'Help yourself - just one each, no more.'

A stunned silence met Jim's monstrous proposal. Nobody spoke or even moved. 'Come on,' said Jim, impatiently. 'I ain't got all night!'

Eventually, the tearaways' spokesman found his voice. 'You must be mad!' he expostulated. 'We ain't having none of those!'

'Well,' said Jim, thoughtfully, 'you'd fucking better. You see, there's a loaded shooter down the bottom, and the last one in, gets it!'

During the ensuing, feverish scramble, two of the gang members actually had a fight concerning the ownership of a meat cleaver.

Not only did every single one of them plead guilty to possessing offensive weapons, but now that Jim had waved the big stick at them, their behaviour changed dramatically and their unpleasant habits were seen in Dalston no more.

Could this happen today? No, it couldn't. Tough old tecs like Jim West have no place whatsoever in today's society.

Because, you see, if they did, crime would come spiralling downwards, the tearaways, instead of being cosseted by mealy-mouthed Social Workers, slimy solicitors and militant action groups, would be too terrified of putting a foot wrong, and decent, hard-working men and women would be able to walk the streets in comparative safety.

And that, of course, would never do.

The Frustrated Bricklayer

Robbery, in its simplest form, is stealing, and at the time of doing so and in order to do so, putting a person in fear of being then and there subjected to violence. It is a tremendously serious offence and despite any jokey references which might be made about it on some of the more gormless television programmes, don't let anybody tell you different. Robbery is punishable on indictment (as is attempted robbery, conspiracy to rob and assault with intent to rob) with a maximum of Life Imprisonment.

When robbers confess their crimes, they always do their best to minimise their role. I have seldom known different. They'll tell you that they were driving the car, that they were only the look-out or that the gun which they had wasn't a real one. Whoever was beastly to the victims, it certainly wasn't them. If they are placed in a position where the evidence irrevocably puts them holding a gun at the scene of the robbery, still they seek to portray themselves in the most favourable light. They will tell you that they merely strolled into the building society and said in a pleasant but no-nonsense voice, 'All right, love, just put the money in the bag. I ain't going to hurt you. Now come on, be sensible.'

Just to put the record straight, robbers don't behave like that. The concept of robbery is surprise, disorientation and terror in that order with gratuitous violence as an acceptable option. So what happens is that a group of shoppers, tradesmen and old-age pensioners are waiting to be served in a building society when all of a sudden the door bursts open and in rush two or three bulky masked men, brandishing shotguns. They are bulky, firstly because of their physical size and secondly because they have a fresh set of clothing on underneath their 'working clothes' so that afterwards, they can strip off the outer layer of their garments and thus facilitate their escape. Whether the sawn-offs are used or not, I have never known a time when they have not been loaded. Invariably, a shot is discharged into the ceiling and the terrific noise in this confined space plus the crashing of the falling plaster freezes customers and counter-staff alike.

The demand is then made for the money but also it is often accompanied by irrational and contradictory screamed commands - 'Shuddup!' 'Siddown!' 'Don't look at me!' 'Stand up!' and all of this is done to terrify and disorientate the victims. The first of the standard operating procedures used by the Second World War Special Air Service when they burst into a German Mess Room was to shoot the first man who moved, whether he was hostile or not. This was because he had recovered from the shock and had started to think for himself. The second was to shoot the man closest to you since he was likeliest to cause the most trouble. Although shooting victims is still mercifully rare in this country, the same principal applies to robbers because anybody - pensioner, housewife or child - who looks as though they will present the slightest challenge to the robbers is in grave danger of getting a savage beating. At the very least, shoving the business end of a sawn-off shotgun into a customer's mouth is regarded as a suitably cautionary warning for the rest of the victims.

I've seen victims of robbery all through my service, hundreds of them and never more so than when I served on the Flying Squad. These would be ordinary, decent folk who were subjected to minutes or sometimes even hours of pure, concentrated terror and it took many of them months, often years, to recover from the shock. Some, I know, never did.

A family was taken hostage and held, overnight in their own home by a gang of thugs who threatened them at gun-point and tied them up. The following morning, the father was taken by two of the gang to a security company where he was the custodian. They strapped a very convincing imitation bomb to him and he was ordered by the gang, who controlled his movements using a remote control device, to open the vaults. Any attempt to unfasten the belt or to warn his workmates, they told him, would result in the bomb's immediate detonation. Thus they were able to steal £480,000, which represented a very nice three-way split.

A three-way split of a different kind was experienced by the family who had been taken hostage. The daughter eventually managed to come to terms with her trauma with the help of a Victim Support Group; in fact, she later formed her own group, which was highly successful. However, the wife of the custodian was so profoundly shocked that she was unable to provide the police with a witness statement and she later died, never having spoken one word about the events of that night. Shortly afterwards, the custodian also died, his daughter convinced that the shock of the attack had considerably shortened his life. I do not doubt for one second that she was right.

The undoubtably reformed criminal, Francis Davidson 'Mad Frankie' Fraser once described receiving a flogging in prison as 'having the bollocks knocked out of you.' I should think that's just how robbery victims feel. Mind you, this often works both ways. One of the more spectacular Flying Squad duties is a piece of pro-active policing, known as 'The Pavement Job'. This is no more than a sophisticated ambush. It occurs when the Squad receive information regarding the time and location of a robbery. The area is staked out by Flying Squad and often Firearms Unit officers, secreting themselves in all manner of hiding places. And then, hopefully, just as the robbers are about to attack, the

Flying Squad get in first and nab them. Now, although Squadmen have to move very quickly indeed on an ambush, they are assisted to a certain degree by the robbers themselves. You see, whilst they are preparing to attack the prize, many professional robbers act in a very professional way indeed. If a bank is going to be attacked at 9.30 in the morning, they will often show up at 4am to 'walk the plot' to ensure that there is no possibility of an ambush. They will drive around and around the plot before a security wagon arrives. In the minutes before it arrives, they will be looking all around, up and down the street and up at the buildings. But - when the moment comes when the prize is in front of them and they go for it, they suddenly get tunnel vision. They can see only the prize, nothing else; in short, they're blinkered.

And when they're suddenly pounced upon, brought crashing to the ground and feel the stubby end of a Smith & Wesson Model 64 stuck in their ear, they experience the same sort of trepidation that their victims feel. Quite often, it can take fully 30 seconds before they're composed enough to start whining for their solicitor. I can remember sprinting down Shoreditch High Street, following a gang's unsuccessful attempt to rob a rent collector only to see one of the robbers hit the pavement with a resounding Thump! courtesy of a well-timed rugby tackle from the late Detective Inspector Cam Burnell. I suddenly saw a column of what I believed to be smoke rising from the body of the robber and thought that Cam had unfortunately shot him, although I was unable to comprehend why as I had not heard the sound of the gunshot. Getting closer, I suddenly realised that because this was a cold November day, what I thought to be smoke was in fact steam, rising from the robbers trousers where the shock of being so boisterously apprehended had caused him to wet his pants. On another occasion, a robber who was just about to fire a Hilti gun (an industrial tool used for firing bolts into concrete) into the armoured window of a security van, (thereby running the possibility of slaughtering all of the occupants) was most put out to find that a detective's revolver was pointed straight between his eyes. 'I want my Mum!' he wailed. Bless his heart.

So that's what robbery is. But Judges have wide-sweeping powers when it comes to sentencing, and it used to infuriate me when thoroughly dangerous young men, convicted of robbery, swaggered free from court, proud possessors of a 'get out of jail' 2-year Probation Order.

That was the stock prescription of one of the Old Bailey's dottiest

Judges who, like Father Flanagan in *Boy's Town* felt that there was no such thing as a bad boy. I thought he was certifiably insane and I loathed him. As soon as the Station's teleprinter started chattering out the names of runners and riders for the following day's attendance at the Bailey, I would groan if I saw that I was appearing in his court and would try (always unsuccessfully) to invent reasons why my case should be moved to another court. Of course, defence lawyers adored him. 'What an irrepressible, eccentric old darling he is!' they would chortle, once justice had been well and truly stuffed.

But if I paint a picture of doom and gloom about robbery and all its aspects, please remember that there are always two sides to every coin, as the story which follows illustrates and which includes an account of the Judge who was as bonkers as conkers.

Jim Jarvis, who was my Detective Inspector at Forest Gate, had just finished a robbery case at the Old Bailey, in front of - guess who? Yes, you're right. The young felon had walked out of court with Jim, having received his statutory 2 years Probation Order, and had, in fact, travelled back on the same tube train with him, in order to get his personal property back from the Police Station. Restoration of prisoners' property was always delegated to those of lowly rank, so I collected young Johnny Wilkins' belongings and tipped them out on to the table, so that he could check them, before signing for them. One of his possessions was a large and very distinctive penknife.

'What do you carry that around with you for?' I asked.

'I just do,' was the ambiguous reply. 'No offence, is it?'

Well, it wasn't then, and I don't suppose it is now, so he got the knife back, and that was that.

A few weeks later, I was called to an off-licence, to deal with an allegation of attempted robbery. A little old boy, who was a wonderful East-End character, ran the shop.

'Little barstid comes in 'ere yesterday,' he croaked. ''e says to me, "I want 20 quid off you each week, or I'll cut you up." 'Wot!' I says, 'Piss orf!' and I didn't think no more abaht it. Bugger me, if 'e don't come back in today, and says, 'Where's that dough?' 'e's got a bleedin' knife in 'is hand. 'Fuck you!' I says, and threw the bleedin' till at 'im. He cut me across the 'and, and run orf. Made 'im drop the knife, though.'

And from under the counter, he handed me a rather large penknife, that looked awfully familiar...

It didn't take long to find young Mr Wilkins. He was in a local cafe with some of his cronies. 'Right, get up, Johnny,' I said. 'You're arrested for trying to rob the off-licence in Odessa Road, today.'

'O.K.,' replied Johnny, and as his courageous colleagues slunk away, he came along as good as gold. At the Police Station, I asked Johnny if he'd like to make a written statement about the offence. 'Sure, why not?' he replied. And, at his dictation, I wrote down a confession, which concurred with the account given by the off-licensee. At the conclusion, before asking him to certify the statement, I said to Johnny, 'Anything else you want to say?'

'Yes,' he replied. 'Can you put down, 'I know I've done wrong, and I hope I go to prison for a long time.'

I did so, and afterwards I said to him, 'That was a funny thing to say, about wanting to go to prison.'

'Well,' he replied, 'I hope I do. Borstal would do me, really. I can't get a job, and while I'm out on the streets, robberies are an easy way to get money. If I go inside, I can learn a trade. A bricklayer, that's what I'd like to be.'

In due course, up the steps at the Bailey went Johnny. And who did he go in front of? Dead right. Johnny pleaded guilty to the counts of blackmail, attempted robbery and inflicting grievous bodily harm contained in his indictment; and it is interesting to note that with regard to these three offences, the maximum penalties respectively are: 14 years Imprisonment, Life Imprisonment and Life Imprisonment. I thought to myself, not even Father Flanagan here, can fail to send Johnny down for Borstal, at the very least. I was in the witness box, giving details of Johnny's previous history. In the middle of it, that silly old bugger of a Judge interrupted me. 'I see you took this statement under caution from this boy, officer,' he squeaked, in that ridiculously high-pitched voice of his.

'Yes, m'Lud,' I replied.

'And here, you have him saying he hopes he will be sent to prison for a long time,' he continued. 'That was an odd thing for him to say, wouldn't you agree, officer?'

'It was, m'Lud,' I nodded.

'Did he, in fact, say that?' inquired the Judge. And before I could answer, he suddenly screamed at me, '*Well, did he?*'

I could feel my face reddening. 'Yes, he did,' I replied, shortly.

'Well,' replied the obviously disbelieving Judge, giving me a very funny sideways look. 'Well. An extremely strange thing to say, I'd have said.' And then, turning to the prisoner, this amazing old fool said, 'I feel there is much good in you. Your pathetic honesty in pleading guilty has saved you from a prison sentence, today. I want this Probation Order to have a chance to work. Two years' probation, to run concurrently with the previous order.'

I was absolutely furious at the way that I, not to mention justice, had been treated by the Judge. I stamped out of court and generally threw my toys about. 'Stupid old git!' I said to the court usher. 'Has someone got to get themselves bloody killed, before that dribbling lunatic will put them away?'

The usher tut-tutted, and shook his head, not so much in agreement with my sentiments, but in an attempt to warn me that the Judge had followed me out of court, and was now standing right behind me, obviously having heard every word that I'd said. I was in no mood to apologise and just glared at the old idiot, who glared right back at me, and then stumped off. I was extremely lucky. That lunatic could well have reintroduced transportation (he was quite capable of it) and then I'd have been writing this from Brisbane.

The only person who consoled me was Johnny Wilkins. 'Funny old geezer, that Judge, weren't he, Mr Kirby?' he said, as we took a glass in *The Feathers.*

'Funny ain't the word for him,' I snorted, and bought Johnny the other half. 'I'd like to make him eat his fucking wig.'

'Don't worry, Mr K,' said Johnny. 'I'll break the Probation Order, and then you'll have to come and nick me, won't you?'

'Yes,' I said, brightening up considerably. 'There is that to it.'

And that's exactly what happened. Newham Probation and After-care Service waited in vain for Johnny to show up, and in the end, they obtained a warrant for breaching the Probation Order. Hardly was the Magistrate's ink dry on the warrant, than I was round to Johnny's lodgings.

'It's alright, Johnny, I've got it,' I said, waving the warrant.

'Cor, thank Christ for that!' replied Johnny. 'I thought they'd forgotten about me.'

Back up the steps went Johnny. I saw him in the cells, just before he was arraigned. 'Think they'll put me down this time, Mr Kirby?' he asked.

'I bloody-well hope so,' I replied. 'I have got other people to arrest, you know.'

Johnny admitted the breach of probation to the Recorder of London, the late Sir Carl Aarvold OBE, TD, in No. 1 Court at the Old Bailey. His astonished defence Counsel told the Recorder, 'This extraordinary young man really wants a custodial sentence, My Lord. This is contained in the statement which he made to the officer in the case and now he's verified it to me, as well!'

Sir Carl raised his eyebrows. 'Really?' he said. 'Well, better accommodate him, I suppose.' And then, as an afterthought, he added, 'How much does he want?'

The Recorder sentenced an overjoyed Johnny to a term of Borstal Training and I had the grace to blush as Johnny was led down to the cells, waving and shouting, 'Thanks, Mr Kirby!'

I never saw or heard of the strangely likable Mr Wilkins again. By the time he was released, I was attached to the Yard's Serious Crime Squad, and was whizzing about all over the place. But I do hope he got his bricklayers' course.

Q Cars

I can't in all honesty claim that Trenchard was before my time, because at the time of his death in 1956, a despairing schoolmaster was busily writing into my report book, 'unless he makes a sustained effort next term, I really do not know what will become of him' - remarks which were to mortify my mother, infuriate my father and to leave me, I regret to say, in a state of total indifference.

But from what I've read and heard about him, I don't think I'd have been too enamoured with 'Boom' as he was disrespectfully known, due to his habit of bellowing orders. Trenchard – or to give him his full title, Air Marshall Lord Hugh Montague, 1st Viscount Trenchard, GCB, OM, GCVO, DSO – was Commissioner of the Metropolitan Police from 1931 to 1935. In four short years, he completely transformed the Force. He created the Map Room and a much-needed statistical department. The new Information Room linked the cars which were equipped with radio across the capital. Police-related schools were set up; one for wireless training, a driving school and a detective training school as well as a forensic laboratory. Police Married Quarters, Section Houses and canteens were either substantially renewed or completely rebuilt. Each of the four police areas were provided with sports grounds. Trenchard brought about more much needed changes and innovations in an incredibly short space of time, far more than any other Commissioner, before or since. And yet, he was almost universally hated.

To start with, Trenchard was practically illiterate. He found it almost impossible to convey his ideas to paper; assistants had to do it instead and then only after they had deciphered his scribblings and managed to deduce orally what was required because Trenchard was as incoherent verbally as he was illiterate. He was a Blimpish sort of character, who addressed subordinates as 'My Man' and either conveniently forgetting, or more likely never knowing in the first place that the rank and file are the backbone of any Police Force. If he disdained the constables and sergeants of his Force, he loathed the Police Federation, set up 12 years earlier and came to the conclusion that only by way of introducing an 'officer class' into the Force would the post of senior officer be filled with 'the right sort of chap'.

It was a disaster. Hendon Police College opened its gates in 1933 and the aspirants were a succession of young men from public school and University who, after a successful 2-year course, emerged with the rank of Junior Station Inspector. This rank carried one pip on the officer's shoulder and an enormous amount of derision. Many of the JSIs (or 'Jessies' as they quickly became known) had little or no conception of street duties in the capital and everybody breathed a collective sigh of relief when Trenchard's successor closed the college at the outbreak of the Second World War. Trenchard also introduced short-term contracts, which meant that police officers could leave after 10 years' service clutching a gratuity, effectively reducing the number of officers who continued to collect a full pension. Of course, many of these officers went on to join provincial police forces, who were delighted to welcome fully-trained, experienced police officers to whom they too would not have to pay a full pension.

Morale comes and goes in the Metropolitan Police; but arguably, it never plummeted lower than during Trenchard's reign until the 1990s.

Strange that so much unhappiness could be caused by a man who engineered such impressive innovations; amongst which I include the 'Q' Car.

These were named after the 'Q' ships, used in the First World War, ships which masqueraded as innocent-looking tramp steamers but which, to the surprise of the enemy 'U' Boats, were suddenly transformed into fast-moving, fully armed vessels.

The 'Q' Cars, launched in June 1933, were based on the earlier Flying Squad vehicles, and were used in much the same way as their counter-parts, except that they were manned by Divisional Detectives who had an intimate knowledge of their own manor. These cars which included a Hillman Wizard, a Humber Snipe, an MG Mark One and a Rover Meteor, first drove out of Vine Street Police Station into the heart of London's West End.

The very first 'Q' Car was crewed by an up-and-coming young detec-tive named Jack Capstick, who later became known to the underworld as 'Charlie Artful' - one of my Scotland Yard heroes. I remember seeing one such crew of a 'Q' Car in the late 1960s, when I was a Police Constable. The driver was 'Chiefy' Southern, a massive crop-haired Ilford Police Constable. He looked intimidating in uniform; now, in plain clothes he looked incredibly frightening, like an under-employed KGB executioner. As for the rest of the crew, they were unknown to me; certainly they were from elsewhere on the Division. I looked at them and their sleek fast car goggle-eyed. I thought they were Gods who walked the earth, and felt in my heart of hearts that I could never, ever, aspire to be like them. It would be all I could do, I thought, to perhaps hitch a lift in the uniformed wire-less car or the van, in the dim, distant future. I didn't realise then, of course, that within two years, I would have been posted to three consec-utive tours on one of these 'Q' Cars (each tour lasted thirteen weeks, in those days) prompting my dear, despairing wife to inform me that if I ever mentioned the term 'Q' Car again, it would result in my being imme-diately (a) emasculated and (b) divorced.

In my younger days, there were two categories of 'Q' Car, which ran consecutive shifts to each other, i.e. 10am to 6pm and 6pm to 2am, thereby effectively giving the Division a 16-hour cover. One car was run by a Uniform Sergeant in plain clothes who had shown a propensity for crime fighting, the other by a Detective Constable or Detective Sergeant. In both cases, the rest of the crew consisted of an Aid and a Class I or Class II uniform driver, also in plain clothes.

These high-powered, unmarked cars – Rovers, Triumph 2000s, Ford Zephyr Zodiacs, Jaguars – had their two-way radios concealed either in the glove compartment or behind a mock facia of a car radio. A gong for stopping vehicles was usually operated by pressing the cigar lighter. My favourite 'Q' Car was a massive 3294 cc Vauxhall Ventora Saloon; the driver took it up to 115 mph on the A127 London to Southend road which convinced me that we were capable of catching anything on the road. Never constricted with crime book investigations, a 'Q' Car was a complete self-contained crime fighting unit, ready to go anywhere, anytime, to arrest the thieves, receivers and tearaways of the District. Well, that was the theory. I remember one of the Aids suffering miserably at the hands of a useless, work-shy, drunken Detective Constable, who thought the late-turn 'Q' Car shift was best served by spending the entire 8 hours in an alcoholic haze, in a local club.

The most famous 'Q' Car, Foxtrot One-One, became associated with one of the most infamous crimes in police history, when, on 12 August 1966, in Braybrook Street, Shepherds Bush, the entire crew were murdered by three gunmen.

I loved 'Q' Cars. To the young, keen-as-mustard embryo detective, it was the best job in the world. Apart from those three tours as an Aid when I crewed Kilo One-Two, I did another tour when I was a Detective Constable on Kilo One-One and another when I was a Detective Sergeant on Juliet One-One, plus lots of filling in, relieving for other officers who were sick or at court. It was very tough work. The hours very often exceeded the eight hour tour and during the late shift, court had to be attended with the prisoners of the previous night. By the time court had finished, there was often just time to get home, have a quick bite to eat and a wash, and I was off to work again. But I wouldn't have missed it for the world. On the rare occasions that I wasn't at court, I'd be sitting at home, hardly able to wait until it was time to go on duty again. I was extremely lucky, because in my early days I was working with keen, experienced officers, including Ron Hughes-Whiffin, who had come to the Met on the amalgamation with Essex in 1965. I have seldom met anyone with such an extensive knowledge of local criminals, nor such dedication. Ron once spotted a car belonging to a fraudster who was circulated as being wanted. He had an instinctive feeling that the fraudster would return to it; and when he did, 37 hours after the observation commenced, Ron was still there to feel his collar. Another was Dave 'Sandy' Sanderson whom I still see to this day. Sandy gave me a pep-talk before we set out on our tour and it made such an impression on me that

I can still remember it, over 30 years later.

'We're going to have a good time on this tour,' he said.

'We're going to have a few nice pints and a few nice meals. We're also going to nick a lot of bodies. What we're not going to do,' he continued, 'is take so much as a ha'penny off those villains and I'll tell you why. At any time in the future, I want to walk into any pub, club or scrap metal yard and say, 'Oi, you, you're nicked' without having them say, "What's the matter, didn't I pay you enough last time?" No, young Richard, we're going to nick 'em.'

And that's just what we did. In just one of those tours, we made 66 crime arrests.

When I ran 'Q' Cars of my own, I insisted on selecting my crew, rather than taking what was given. On Kilo One-One, I had a splendid Police Constable named Dennis Tuff as the driver and the Aid was Alex Baxter, who later got charged (and acquitted) with Grievous Bodily Harm - he was a good bloke, too. I was asked to run Juliet One-One when I was a Detective Sergeant, and again I had no difficulty in choosing my crew - the driver was Kenny Bowerman, who, like my old chum, the late Terry Brown from the Serious Crime Squad, had been awarded the George Medal for their part in arresting Walter 'Angel Face' Probyn, during a shoot-out in Burdett Road, Limehouse, in the mid-1960s. The Aid was Peter Kingston, who was later one of the leading lights of the 'J' Division Crime Squad, and who, years later, was posted to the Flying Squad on my recommendation.

Whilst we were on this 'Q' Car tour, we received a request from Norfolk police to arrest a well-known local villain, one Harry Gubbins, who had stolen a lorry-load of batteries, which he had been contracted to drive from Norwich. We went round to Harry's council house, banged on the door, and shouted, 'Open up - police!' We were rewarded by a blue flash, and a loud 'BANG!' followed by a cry of, 'Oh, fuck!' as the inhabitants had swiftly but clumsily tried to disconnect the power line which they had been using to siphon-off their next-door neighbour's electricity supply.

Harry, a tall, cheerless character, was no trouble at all. His wife, however, was a different matter. Her screeching voice and her absolutely non-stop flow of invective, followed us all over the house, as carefully picking our way through the darkness by torchlight, we went from room to room, retrieving cartons of the missing batteries. As we went upstairs, she shrieked, 'You won't go into that back bedroom! Inspector O'Connor of the Flying Squad didn't have the arsehole to go in there! Go on! You fucking go in there! Mungo'll have you!'

From within this room came the most dreadful, roaring, snarling sound. Not only the bedroom door, but also the lintel and frame was bowed outwards by something inside, which was very large indeed, trying hard to get out.

I turned to the lugubrious Harry. 'Any more batteries in there, mate?' I asked, casually.

He matched me, stare for stare. 'No,' he replied, ingenuously

'O.K.,' I said, and together, we walked back down the stairs.

'Told you!' shrieked his wife. 'None of you Old Bill have got any bleedin' guts! You're all shit-scared of Mungo!'

As we beat a hasty retreat away from the awesome Mungo, and Harry's equally awesome wife, Mrs Gubbins turned her attention to her husband. 'And you, you shit!' she bellowed, 'you're not even a good thief! Go on, fuck off!'

The shock absorbers of the 'Q' Car groaned as we loaded the batteries into the boot, and as cries of, 'Wankers!' and 'Call yourself a thief?' followed us, curious neighbours spilled out of the adjoining dwellings, in order to advise Mrs Gubbins on how best to insult us.

As we drove through the night to Loughton Police Station, the unsuccessful thief turned to me, sighed, and said, 'Do you know, Guv, it's almost worth getting nicked, just to get away from that!'

I wish I could report a happy ending to this tale, but, alas not. The jury at Norwich Crown Court decided that Harry's desperate, implausible story of keeping the batteries safe in his house, because his lorry had broken down, was quite acceptable, and to his horror, acquitted him, leaving him to be reinstated in the bosom of his family!

Disappointment

Have you noticed what a misused word 'disappointment' is? 'Fail to fulfil desire or expectation,' says my *Concise Oxford Dictionary*, but that instructive book was published prior to the invention of appeasing police-speak. When something went catastrophically, staggeringly wrong in the Metropolitan Police – which happened, on average, about once per week during the 1990s – the inevitable senior officer would appear on television, smile wetly at the camera and say, 'The action of these officers...(and here, he'd pause for a forlorn sigh)... disappointed me.' Now, of course, what he meant to say was, 'I was absolutely bloody furious!' but naturally, he wouldn't, in case it interfered with the caring image he was trying to promote. Let me tell you about the time that I felt disappointed, but in order to do so, I need to introduce the Serious Crime Squad.

Police Forces all over England - particularly the Metropolitan Police - have always been good at producing *ad hoc* squads. The late Gerald MacArthur MBE did it when he formed a squad to investigate the Great Train Robbery; and in order to prove that lightning can indeed strike twice, led the very successful investigation into the activities of the Richardson Brothers. The legendary John du Rose OBE, the Deputy Assistant Commissioner who was known as 'Four-Day Johnny' because of the speed which he applied to the successful solving of murder cases, had built up a formidable reputation after smashing the power of the Messina brothers who controlled vice in the West End of London during the 1950s.

Put in charge of the Kray brothers investigation, he wisely appointed Leonard 'Nipper' Read QPM for the day-to-day running of the team. At the conclusion of these investigations, the squads were largely disbanded but, thank goodness, someone with rather more than an ounce of common sense realised that a vacuum would be created if a dedicated squad was not formed to combat the gangs which were ready to step into the shoes prematurely vacated by the brothers Richardson and Kray.

So it was that the Serious Crime Squad was formed in the early 1970s. It was 7 Squad of COC1 Department at the Yard and its chief was a hard-boiled, East-End detective named Bert Wickstead QPM. Also known as 'The Old Grey Fox', Wickstead was a shrewd investigator who believed in backing his men to the hilt and who had a loathing of criminals. They, in turn, were terrified of him. Under Wickstead's rule, the Dixon brothers, the Tibbs family and the West-End's 'Maltese Syndicate' were just three of the gangs who were wiped up. Many old-time senior police officers were often described as being 'blunt' in their manner of dealing with people. To describe Wickstead thus, would have been tantamount to an impertinence. Flamboyant, larger than life and an ace manipulator of the press, Wickstead could be staggeringly rude and in true democratic fashion, distributed his brashness equally to all who crossed his path. Like 'Nipper' Read before him, Wickstead forswore the Yard as the HQ of the Serious Crime Squad and took over the old Married Quarters at Limehouse Police Station, right in the heart of the capital's East-End. He was prudent to do so.

The late Wally Virgo, then the Commander of C1 (later sentenced to 12 years imprisonment for corruption, before having his conviction quashed on appeal) paid him a visit with an infamous proposal concerning the activities of Wickstead's squad. Thereafter, instead of the Serious Crime Squad's correspondence being sent through the internal dispatch system to C1's Commander, it was delivered by hand to the Deputy Assistant Commissioner (Operations) who, at that time was the highly respected Ernie Bond OBE, QPM and one of the 'originals' of Stirling's wartime Special Air Service. This by-passing of the Commander of C1 lasted for several years and produced understandable angst among the honourable Commanders, who succeeded Virgo.

Wickstead was promoted to Commander and in 1974, he was succeeded by Detective Chief Superintendent Len Gillert QPM. Gillert ensured continuity by wisely retaining many of Wickstead's original staff (including Detective Sergeant Bill Waite, a veteran of the Richardson and Kray enquiries who was later the recipient of a very well deserved BEM) and commenced his own investigations into the world of organised crime.

With just two years' service as a Detective Constable under my belt, I was posted to the Serious Crime Squad. I was thrilled at being selected and, in the years that followed, I learnt so much about major investigations (particularly from Bill Waite) that this stood me in good stead for the rest of my career. One of the people that I worked with was Colin Geater, a sound detective and an affable companion. We had previously worked together on 'K' Division and had discovered that we both approached police-work with a combination of humour and pugnacity in more or less equal proportions. In fact, Colin and I had just been commended by the Commissioner, the Director of Public Prosecutions and the Trial Judge at the Old Bailey for our part in smashing a gang of international swindlers. Coincidentally, our next job involved another bunch of continental crooks but no commendations were forthcoming on this one. However, we thought that we'd got a result simply by escaping with our lives, for Colin and I, two French police officers and a car-load of German tourists had collectively looked into the face of death and were able to walk away unscathed. This is what happened.

The job itself was typical Serious Crime Squad fare, with the usual cast of exotic characters. A gang of fraudsters from Italy and France had carried out a series of frauds, including one major, sophisticated share swindle. After the ringleader and three of his associates were arrested, they managed with some outside help to extricate themselves from the cells at the Magistrates' Court and escape. Two of the rest of the gang had previously worked for the real-life French heroin importer who had been portrayed by the actor, Fernando Rey in the film, *The French Connection*. The female gang member could not reconcile herself with sedately driving through the London streets and drove as though she were back home in her native Milano. It made surveillance tricky, to say the very least, and on one occasion, she was tearing through the Brompton Road during rush-hour at 50mph when suddenly she saw something that she fancied in Harrods' window. Slamming on the brakes, she brought the car squealing to a halt and completely ignoring the horn-blowing, tyre-screeching, shouts and curses from all around her, she swept imperiously out of the car, leaving it in the middle of Brompton Road with the driver's door wide open, the keys in the ignition and the engine still running. Her return to the vehicle coincided with the surveillance team's heartbeats returning to normal and she led a procession of assistants who were carrying her purchases to the Alfa Romeo which they deposited in the boot. Giving a flamboyant wave and shouting 'Ciao!' she got back into the car, crashed it into gear and with no indication whatsoever, roared off, leaving her driver's door to slam shut by means of the car's acceleration. The surveillance team who, by this time, were seriously considering demanding danger money, grimly forced their way through two dozen furious motorists to take up the pursuit.

One of the worst members of the group was a Frenchman who was involved in a Gallic 'long-firm fraud' (see page 187) and had made a spectacular departure from his homeland after shooting a Parisian Gendarme in the face. With his arrival in London, he followed the lead of other members of the gang and obtained both solace and implied respectability in the arms of a top model.

The most shocking gang member returned from a dubious business trip abroad and amorously celebrated his return with his English girl-friend, who was tall, leggy, blond and who sported a hyphenated surname and an address in Sloane Street. During their passionate reunion, he murmured that he had brought her a special momento but teasingly refused to reveal the nature of this mystery gift until later. She was somewhat less than pleased when she discovered that this secret souvenir from lands far away was, in fact, a dose of syphilis and in an understandable fit of pique, became my informant. She did provide me with some useful intelligence about her former inamorato but in time, revenge turned into remorse and she committed suicide; one of several 'Sloaney' casualties. They were basically nice, if somewhat naive girls, bowled over by the charm of these Latin rotters. Yes, as I say, a typical Serious Crime Squad job.

I mentioned the pistol-packin' Parisian who was involved in a fraud which affected the wine trade. Another person, whom I suspected was also deeply involved, was a French national and therefore, a deftly worded report to the Director of Public Prosecutions resulted in Colin and me, armed with *Commissions Rogatoire*, flying to Paris. There, we were met and taken to the headquarters of the Police Judiciare on the Quai des Orfevres where we were introduced to a semi-circle of detectives. We worked our way round the group, shaking hands and were being greeted with a chorus of 'Enchanté' or 'Bonjour' until we got to the very last person, who was an attractive young woman. 'Ow air yew?' was the way that she greeted me in a thick, almost incomprehensible accent as we shook hands. 'How do you do,' I replied. 'I'm so glad you speak English. Tell me, do you work in the office?' Her jaw dropped, since this was clearly too much for her to comprehend. 'Quoi?' she replied, which is a rather rude query, the equivalent of, 'Wot?' 'I'm so sorry,' I said. 'I was talking too quickly. Do - you - work - here?' I continued, slowly. 'With - these - men?' I added, pointing to the assembled detectives. Suddenly, comprehension dawned. 'Ah! Je comprends!' she cried. 'Mais non, je suis - er - 'ow do you say eet? I am - er - the interpreter!' I heard a sigh from Colin. 'Oh, good!' he murmured sarcastically.

To our great good fortune, we chanced to meet a young Inspector, an ex-Para and all-round good guy. His overriding ambition was to fornicate for France but as a sideline, he was also the German interpreter. When Colin and I also discovered that he spoke English rather better than we did, we dismissed the young woman and gleefully co-opted him onto the team. We energetically carried out our enquiries in Paris - I seem to remember that these had to do with the shot Gendarme so there was great enthusiasm from our French colleagues. The time passed quickly with a great deal of hard work, terrific meals and the consumption of so much

Pernod that I have never been able to touch a drop since. You're thinking
that things were far too good to be true, aren't you? You'd be right. The
shit-house was right around the next corner.

Our next enquiry was south-east of Paris and you will excuse me if I
neglect to mention the name of the provincial town that we had to visit,
because I've got some fairly hard things to say about it and some of its
inhabitants. First though, we went to the regional headquarters in Lyon
where we met the Chief of Police and our credentials were duly checked
and certified by the Examining Magistrate. We were provided with two
detectives to accompany us to the provincial town and act as liaison. One
of them spoke fractured English, the other did not. Both were a glum,
taciturn pair and Colin took an instant dislike to the former; and me, to
the latter. It was explained to us that Colin and I would be booked into a
hotel in Lyon overnight and then, first thing in the morning, we would all
set out, by car, to the town. It was a considerable distance away and by
the time we had arrived and carried out our enquiries, it would be far too
late to return and therefore, we would stay the night in the town and then
return to Lyon the following day. At this, the English speaking officer
exploded with temper. As far as I could make out, the following evening,
he had wanted to attend a fairly important football match and now,
because of these damned foreigners, his plans had been put into disarray.
The senior officer coldly made it quite clear that a sensible career move
for him, would be to shut his trap, before he, the Chief, was embarrassed
any further in front of his English companions and to get on with it. At
this, the football fan flounced off in a massive temper tantrum and the
stage was set for disaster.

The following morning, we set off and the journey took simply ages.
When we arrived, the town was a ghastly place - a dusty, grubby, fly-
blown dump. Off we went to the local Police Station, where our mission
was explained to the local detectives who looked suitably unenthusiastic
about assisting us. Have you noticed, with outlying stations in the Met,
the less they do, the less they want to do? It's like that in France, too. But
I sensed it was something more, in this case. There was a long, muttered
conversation between the two detectives from Lyon and the locals, inter-
spersed with sly, crafty looks in our direction. Eventually, the football fan
sauntered over. He attempted to look regretful, but he was hard-pressed
to keep the look of cunning triumph out of his eyes.

'Theese man, you want,' he said. ''e is not 'ere. No one has 'eard of 'eem.'

'But this can't be right,' I replied. 'Look - I have here his name, address, the name and address of his haulage company and his telephone number.' There was a further muttered conversation between the two groups. Finally, the football fan strolled back to us, lit a Gauloise and kindly blew a cancerous lungfull in my face. 'Theese mens,' he said, pointing to the locals, 'they do not know the man 'oo you look for. They say, tell them what it is you want 'im for, and if they can find 'im, they will ask 'im.' He gave a Gallic shrug. 'They will telex you with the answer in England,' he added.

It did not require advanced intelligence to realise that we were being given the massive run-around, and not just because our little chum could get back to Lyon to watch his bloody football match. I was furious.

'Right, you,' I said. 'You translate what I say, you understand?' He nodded, grudgingly. 'This address,' I said, showing the locals the name and address of the haulage company, 'is in the same street as this Police Station, is it not?' There was surly agreement. 'And if I'm not mistaken,' I continued, pointing out of the window, 'that's his haulage yard across the road and those are his trucks.' Again, there was grudging assent. 'So if you don't get out there and bring him in right now,' I snapped, warming to my task, 'I'll bloody-well go in there and arrest him myself!' This caused a bit of consternation since, for some unaccountable reason, continental police officers and their Examining magistrates do tend to get a bit shirty about Scotland Yard detectives making arrests on their patch - in fact, I was still the subject of conversation in the Bundeskriminalamt Headquarters after carrying out a spectacular arrest at the Kempinski Hotel in Berlin, a couple of years previously.

So the haulage owner was brought in. He might well have been kith and kin to the French detectives; he complimented a shifty group of characters. The interview was clearly not going to be the cut-and-thrust routine that was the norm, during those halcyon pre-PACE days, oh dear me, no. One of the detectives produced a portable typewriter and thrust an official form into it - it caused a ripple of amusement between Colin and me, since its official title was 'Proces-Verbal'. The stilted interview commenced - English/French, French/English - whilst a synopsis was laboriously tapped out on the typewriter. Very unsatisfactory and unhelpful and that was that.

In securing accommodation, we now discovered that the French detectives were provided with a niggardly subsistence allowance. Not only were they not going to exceed that allowance by one centime, these two mean bastards were going to try and actually make a profit. We booked into a seedy, charmless hotel (although in fairness, I believe it may have been the town's only hotel) and went in search of a restaurant. Our colleagues idea of an evening's haute cuisine was a cheerless fast-food restaurant and we sat down to a plate of unappetising grey chicken which was also, unsurprisingly, extremely cheap. The Frenchmen kept smacking their lips and crying, 'Delicieux!', as though they were actually enjoying it. If they were trying to get their own back over the missed football match and my performance of the afternoon and were also trying to wind us up, they were doing quite well. Now, you may be asking, why didn't Colin and I simply say, 'Now look, boys, this evening's on us,' and gone out for a slap-up meal? Well, yes, I agree, we could have done, but the thought of even attempting to be pleasant to this pair of creeps would have been unbearable. Sticking hot needles in my eyelids would have been an acceptable alternative.

Back we went to that dingy hotel, which Colin was later to describe as being 'wall-to-wall squalor'. That night, my sleep was thoroughly disturbed by the appearance of a huge winged insect - it had a body about the size of a thrush - and it droned relentlessly round and round my room, occasionally crashing into the walls. I cowered miserably under the bedclothes - I was not so much afraid of getting stung, as I was at the thought of it dragging me off to its lair. Agonisingly slowly, the night came to an end and after a truly ghastly breakfast which was only enlivened by the thought that the croissants might have possessed some antique value, we set off on the road back to Lyon.

Colin and I sat in the back of the car and I consoled myself with the forlorn hope that I might be able to catch up on some of the robbed sleep of the previous night. The non-English speaker was driving and of the two, he was by far the worst driver. He was erratic, his gear changes were appalling and, as I was soon to discover, his road sense and judgment were non-existent. We were travelling along a long, straight and very narrow road. There were just two lanes of traffic; the one upon which we were travelling and the one catering for vehicles travelling towards us. And then the driver had to brake sharply, because we had joined the tail-end of a line of trucks which was so long, it stretched out as far as the eye could see. This was not to the driver's liking. He pulled out to the left, on the wrong side of the road, crashed down into third gear, stuck his foot down and off we went. As we sped along, I glanced nervously at the ponderous trucks on our right. They were nose-to-tail and if a car should come towards us, we really would have no place to go.

And then, in the distance, I saw a dot, a dot which grew larger with every passing second. It was another car, closing with us very rapidly indeed, quite possibly travelling as fast as we were; and if this were so, I would estimate that our total speeds as being 150 mph. I heard the sound of a horn blaring out - obviously, the other car's - and as I looked again, desperately to my right, I saw that the position was still unchanged. There really was nowhere to go. The approaching car, a large Mercedes with German number-plates was now very close indeed and it was this stage that I felt disappointed. I was quite calm; I didn't feel scared and I was way past anger because things were happening so fast. I just remember feeling disappointed and pretty fed-up that I was never going to see my wife and family again and all because of this garlic-munching cretin, seated two feet in front of me. It was then that the miracle occurred. The driver of the truck to our right had seen our predicament and had slowed, so that he was able to produce a space between his truck and the one in front and our driver slipped into that gap. The Mercedes missed us, literally by inches. The driver's face was a mixture of fear and fury and that, together with the look of terror on his young family's faces occasionally revisit me in my nightmares. I slumped back in my seat, my face dripping with sweat and glanced at Colin. His complexion resembled that of a certain well-known Transylvanian nobleman, prior to that worthy Count refreshing himself with an evening glass of gore. I made a weak joke, in a very shaky voice, to that effect. Colin later remarked that he thought that I was providing therapeutic counselling for him, because my complexion looked worse!

We eventually got back to our hotel. I'm sure we didn't bid farewell to our hosts; it's quite possible that any attempt at conversation would have dented *entente-cordiale* to such an extent that the Channel Tunnel might never have been built. All Colin and I wanted to do at that moment was to have a large drink apiece and take the opportunity to stop trembling. After a bit, Colin said, 'I've got a pox of this trip.' 'So have I,' I agreed. 'Let's go home.' So we did.

During our trip, Colin had been promoted to Detective Sergeant and had been posted, so he left the Serious Crime Squad immediately upon our return. I wrote out the report to the Director of Public Prosecutions and put in a couple of scathing paragraphs concerning the honestly and integrity of the provincial town's detective force. I handed the completed report to our much-loved Detective Superintendent, George Atterwell and I waited outside his office whilst he read it. I knew when he had reached the offending paragraphs, because I heard a loud 'Pop!' as his pipe fell out of his mouth and hit his desk top. 'Dick, you bloody idiot!' he shouted as I wandered into his office, failing at an attempt to promote a look of injured innocence. 'You can't say this! It'll cause a diplomatic incident!' I changed the paragraphs, of course, not to save a diplomatic wrangle but because to have upset George was unthinkable; and anybody who served with that great man will know exactly what I mean.

I got on with my career and I had a wonderful exciting time, investigating the best cases with the finest men and women who made up what used to be the finest Police Force in the world - and I pray to God that one day soon, it will be again. I had been on overseas investigations before and I was destined to go on several more afterwards, but that one in south-east France, believe me, was the pits.

Eventually, I retired and a few years later, Colin followed me into retirement from a career that was so distinguished that I thought that he merited an award in the Honours Lists; but then, I was just a Detective Sergeant, so what would I know?

And then, one day, I was sitting at the breakfast table, reading the *Daily Telegraph* and as I casually glanced through the foreign section, I suddenly hooted with laughter so loudly that my startled wife dropped a cup and saucer. The reason for my amusement was that I had just read the name of that grubby town where Colin and I had travelled to, twenty years before, which had been policed in such a useless manner. Apparently, a black rock festival, together with several hundred noisy fans had suddenly and inexplicably descended upon the town causing the population, according to the report, to be 'stunned'.

And possibly, just a little 'disappointed', as well!

Penal Pete and Friends

I worked at twelve of London's Police Stations and attended eight different Magistrates' Courts during that time. Then, with the Serious

Crime Squad and the Flying Squad I found myself at many other Magistrates' Courts all over London, the Home Counties, Scotland and Northern Ireland.

The reason for this idle boast, is to tell you that from my own dealings with a vast number of Magistrates – whether Lay, Stipendiary or Resident – some of the most wonderful characters have emerged. It is true that some of the Lay Magistrates (or Justices of the Peace) are vilified by police officers for their inability to use even a modicum of common sense during cases or because they allow themselves to be thoroughly bamboozled by a slimy solicitor for the defence, who can well and truly pull the wool down over their eyes.

But not all! Who can forget Barking Magistrates' Court's Dorothy Revvington; indeed, who would want to forget her? Not me, for a start. I became this dear lady's number one fan after she imperiously threw out a charge of Assault Occasioning Actual Bodily Harm, which had been spuriously brought against me.

Move half-a-dozen miles to the east, to Havering Magistrates' Court. There on the bench, in the 1970s sat the late Fred Taylor J.P. who was known to strike terror not only into the hearts of many a tearaway but also those police officers who had failed to properly prepare their cases. In his youth, Fred had been a good, all-round sportsman, and had run marathons with the Haringay Harriers. He was to serve for many years on the bench and also on the Appeals Committee at Snaresbrook Crown Court. Fred could be impatient, irascible and often downright rude.

He also possessed a very strong sense of public duty, was impossible to fool and also had a heart of gold, which he kept meticulously hidden!

I was a Temporary DC during the early 1970s and one summer morning, my partner and I were stealthily creeping out of Romford's CID office before we could be lumbered with taking exhibits up to the Lab when the telephone rang.

I answered it, to learn that a store detective in the town centre had spotted a large West Indian lady attempting to steal from a shopper's bag. Lightning looked slow by comparison, as we flew into the shopping area where we located the store detective who swiftly pointed out the suspect to us. After a short surveillance, the suspect obliged us by attempting to 'dip' two more shoppers' bags and she was duly swagged off, volubly protesting her innocence.

At the Police Station, a search at CRO revealed that she had an enormous amount of convictions, almost exclusively for the same type of offence and we were to discover that her photograph graced the pages of the Flying Squad's 'Book of Dips', so this was indeed a prize knock-off. Refuting all of the evidence, she was duly charged with being a Suspected Person (Dips) with three cases of attempted theft, as an alternative.

Now, to the most simple-minded of Dippers (or Whizzers) it was hugely preferable to plead Guilty to being a Suspected Person, because on this purely summary offence, the maximum penalty was three months imprisonment. Even if she had been sent to the Crown Court for sentence, for being an incorrigible rogue under Section 5 Vagrancy Act 1824, the maximum sentence was 12 months imprisonment, whereas the maximum sentence for attempted theft was 10 years. This lady, however, would have none of it and by electing summary trial, came to appear before Fred Taylor.

Having heard all of the evidence from the prosecution, wild allegations of police misconduct from the defendant and a simpering plea from the defence Counsel that she be given the benefit of the doubt, Fred took all of two seconds flat to find her guilty. 'Anything known?' he inquired tersely. 'I beg your pardon,' said the prosecution Counsel, 'but what is it that Your Worship has found the defendant guilty of?' 'What?' testily demanded Fred. 'I dunno. Everything.' 'Your Worship,' patiently explained the Counsel, 'She cannot be found guilty of everything. The suspected person charge is an alternative to the three cases of attempted theft.' 'Oh, Christ,' replied Fred, wearily, 'Look, what do you want her found guilty of?' 'The three charges of attempted theft,' smoothly answered the counsel. 'Right, that's what she's guilty of, then,' replied a relieved Fred. 'Anything known?' As I read out her staggering list of form, her defence Counsel who had decided that Fred was the Magistrate from Hell, stood there, dumbly shaking his head from side to side, rather like a very old boxer, who over a period of years in the ring, has taken an enormous amount of punishment.

Fred swiftly committed the defendant in custody to the Crown Court for sentence and in the fullness of time, she appeared before His Honour Judge Peter Mason QC who, not for nothing was known as 'Penal Pete'. He smartly disposed of the case and we left the court as did the defence Counsel. 'You know,' I heard him say to his instructing solicitor, 'Penal Pete always gives three years for this sort of offence. In this case,' he continued, 'I did rather hope it would be probation, rather than imprison-ment!'

Back to Havering Magistrates' Court, where I'd arrested four young tearaways for a minor theft. All of them had made a real effort to be prop-erly 'booted and suited', since it was not unknown for the immaculate Fred to send a scruffy defendant home to change, before appearing in his court. The four of them pleaded guilty and after I'd given the facts, Fred fined each of them £20. 'Can I 'ave time to pay, yer Honour?' asked the first defendant. 'Seven days,' replied Fred. 'Time to pay, please, yer Honour? asked the second and third defendants. 'Seven days,' replied Fred, to each of them. Hoping to bring a little brevity to the proceedings, the fourth defendant said, 'Can I 'ave time, yer Honour?' With a rare flash of humour, Fred replied, 'Only if you don't pay!'

On another occasion, Fred had called an adjournment in the middle of a case and, to me at least, it was clear that the Bench was going to take their customary 20-minute coffee break. I too was enjoying a cup of coffee next door in the canteen at Romford Police Station, when suddenly, the Court Inspector came flying up the stairs. 'Fred's back!' he gasped. 'Get back to court quick and tell him something convincing! He's raving!' I rushed back to court, to find Fred quietly fuming. 'I'm so sorry, Your Worship,' I said. 'I'm afraid I had to answer an urgent call of nature.' 'Really!' scoffed Fred, disbelief written all over his face. 'Just as well I called the adjournment when I did!'

But inevitably, the last word has to be Fred's. He demonstrated it, in stunning style, when a miserable creature from a nearby sprawling council estate appeared before him. She had been charged with three specimen offences of obtaining benefit by deception from Social Security and after pleading guilty, asked for an enormous number of similar cases to be taken into consideration. After the brief facts had been given and a speech whined in mitigation, Fred exploded.

'I've had enough of this sort of behaviour!' he roared. 'I'm going to set an example to deter others from committing this type of crime! For the first offence, three months' imprisonment!' 'Oh!' gasped the defen-dant. 'For the second offence,' thundered Fred, 'three months' imprison-ment consecutive!' 'Ah!' cried the defendant, clutching wildly at her clothing, which had almost been fashionable when she had shoplifted it three years previously. 'And for the third offence,' bellowed Fred, 'three months' imprisonment consecutive, making nine months' imprisonment in total!' 'Aaahh!' shrieked the defendant and slumped to the floor, in a dead faint.

A court usher took hold of her ankles, a probation officer slid her hands under the unconscious prisoner's armpits and with considerable difficulty, she was carried to the cells. The deathly silence that had descended on the court was broken when Fred leant over the bench. 'By the way,' he said conversationally, 'when she comes round, tell her it's suspended for two years!'

Maniacs of the Manor

My introduction to one particular thug, whom I shall re-name Harry Thompson, occurred in a back garden in the early hours of a wet February morning, over 30 years ago. Before I had the opportunity to extend a proper introduction, a textbook right hook flashed out from Harry, connecting very smartly with my left eye. Anxious to consolidate this new alliance, I sticked Harry so hard that the top of his head suddenly resembled a canoe. The preliminary courtesies over, we tottered off to the local nick.

Later that morning at the Magistrates' Court, Harry, by now rather more sober than he had been a few hours previously, presented a shame-faced, contrite appearance, not through remorse at having provided me with a classic 'shiner' but because he now realised that, due to his impetuosity, he was now in imminent danger of 'collecting a carpet' (or to the uninitiated, three months' imprisonment).

Still, the drama of the courtroom was lightened with a little humour, when a fairly pristine Chairman of the Bench, who had never seen Harry before, demanded to know if the prisoner required an interpreter, since he had mistaken Harry's bandages for a turban.

Harry pleaded Guilty to his misdemeanours and with a cunning born of years of experience, apologised, through the Bench, to me for his rash and unbecoming behaviour. After taking everything into account, including Harry's remorse, and his previous, which many a defence Counsel would despair of, the Beak sternly admonished Harry for his misdeeds and fined him, giving him seven days to pay.

The Chairman then complimented me for my promptness and diligence, although to this day I have yet to discover whether he was referring to my spotting Harry up to no good in the first place or for my spirited counter-attack. Outside the court, Harry and I shook hands and I was formally pronounced a 'toff and a gent.' We then went our separate ways, me to have soothing ointment applied to my bruised eye and a scolding from my despairing wife and Harry to his local, to demand that the licensee should contemptuously flout that section of the licensing Act which governed opening hours.

It might appear that I am portraying Harry as a lovable sort of rough diamond. Well, I am not. I have always had an aversion to violent criminals, not only when it's parts of me that they want to re-shape with malice afore-thought but for the sake of anybody else unfortunate enough to cross their path. And yet people like this become folk heroes. The Krays are an obvious example, but there are many others.

Billy Blythe, a tiny man with a satanic temper, had an appalling record of violence. Having striped DI Peter Vibart of the Flying Squad with a razor in 1945, Blythe went on to take part in a shocking attack on Jack Spot, which was witnessed by Spot's wife. Spot received 78 stitches and Blythe received five years - and yet, when he died, four months into his sentence at the tender age of 39, the *Daily Mirror* reported that this was the biggest, most attended gangland funeral, ever.

None of these men could be considered tall. Wassle Newman was a bully who measured no more than 5' 7" but he threw housebricks into the air and hit them with his bare fists on the way down, to toughen his hands. Jack 'Dodger' Mullins was even shorter, but served enormous sentences for sheer brutality and was a leading light in the Dartmoor Prison riot of 1932. Wearying of a tiresome girlfriend, Mullins pushed her out of a window and although it was mischievously alleged that the police officer who apprehended him for his outrage broke Mullin's nose with a knuckleduster, it did little to curb his lawless ways.

An East End fish and chip shop proprietor had the staggering impertinence to suggest that Jimmy Spinks should actually pay for his supper and as a mark of his displeasure, Spinks picked up the shop's cat and casually tossed it into the fryer. And in the most appalling of cases, an armed robber, at one time a household name, was leaving a freshly plundered bank en-route to the waiting getaway car when an eight year old girl stepped into his path. Without pausing in his stride, he levelled the sawn-off at her, pulled the trigger and blew her out of the way. She did not, of course, represent any conceivable threat to him, nor was there any risk of her identifying him at a later stage, since he was still masked. She was shot simply because she was in his avenue of escape. And yet it defies logic that this man, and others I have mentioned, were venerated by their contemporaries.

Ah, well. Back to Harry Thompson. At the time of our preliminary encounter, Harry was about five years older than me. He was also about five times as strong. Superficially, both of us appeared fairly similar in appearance, short and stocky, but it was not until Harry was viewed in profile that it became apparent that he was twice as thick as me. Harry had trained to be a professional boxer until the promoter realised that he had a homicidal maniac in the ring and promptly washed his hands of him.

Prior to that, Harry's National Service had been auspicious purely from boxing for the platoon and then the battalion. But as his lunatic temper came bubbling to the surface and he started behaving as violently out of the ring as he did in it, he rapidly fell out of favour with his Commanding Officer and a spell in military prison followed. Harry was one of the few people ever to escape from such an establishment and not by stealth or guile, either. He simply took on all-comers and irrespective of whether these barriers were in human form or were inanimate objects such as doors, he just punched, head-butted or kicked his way through them.

In one of our quieter moments, over a glass, I once asked Harry why he had never vented his aggression by joining the Special Air Service. His reply was illuminating. 'I did, Dick,' he answered, 'but they chucked me off selection, 'cos I was too thick.' Just for once, Harry was being candid with me.

Harry was not a good thief. He did not have the intellect. Seldom did he have accomplices, because the local tearaways knew of his predilection for gross violence. No, violence was in fact Harry's *raison d'etre* and it was the one thing he was good at it. The following story was recounted to me one night by a scrawny little sneak-thief. One evening he had gone to a party, held in a local council flat when to his horror, he had encountered in the hallway a local tough, together with four of his friends, to whom the little thief owed money from a card game. The tough grabbed hold of the little thief and started slapping him around, ably supported by his friends, and the thief knew this was just a prelude until the curtain went up on a full-scale beating.

Just then, the door to the living room opened and Harry Thompson, who had been enjoying a drink with some friends, emerged into the hallway. He mildly observed that odds of five to one were hardly sporting, to which the tough replied that Harry might well find life a little easier if he were to keep his broken nose out of other people's business.

The little thief told me that as he saw Harry shrug his shoulders and give a sleepy smile, he thought that Harry had thought better of the whole business, but as Harry stepped forward and squared up, he realised he was wrong. The five of them promptly charged down the narrow hallway and Harry let loose five crippling punches, one for each of them. It was all that was needed. Now, that's what I call style; but Harry, being Harry, had to devalue matters by stepping over the sprawling bodies, unzip his fly and contemptuously urinate over the unconscious tough and his comrades.

So as the years went by, Harry notched-up a staggering 87 convictions, almost without exception for violence. From time to time, I bumped into him and we would be gravely courteous to each other. On one occasion I had to arrest him, having tracked him down to a pub which was so renowned for violent disorder, that when the uniform were called, they would park the wireless car and the van a block away. On the only occasion they did not, all the windows of the vehicles were smashed.

I entered the pub alone, not out of bravado, but because I knew full well that the presence of two or more officers would be regarded as an provocation by the regulars. There was Harry, surrounded by his cronies. I could not have been more considerately treated if I had attended a garden party at Buckingham Palace. Harry quickly finished his drink and accompanied me to the 'Q' Car, parked a sensible distance away. But when you think about it, Harry didn't need to act tough with me, in order to impress his mates. He had a reputation for toughness that had been put to the test, and had not been found wanting.

On the last occasion that I saw Harry, I was attending a Magistrates' Court in order to obtain a remand on a Flying Squad case. I saw Harry's name in the lists and when I went into court there was Harry, considerably older now, his once-handsome face now grotesque through serious drinking. In addition to the drink, age had slowed his reactions, so that up-and-coming tearaway's punches were now landing first and these, too, were giving his face a lived-in look.

Still, some of the old magic was still apparent, because the three PCs to whom Harry had handed out lots of punishment were glowering at him from the other side of the otherwise deserted courtroom. Perhaps I knew that this would be the last time that I might see Harry, so I put my misgivings about violent criminals to one side and we greeted each other like long-lost brothers, shook hands, beat each other on the back and had a little spar.

After a few words, during which Harry declared that I was still 'a blinking toff,' I realised that my case was just about to be called in an adjacent court, so I bade him farewell and made for the door.

'Blimey, Sarge!' exclaimed one of the PCs who had witnessed our reunion. 'He's not a mate of yours, is he? He's a bleedin' animal!' 'Harry?' I replied, looking across the courtroom at my old adversary, I could just make out a familiar scar on his forehead. I shook my head. 'No,' I said to the perplexed PC. 'It's just a question of knowing how to handle him!'

Randall Jones: one of the Finest Detectives

'Cast not a clout till May be out' is an old English proverb, and what it means is that you shouldn't cast a clout (or take off a layer of clothing) until May is out; in other words, until Summer starts. This interpretation may not have occurred to one young East Ender; it certainly didn't apply to the behaviour of some of the Spanish Police in the 1960s!

But I'm getting ahead of myself.

This thought and many others crept into my mind the other night as I sat back in my armchair, sipped a glass of scotch and stared into the fire. The flames from the fire leaped and as the coals blazed and glowed, the memories came tumbling back from those days when police work was actually fun, the CID was staffed with real detectives and political correctness had never been heard of.

One of those memories concerned Randall Jones, whom I consider to be one of the greatest detectives that I ever had the pleasure of working with. Tall, Welsh, quietly spoken with a florid complexion, he was a veteran of the Flying Squad and the Regional Crime Squad; and due to his expertise both in the ring and on the rugby field, he was as hard as bloody nails. He was an extraordinary man in many ways. I think that two of his most outstanding attributes were his compassion and his generosity for his subordinates.

In those days before overtime was paid to the CID, detectives, particularly young detectives, were expected to work very long hours and were suitably admonished by the First Class Sergeant if they did not. When you worked for Randall Jones, yes, you worked very hard and for long hours too, but when it was possible to have an early evening, then he would encourage young married officers (such as myself) to go home to spend some time with their families. This in itself was extraordinary, because Randall loved to have a drink with the chaps and really, by sending you home, he was depriving himself of company. But what was astonishing was the fact that he should have such an insight into the problems of young married couples, because Randall was a bachelor and got married only at the end of his service.

When my car developed a fault that necessitated it being kept by the garage overnight, Randell immediately handed his car keys to me, so that I might get home and return to the office in the morning. If my paperwork failed to reach Randall's high standards, my imperfections were gently pointed out to me and alternatives suggested. And at the conclusion of an inquiry, when we presented Randall with an exquisite Meerschaum pipe, he wept, telling us that we had been excessively generous, it was far too beautiful to smoke and that he would keep it in his cabinet!

In the event of trouble, if you were in the right, Randall would back you to the hilt and was outspoken in your defence to the point of recklessness, where disapprobation from the most senior of officers could have seriously curtailed his career. He had no time for officers of his rank who failed to back their men and was liable to openly describe his contempt for them.

Randall was a master investigator, knowing detective work inside-out and in addition, he knew criminals, their habits and haunts as few other detectives did. His informants were of the highest calibre and he treated them, as he did everybody else, very fairly. Well, almost everybody. Randall's dark side revealed a loathing for violent criminals and they, in turn, were terrified of him. The way that Randall dealt with some of the capital's more violent inhabitants are known to many, but these accounts are whispered, rather than uttered and they have no place in this narrative.

On a rather lighter note, I was involved in the investigation of a blackmail case and during the course of it, Randall had dealings with one of these hoodlums.

I spoke to the criminal's girl-friend a few months later. She told me that since his meeting with Randall, her boyfriend had started having terrifying, recurrent nightmares and was leaving quite a lot of his hair, which had started to come out in tufts, on the pillow. And he was just a witness for the prosecution!

Randall rose to the rank of Detective Chief Superintendent, but with a very distinguished career behind him, he sadly died, having seen only a few short months of retirement. I find it impossible to say how much I admired him. All I wanted to do was model myself on him, so that one day, I might turn out to be almost as great a detective as he had been. It didn't work, of course and anybody who knew him will tell you why. There was only one Randall Jones. He stood alone.

This, rather neatly, brings me to the point of this particular story, because I was a junior DC on a murder squad, which was headed by Randall in the early 1970s. The murder had occurred in London's tough and colourful East End but in stark contrast to the same area today, in those days if police said that they wanted assistance from the general public, they got it.

I was deputed to interview a young man, who in response to the police request, had walked into the police station to tell me that although he had been in the general vicinity at the time of the murder, he had neither heard nor seen anything suspicious. I therefore took a negative witness statement from him, thanked him for his time and he left the police station. It was then that the result of the routine search that I had requested at Criminal Records Office came through; it transpired that he was circulated as being wanted by Interpol. I swiftly despatched a brace of Aids to intercept him twixt police station and home and scrag him back in.

Having accomplished their mission, the suspect was casually deposited into the cells (as suspects were, in those halcyon pre-PACE days) and the Aids wandered off, quarrelling amongst themselves as to whose diary he should appear in the back of; and if you think that's poor English, you know I'm sure exactly what I mean.

I went down to the cells, where I confronted a very angry young man. 'This is a nice thing!' he cried. 'I come in here to help you out and I get chucked in the cells like a common criminal!' 'You're here, because you're circulated as being wanted for failing to appear,' I replied. Genuine bewilderment flooded over his face. 'Failing to appear?' he echoed. 'That's rubbish! I've never been in trouble with you lot in my life! Where am I supposed to have failed to appear?'

'Spain,' I replied, and the perplexity was swept from his face, as though it had been wiped with a cloth, to be replaced with a look of absolute terror. 'Spain!' he screamed. 'Don't send me back there! Oh Christ, you can't ! I've got to get out of here!' And with that, since I was the only barrier in the cell doorway standing between him and freedom, he launched himself at me. I had to severely rebuke him for his outburst and eventually, he sat trembling on the edge of his cot. 'Just sit there and take it easy,' I said. 'I'll see if I can find out a bit more about this.' He nodded dumbly, looking at me with blank, unseeing eyes.

'Yeah,' I've got it here,' said the laconic Detective Sergeant, telephoning me from the Interpol office at the Yard, having checked the reference number I had given him from CRO. 'It's a warrant from Torremolinos for theft of a purse.' 'So when do I get to take him over there Sarge?' I said excitedly. 'What do I have to do now?' My naive remarks enriched the DS's otherwise boring existence at the Yard, because for nearly a full minute, he was convulsed with laughter. 'You don't, you chump,' he laughed. 'It's just a local warrant. What it means is, if he ever goes back over there, he can be lifted, but not otherwise. You won't get a trip out of this one!' 'But' I said stupidly, my dreams of far off sunny beaches suddenly dashed, 'but I've got him in the cells.' 'Take my advice, tell him to f**k off and not to do it again!' He was still laughing when he put down the telephone.

I was smarting from being jeered at as I returned to the cells, but when I saw the pitiable look on the face of the Spanish suspect, looking at me in much the same way as a condemned man might regard the prison Governor, in the forlorn hope that he might be carrying a stay of execution, I felt so sorry for him that I promptly repeated the news that I'd received from Interpol. The poor chap all but kissed my hands as he snuffled out his thanks. 'Now, look,' I said, 'Of course you're free to leave any time you like, but if it's not too much trouble, why were you in such a state about this business?'

The young man wiped his eyes. 'I went to Spain with some mates in June, oh, about five years ago,' he replied. 'One night we all went out to a nightclub. We all had a few drinks and then, all of a sudden, this girl who was sitting near me reckoned that she'd had her purse nicked. The next thing I knew, was the local coppers came and dragged me outside.'

I nodded, encouraging him to continue. The local coppers that he was referring to, would, in those days, have received their pay cheques from General Franco. 'It doesn't make any difference now,' he continued, 'but it's God's truth, I didn't nick that girl's purse and I don't know who did. But those coppers dragged me down the nick and gave me the treatment. Christ, was it rough! Boots, fists, rifle butts, the lot! After a couple of minutes of this, I'd have stuck my hands up to nicking the Crown jewels! 'Alright, leave off! I said, when they ran out of breath. You want a confession? Alright, I'll give you one!' One of them, a horrible looking bloke, with a tooth missing, grinned at me. 'A confession, Senor?' he said, 'We don't want no steenkin confession. We doin this, because we like eet!'

I shook hands with the young man at the door of the Police Station and I saw him no more. But, do you know, as I gazed at the orange sun sinking out of sight behind the Beckton gasometers, I contemplated the two different police cultures and I consoled myself with the thought that the young man would have considered Randall Jones to be a pussy cat!

A Savage Tribe

I enjoyed a triumphant tour on the Flying Squad at the Yard in the early 1980s. I had the best officers on my team and between us, we had the best informants, the best jobs, the best arrests and the best results. Then disaster struck. I was temporarily promoted to the rank of Detective Inspector and it went straight to my head. You may not be unduly surprised to learn that senior officers do not appreciate being forcefully told what to do by jumped-up junior officers who have got far too big for their boots and I was promptly posted. In those days, it was usual, once an officer was to be posted off the Squad, to be given a choice of perhaps three stations where vacancies existed. This courtesy was by-passed in my case and I was sent straight to 'N' Division.

Let me fully explain the misery of my self-inflicted misfortune. 'N' Division was part of 3 Area, which represented one-quarter of the 900 square miles of the Metropolitan Police District. It was situated in the North-west corner of 3 Area and I lived in the South-east corner. It took three changes on the tube system and a bus either end to complete my journey to work, which would take me an hour and three-quarters, on a good day. 'N' Division covers Holloway, Highbury Vale, Kings Cross,

Islington and Caledonian Road Police Stations and its boundaries touch Haringay in the North, Clerkenwell in the South, Camden Town in the West and Hackney in the East. It was a cheerless place, with a huge indigenous population swollen with large numbers of Afro-Caribbean and Greek families. It was famed for its social deprivation and the crumbling tenements were filled with some of the worst and most unscrupulous criminals in the capital. It was a good place for an up-and-coming young detective to 'make his bones', but I'd just turned forty and much as I liked hard work, I could have done without spending eight hours per day in these depressing surroundings whilst being further burdened with the best part of four hours travelling.

'You'll hate it here,' was the gloomy, departing prognosis of the 'N' Division Commander as he sent me off to Holloway Police Station. The Chief Superintendent was equally welcoming.

'I'll give you a tip, to make your life here a bit easier,' he said, and I leaned eagerly forward in my seat, to capture these pearls of wisdom.

'Don't fuck the typists,' he said, frowning. 'They're all Greek and they've all got Greek boy-friends, brothers and fathers and I don't need that sort of aggravation. All right. That's it. Hop it.' So this was to be my celibate world for the next two years; and at the end of that time, almost to the day, the Flying Squad felt that I had exorcised my bolshie demons and welcomed me back to the fold and there I stayed for the next six years of my service. But that was in the future...

I'd been asked to help out with a routine arrest of a youngster, named Gary Savage, for burglary by one of the Detective Constables at Holloway Police Station. He gave me the details and although I didn't personally know any of the genus Savage, I was aware that they were trouble. And for those of you who don't know the meaning of the word 'trouble' in this particular context, it means that the attendance by police to such a families address, for any reason whatsoever, would result in both screeching abuse and physical violence from the occupants.

I spoke to the Detective Inspector about it. 'I want to take a heavy team round there, early in the morning,' I said. As he pursed his lips and started to shake his head negatively from side to side, I continued, 'Look, it's been my experience from the Flying Squad, that when you go to nick someone who's going to be aggravation, if you go team-handed, they can see that you mean business and generally, there won't be any trouble.'

The Inspector, whose head had continued shaking to such an extent that I had begun to suspect a mild form of Parkinson's Disease, replied, 'Can't afford the overtime,' as though it were coming out of his own pocket.

So, with plenty of misgivings, I, together with the Detective Constable plus one other officer went to the address the following morning. The Uniformed branch at Holloway had an operation of their own that morning so they were unable to spare any of their troops. I pulled up my coat collar against the chill wind that blew down those mean Islingtonian streets as I got out of the CID car, and looked up at the grimy facade of the young burglar's family hovel. My apprehensions were well-founded, because the inevitable happened. The front door was opened by the family matriarch and with a skill, born of years of experience, immediately identified our profession.

'Wot?' she demanded aggressively.

The Detective Constable spoke first. 'We want to speak to Gary, Mrs..'

'Why?' interrupted Mrs Savage.

'It's about a burglary.'

'Wot burglary?' snapped Mrs Savage. Just then, a rat-faced 17 year old appeared beside his mother.

'Hello, Gary,' said the Detective Constable.

'Say nuffin,' interjected Mrs Savage and continued, 'Wot burglary, then?' The Detective Constable sighed. 'A burglary at Parkin's Tobacconists...'

'When?' cut in Mrs Savage. 'Last Thursday,' replied the young detective, grateful that he'd been allowed to actually complete a sentence without interruption. Mrs Savage turned to her rodent-faced offspring. 'Did yew do a burglary at Parkin's last Thursday?' she demanded. It is difficult to put into words how cunning, evasiveness and imbecility could cross somebody's face in a period of 15 seconds, but Gary Savage achieved this, before he finally answered, 'Nah.'

'There you are,' said Mrs Savage triumphantly, as though a lorry load of archdeacons had alibied her son. 'e didn't do it. Now fuck off!' As she went to slam the door, the Detective Constable stopped her and said, 'Gary's under arrest, Mrs Savage and he'll have to come to...' and that was as far as he got. Spinning round, Mrs Savage shrieked, 'Johnny! Harry! Billy!' and down the hallway rushed three of Gary's siblings, the whole family flung themselves at us and a full-scale riot developed. Eventually, the family was hauled down to the Police Station and were charged with assaulting the police.

I was aching all over from the bashing that I and the others had so unnecessarily taken and I was furious, absolutely hopping mad. With hindsight, it's foolish to interview anybody in that state, because you're obviously not in full control but at the time, I was so angry that I got stuck in straight away.

I pointed an accusing finger at a spot right between my adversary's eyes. 'You, mister are a wanker,' I said with sure and certain authority. He started to open his mouth to protest against this slur but I anticipated this and I stopped him with a gesture. 'Don't tell me you're not,' I said, fiercely. 'You've got no guts at all. D'you think it's clever, me getting knocked about? Do you? Now it's just the two of us, how'd you fancy a pop at me? Just us two? Right now?'

My opponent dumbly shook his head. 'It would make good sense if you were to stay out of my way, in future,' I said quietly. 'You follow?'

He nodded. I jerked a thumb in the direction of the door. 'All right,' I said. 'Get out.' The white-faced Detective Inspector was silent for a moment. 'Actually, it is my office,' he said, humbly. Of course, he was quite right, so feeling rather foolish, it was me who had to leave.

Now, you may think that this was pretty beastly behaviour to my senior officer and you might be right. He could have used my intemperate words as evidence against me to support a charge on a discipline board (if the rest of the CID office hadn't been momentarily struck deaf, dumb and blind) but I really didn't care. I have already said that Holloway was the dreariest posting of my career and this was just one of the disturbances I had with various of the personnel, in an effort to get myself kicked off the division. But it was an empty victory; my behaviour to that, or indeed any other officer, did nothing to shift me from this vale of tears and I had to accept and serve my full two-year banishment.

But whether you think that my conduct to the Detective Inspector was reprehensible or not, you may agree with me that thanks to his lack of leadership, his inability to second-guess the behaviour of criminals and his parsimony with the station's budget, he had put all three of us in an untenable position; and that was only the beginning of the trouble.

At this time, Islington Council was fully in the grip of the so-called Loony Left. They had abolished black bin-liners, having decided that these were an affront to the black population, nursery nurses taught their small charges the words of, 'Baa-baa, black sheep' at their peril and the

African dance classes, mainly attended by middle class, middle-aged white women desperately in search of cultural harmony (so they said) and the lesbian self-defence classes were thriving. They had recently formed a so-called Police Consultative Group, funding it with sixty thousand pounds'-worth of the ratepayers money and until one of its leading lights absconded with the group's entire funds, they were rightly considered a thorn in the side of the police at Holloway. There was no consultation; their role seemed to be purely to attack police actions and policies for any reason, for political gain. This case was Heaven-sent for them. They championed the Savages' cause, ostentatiously appeared at every court appearance and ensured that the Detective Constable was summoned for Assault Occasioning Actual Bodily Harm; which, if proved, was punishable with a maximum of 5 years' imprisonment.

Stipendiary Magistrates could be rude, impatient and irascible - they were also outstandingly fair and difficult to fool and in consequence, our day in court was priceless. The eldest son, Billy, who had been charged with assaulting me, was in the witness box. There is an art to giving evidence and, in common with many of life's qualifications, this ability had passed Billy by. In a forlorn effort to appear truthful, he was trying to portray himself as a bashful intermediary, his family as genial members of society and me, as a despotic monster.

'That Kirby just pushed his way in, Your Honour,' he earnestly told Mr Rollins, the Stipendiary Magistrate, 'and my Mum, she goes, "Excuse me, can I help you, officer?" really polite, like. And that Kirby, he didn't say nuffin', he just punched her right in the face, breaking her nose and blacking her eyes. And he went over to where she was lying on the floor, with blood all over her face, and he kicked her teeth in. Oh, yeah, and all her ribs as well. So I goes to him, I goes, 'Excuse me, officer, but would you mind not belting my Mum, like that?'

'Indeed?' exclaimed Mr Rollins, incredulously. 'And did your mother seek medical aid, as a result of receiving these fearful injuries?'

'Well, no,' admitted the mendacious Billy. 'She ain't one to make a fuss!'

The Flying Door

'That Linval, 'e's well at it, Mr Kirby,' said Sammy the Snout, decisively. I sighed and stirred my third cup of coffee as though this operation could possibly inject some taste into this cup of tepid muck.

Taking my silence as disbelief, Sammy sought to reassert himself. ''e is, I swear it!' he said, eagerly.

I sighed again. This is what happens, I thought, when you try to treat a snout graciously. Whenever Sammy telephoned me with the promise of some information of interest, we would agree the time that we would meet and choose one of two possible locations for a pick-up point. Having agreed upon the location, I would drive there and if I were satisfied that it was safe, I would pick Sammy up and drive to one of several other locations, all of them safe to drive into and quick and easy to drive out of. There Sammy would impart his information and afterwards, I would drop him off at a place of our mutual choosing.

And today? Today, I'd treated Sammy to cups of coffee in a reasonably safe cafe in Camden Town and here he was, remonstrating with me as though he were a CID typist who had actually believed the flattery lavished on her at the Christmas party and who was now catching up with reality.

I surreptitiously glanced around the cafe, in the hope that the clientele hadn't been listening to our entire conversation. Everybody else seemed immersed in their own discussions. I regarded Sammy through narrowed eyes. He was an unprepossessing sight. Thin, to the point of being emaciated, his pointed, pock-marked features were constantly on the move, his eyes flickering from side to side as though anticipating instant recognition and denunciation. From time to time, a grubby fingernail would find itself in Sammy's mouth where it would be furiously worried until he lost interest in it and resumed the hunted examination of his neighbours. I could never be sure if the odd, stale smell of decay which drifted across the table emanated from Sammy's body, which was desperately in need of hosing down, his mouth, the contents of which would have caused the despair of the most talented of dentists or his clothes which the most resolute of the capital's homeless would have haughtily disdained.

There was one thing, though, of which I was certain. Any criminal who might be observing us who possessed even a modicum of experience or intelligence would be in no doubt that he was watching a CID officer debriefing his snout; hence my reluctance to be seen with Sammy in public.

'Sammy, dear,' I said quietly. 'I am aware that Linval's at it. I would like to do something of a positive nature about it; and so, no doubt, would you?' From the glazed look in Sammy's eyes, I saw that I had temporarily lost him. Ever since I had dealt compassionately with Sammy at court on a minor theft charge, he had been as loyal as a dog and although his uses as an informant were fairly limited, he sometimes provided me with a nugget of information that was solid gold. However, intellectual conversation was not really his forte and therefore, I would have to render matters down to a more basic level.

'Sammy!' I said, sharply, to attract his wandering attention. 'You would like me to nick Linval, wouldn't you?'

'Yeah!' breathed Sammy, 'cos 'e's well at it, Mr Kirby!'

This discourse was getting rather repetitive, but still I nodded, acknowledging Sammy's massive contribution to criminal intelligence. 'And having nicked him,' I continued, 'you'd like to see about five years imprisonment stuck up his arse, wouldn't you?'

'Five years at least, Mr K!' Sammy agreed eagerly.

'Well,' I said, 'if you accept that I can't take Linval in front of a Judge at the Bailey and get him down by saying, 'Excuse me, M'Lud, but he's been at it,' you'd better get me something worthwhile on him, hadn't you?'

Sammy nodded dumbly.

'Because,' I said, warming to my task, 'if you think I can convict Linval or anybody else on the fartful you've given me, you're very much mistaken; so if you want a few bob out of Scotland Yard, bugger off and get working!'

'Sorry, Mr Kirby,' said Sammy, humbly, looking for all the world like a pet dog that had just received an unkind clump. I did feel a bit ashamed of myself and because I liked to send my snouts on to the field of battle with their heads held high, I patted him reassuringly on the shoulder. 'Sam, you're my best snout, you know that,' I said quietly. 'Go out there and get the goods on Linval and there'll be a nice drink in it for you, but promise me that you'll watch yourself, because good'uns like you are hard to find.'

Sammy beamed with pleasure. 'Leave it with me, Mr Kirby,' he said and with his tiny chest swelling with pleasure, he walked out of the cafe into the watery light of an autumnal Camden Town afternoon. As I paid for the six cups of tasteless coffee which we'd consumed, I reflected on what Sammy had said and he wasn't far wrong about one thing; Linval Johnson was certainly a wrong'un.

Shortly after arriving at Holloway, Johnson had been pointed out to me as being one of the tight-packed community's more unsavoury residents. He was tall, black and thin and he made a despicable living from attacking women on the streets and snatching their handbags. Off duty, so to speak, one of his more unattractive pursuits was to swagger along Stroud Green Road, and when he spotted a Woman Police officer out on a lone patrol, he'd sidle up to her and murmur, 'Me goin' to rape yuh, bitch!' and smirking at the look of shock on the poor girl's face, he'd saunter away feeling highly satisfied with himself. A couple of WPCs were plainly terrified of him and in fact, one refused to go out on her own at all, following such an encounter. Vermin like Johnson would not have walked away unscathed during my younger days. Still, since we lived in more enlightened times, I had him brought into the Station and just the two of us had an informative little chat. I started off by pointing out the inadvisability of threats and poor manners. Johnson retorted that the WPCs must have misheard him. This, I firmly informed him, was not the case and if there were any reoccurrence, things would go ill with him; and in fairness, I think that that was the end of his unattractive proposals. We then got on to other pressing matters.

I admired his wardrobe. True, his suit of plaid plus-fours, the knee-length tartan stockings and the jaunty Robin Hood hat were not necessarily to my taste but they were undeniably the last word in style. This, Johnson acknowledged with a grin, was true. But from where, I wondered, had the funding come for such fine raiment? Linval was suddenly mulishly silent. Surely not, I probed gently, from pimping, which was his original trade or calling? This produced a massive fit of the sulks, which threatened to curtail our lively social intercourse so I changed tack and suggested that his income stemmed from robbing women of their handbags. This slur was indignantly repudiated but this was the information Sammy had given me and I did not doubt that it was true. The trouble was, Johnson was so difficult to catch. He did not stick to a proscribed area, nor a specified time. He might let three or four septuagenarian ladies, each with bulging handbags, pass him, free from let or hindrance and then savagely attack the fifth unescorted woman who walked round the corner. He always operated on foot and alone. When you consider how much money the average woman carries in her purse, it's not really all that much. No, my pet theory was that Johnson just liked terrorising women.

Escorting Johnson to the door, I bade him a genial farewell, informing him that the next time we met, the encounter would not be nearly so cordial. Adjusting his hat to a jaunty angle, Johnson recovered a little of his *sang-froid* and sauntered off into Hornsey Road, almost colliding with a uniform constable who was about to enter the Station. 'Mind where you're going,' I said sharply to the officer, in a voice loud enough for Johnson to hear. 'He's my best snout!' Although this raised a chuckle from the officer, it was just a bit of casual spitefulness from yours truly. I didn't expect Johnson to make a sobbing confession in reaction to this aspersion; I just wanted him to receive confirmation that I thought he was slime and that I was going to go all out to nick him.

Well, God knows, I tried. I tried with Sammy and I tried with other informants but I never even got close to nicking Johnson and eventually, I went back to the Flying Squad and immersed myself in the world of robbers who usually strike during daylight hours. And then, one day, news came filtering in that had me firstly reaching for the phone for confirmation and secondly for a bottle of Scotch, to pour large drinks all round, as the following story was recounted amidst roars of laughter...

Because of his intimidating height, if it was just the money Johnson was after instead of wanting to terrorise women, all he had to do was grab the victim's handbag. Certainly, there was no excuse for him to spray CS gas into his elderly victim's face, but that's just what he did on this particular occasion and, as usual, only a fragmented description could be obtained from the traumatised victim. Of course, everybody knew the identity of the perpetrator but knowing it and proving it were two completely separate and different ball-games. Not a single clue pointed towards Johnson as being the culprit, not one... well, none, that is, except for Sheila McDonnagh.

Cadaverously gaunt, most of Sheila's dyed blonde hair had been consumed by her black roots and that, combined with a hacking cough gave her the appearance of a tragic heroine, rather like Mimi in Puccini's opera *La Boheme*. At least, that was the perception of the army of Islington's Social Workers, each of whom privately desired to be the first to redeem her from her unworthy life style. Less honourable were the attentions of the more unsavoury of Holloway's criminal element who used her as a tart and also as a minor receiver of stolen property. So when, the following day, Sheila tried to obtain a dress by means of the victim's stolen credit card, she was quickly apprehended. During the interview, she tearfully confessed that she had obtained the card from Johnson the previous evening, just a few minutes walk from the scene of the attack and within minutes of the attack occurring. A little pressure was applied and when a suggestion was made that in return for a witness statement, naming Johnson as her benefactor, a caution might be forthcoming, Sheila remembered Johnson remarking that he had stolen the card a few minutes previously from 'some bitch'. The hunt was now on with a vengeance but the elusive Johnson was always on the move because, as he had previously told me, he operated on the assumption that police were always looking for him.

He was eventually tracked down to an address in north Holloway. Believing that Johnson was still in possession of his CS gas canisters, the officers decided to take no chances. They resolved to introduce a sledge-hammer to the front door of the premises and go in and seize Johnson before he had time to react. But just in case he did have time to resist and use the CS gas on them, the officers had the extra edge of being issued with respirators by PT17, the (then) Firearms Department, in order to give them protection from the gas.

It was a good plan, and it almost certainly would have worked, had it not been for the fact that the house was crowded with so many other itin-erant delinquents of the area, that Johnson had had to make his bed in the hallway, just behind the front door. I suppose it highly likely that Johnson received the same amount of shock as had his female victims, when the heavy front door was smashed right off its hinges and landed on top of him. Having had the added discomfort of half-a-dozen heavy young men trampling on the door that now reposed on top of him in their eagerness to get inside, poor Linval's shock turned to horror when, having rid himself of the burden of the door, he struggled to his feet, only to find himself surrounded by what he thought to be an assault troop from the Special Air Service.

'Fuckin' hell, man!' screamed Linval, flinging his arms up in the air. 'I'm a fuckin' robber, not a terrorist!'

As a badly bruised and a still traumatised Johnson sat in his cell at Holloway Police Station, he should have reflected upon his past indis-cretions and resolved to lead an industrious life in future. In fact, he did nothing of the kind. Whilst one part of his mind was seething at being betrayed, the other was busily concocting a defence which included a cast-iron alibi for the time of the offence. Unfortunately, he was unaware of the existence of Sheila McDonnagh's witness statement and was understandably dismayed at the hilarious reception given by his interrogators when he introduced Sheila as his alibi and was forced to fabricate a further defence.

I regret to say that all of his most impassioned denials went unheeded, the Judge at the Bailey deciding that ladies should be allowed to walk through the streets of Holloway, safe from Johnson's molestations, for the following five years.

A Local Celebrity

Exactly why Julius Wiseman went off the rails, is difficult to say. Certainly, it was not due to social deprivation, nor disintegrating family values. His father was a noted neurosurgeon and his sister was a highly successful and well respected General Practitioner. His uncle was one of the youngest High Court Judges ever to be appointed to the Queen's Bench Division and his mother was a creator of exquisite watercolours. She was also the creator of young Julius, which was not, alas, to her credit.

From an early age, it was evident that Julius was a disagreeable child. Swiftly banishing him to a far-away boarding school (which was almost as difficult to get into, as it was to get out of) the family breathed a collective sigh of relief. Returning home for a mercifully brief period, Julius went up to a redbrick university to read law.

It is from this point that it is easier to chart the sequence of events that was to result in the disgrace, downfall and degradation of Julius Wiseman. The fact that he had sequestrated substantial sums of money from fellow students in order to settle some pressing gambling debts, would have been bad enough. To do so without their knowledge was quite reprehensible. Despite the fact that Professor Wiseman was able to pre-empt criminal proceedings by swiftly reimbursing the furious students, Julius was sent down from university and that was to mark his disgrace. His downfall was provided by a combination of his own criminality, his inability to keep his mouth shut and the intervention of His Honour Judge Michael Stone QC. I facilitated the degradation.

I'm starting to get ahead of myself. Julius, by now, was an arrogant, overbearing reject of the establishment. Instead of capitalising on this, and getting himself called to the Bar, Julius commenced his career of crime by means of a spectacularly planned burglary. He carefully reconnoitred the warehouse that he and his accomplices had decided to break into. The alarms had been noted, and a small fire extinguisher had been provided with which to fill them with foam, to stop them effectively activating. An impressive array of burglars' tools had been obtained. A minutely detailed plan, plus a scale model of the warehouse had been assembled, a van to carry away the booty had been stolen and hot-wired and a receiver had been arranged and a price for the commodity agreed. Timings of police patrols in the area had been put down to the minute, as had the fact that dusk occurred at 9.17pm and that that particular night, would be a moonless one. The break-in was timed to occur at precisely 44 minutes after sun-down and nothing could go wrong.

Everything went wrong.

Besides being a tiresome boy, Julius had always been a clumsy one. As he managed to trip over a dustbin that crashed to the cobblestones with such a cacophonous rattle that practically every light in the neighbourhood came on, two members of Julius' gang panicked to such an extent that they both turned and ran head-first into each other, causing a badly bleeding nose in one case and mild concussion in the other. Those neighbours who were not already leaning out of their windows, rapidly reinforced those who were, after the third member of the gang howled in agony as he was attacked by a disgruntled wire-haired terrier, peeved at having been awoken from a deep sleep, which bit him very viciously in the ankle. In a rare act of compassion, Julius attempted to assist his comrade by kicking the dog away, and was attacked in turn by the dog's owner, a sprightly 74 year-old widow, who savagely coshed him with her umbrella.

At this time, Julius had reasoned, all of the uniformed police officers at the local Police Station, should have been parading for night-duty. So they were, except for the crew of the wireless car who worked a different shift and who, by chance, rounded the corner at that precise moment and nabbed the lot of them. Julius confessed everything to the highly amused CID officers who interviewed him, not out of remorse, but because he was so arrogantly proud of what he set out to do.

In the fullness of time, Julius and his gang appeared at the North-east London Quarter Sessions, before His Honour Judge Stone QC. Michael

Stone was a fair Judge, but not one to be trifled with. Only one defendant in living memory, who, smarting at a bit of unexpected porridge, had dared to wish Judge Stone a speedy departure from this earth, adding that he hoped his demise would be accompanied with screaming torment, through cancer. Swiftly having the impertinent felon dragged back into court, Judge Stone awarded him another 6 months on top, stating it was in recognition of 'your infernal cheek.'

In common with many Judges, having heard the circumstances of the case, together with mitigation from the defence, Judge Stone would write down the sentence that he was about to award in his desk book and then deliver his punishment. Julius was now asked if he wished to say anything before sentence was passed. In retrospect, Julius would realise that what was next to occur would vie for pride of place as being the biggest gaffe in legal circles, since Anne Boleyn had asked King Henry VIII, if he thought the appropriate penalty for adultery was Community Service.

'Yes,' replied Julius, casually, rising to his feet. 'I'd just like to point out,' he continued, 'that you cannot send me to prison for a first offence.'

Judge Stone's eyebrows assumed the shape of crescent moons and shot northwards, threatening to knock his wig off. 'WHAT!' he gasped.

'No,' blithely continued Julius, 'and I'd like to take this opportunity of pointing out the legal precedents, contained in the First Offenders Act of 1958, together with Section 17(2) of the Criminal Justice Act 1948.' On and on he went, causing barristers and co-defendants alike to cringe inside their clothes as Judge Stone's face grew harder and his eyes flintier.

Mercifully, Julius' speech came to an end. 'I see,' said the Judge, quietly, as he drew two decisive lines with his pen through his former (and now revised) decision, which had previously read, '6 months imprisonment, suspended for 2 years.'

'You will all go to prison for 9 months,' said the Judge sternly , adding crisply, 'take them down!'

'Cor, fanks a lot, Jules,' mournfully muttered one of his co-defendants. 'Yeah,' agreed another, adding, 'you prize twat!'

It was an opinion shared both privately and publicly, by a lot of people.

Prison did nothing to reform Julius, but within 15 minutes of entering its' system, he learnt in a rather painful lesson the advisability of keeping one's lippy mouth shut, especially in the presence of people who are your physical superiors. Due to an administrative error (which Julius always maintained, probably quite correctly, was deliberate) he was not sent to a 'soft' first-time offenders prison, but instead spent almost all of his sentence at Wandsworth, probably one of the toughest prisons in England.

Upon his release, Jules harboured a seething resentment of everyone in authority which was to last until his death in a Road Traffic accident on the A406 trunk road several years later. Judge Stone, not unnaturally, came top of the list, but the police ran it a close second. Julius had a distinctive car which he drove to the detriment of all other road users, and he was frequently stopped by police. He had been pointed out to me, as a new Police Constable, as being one of the more loathsome characters on the manor. And whenever he was stopped, Julius refused as a matter of principle to offer his driving documents to the officer stopping him, saying he had left them at home. The officer would duly issue him a form HO/RT/1, which required him to produce his documents at a Police Station of his choice, within 5 days of being stopped. Julius would always present himself on the fifth day, just before the deadline. Because of his hectoring attitude, his public-school voice and his utter contempt for any kind of authority, many uniformed police officers were terrified of him.

On this particular occasion, I was off-duty, and had wandered into a Police Station in order to send a form through the internal dispatch system. As I did so, Julius Wiseman swept into the front office and banged down a HO/RT/1 form on the counter. 'Good morning, good morning, good morning!' he snapped, to the uniformed Sergeant, the Police Constable and the Woman Police Constable, who, apart from me, were the inhabitants of that room. 'Now then, Sergeant, here's another of those ridiculous buff-coloured forms which one of your local cretins have seen fit to give to me, and these,' and with that, he flung his driving licence, certificate of insurance and test certificate across the counter and on to the floor beyond, 'are my documents.' He sneered as the Sergeant bent to the floor and retrieved them. 'Now just get out that damned book of yours and do whatever you've got to do, because I'm a busy man,' he continued. 'Oh, and when you've finished your idiotic scrawling, be sure to give me that form back. It's my sixty-fourth this year and it will form an important part of my claim of harassment that I shall shortly be making to the Commissioner. Get a move on, man, for God's sake!'

'Sorry, Mr Wiseman,' muttered the Sergeant, writing furiously.

'And what's special about today, do you know?' demanded Julius in a particularly hectoring fashion.

'No, Mr Wiseman,' mumbled the Sergeant, scribbling faster than ever.

'It's my birthday, that's what!' bellowed Julius. 'Well? Come on, then! Let's hear it!'

You will forgive me, I know, if I do not reveal the names of the police officers present, nor even the location of the Police Station. Over 30 years have passed by, and yet I still flush with humiliation whenever I think of what happened next. All three officers, looking shame-facedly down at the floor, began more or less in unison, to sing, 'Happy Birthday to you, Happy Birthday to you, Happy Birthday Mr Wiseman...'

I could not believe my eyes or my ears. I choked with rage at the spectacle of the three most miserable specimens of what I considered to be the greatest Police Force in the world humbling themselves before this smirking piece of shit.

I grabbed hold of Julius by his lapels, and dragged him outside. Pushing him against the lobby wall, I seized hold of a handful of cloth at the top of his trousers, jerked him onto tip-toe and demanded, 'Do you know what I like about you, Wiseman?'

'What?' gasped Julius in a strangled voice.

'Nothing!' I replied. 'Now fuck off!' and he scuttled away.

My second shock of the day came as the Sergeant rushed outside and grabbed me by the arm, his white face twitching with a mixture of anger and terror. 'Do you know who that was!' he screamed. 'Mr Wiseman, that's who!'

On Yer Bike!

It had gone midnight when I opened the front door, so I was not surprised that my family had finally given up and gone to bed. God, what a day! I was numb from the cold, tired and hungry. I went into the kitchen, where Max (the late and much lamented Wonder Dog) struggled to an upright position, and summoned up the energy for a wag-and-a-half of her tail, before slipping back into a comatose position in her basket.

I rescued my steak and kidney pie (once succulent and tasty, now a smoking ruin) from the oven and with a skill born of cunning from similar burnt offerings of years past, I took a table knife and made a number of incisions to release the scorching heat from the pie's interior.

Uncorking a bottle of Orvieto, I took my belated dinner into the dining room and moodily consumed it. I swallowed the rest of the glass of wine and was just about to re-cork the bottle, prior to heading upstairs to bed, when I saw a folded copy of the local paper. I had recently enjoyed a little success with a couple of cases in the community. What would the headlines be? 'Local Yard tec smashes drugs ring'? 'Top Romford Cop commended by Judge'?

Not a bit of it. The state of Havering Borough Council's drains were far more fascinating than anything I'd done. I flipped quickly through the pages and I was just about to put down the paper and switch out the lights when, on the back page, I saw an account of a court case. Clinton Curling, described as an unemployed, part-time bricklayer (no, I didn't understand it, either) was the name of the miscreant. 'Curling' was a fairly unusual name, and I looked for his address. Yes, that was it. It must be his son, I thought.

I picked up the bottle of wine and poured myself a generous measure. I put my feet up, and read on. Curling had apparently been brought to notice after the police had been called to the estate where he lived. This was in connection with a matter that was nothing whatsoever to do with Curling, but he had taken this heaven-sent opportunity to inscribe graffiti with the aid of an aerosol paint can, over the whole of the temporarily unattended police car.

Whilst on bail for this matter, he was again arrested, having been seen tampering with car door handles and upon being apprehended, was found to be in possession of a quantity of cannabis. Before being unmercifully shaken to his very core with the punitive sentence of 2 years Probation, Curling told Snaresbrook Crown Court, 'I done it, because I'm bored and because I've always 'ated the Filf.'

I closed my eyes and my mind travelled back over 20 years, to when I received that radio call on the 'Q' Car, to go to Ron's cycle shop, regarding a suspect.

Upon our arrival, there was Ron, the proprietor, together with a seedy, unkempt character named Douglas Curling who was in possession of a bicycle. I was later to find out that although Curling had got an enormous number of convictions, they were all for mean, petty offences and the most he'd served was 2 years imprisonment, for sacrilege - stealing money from a church offertory box.

'This geezer tried to sell me this bike,' said Ron. 'He don't know too much about it, so I thought I'd better phone you.'

Thanking Ron, we provisionally questioned Curling, and although he appeared rather apprehensive, he stated quite categorically that this was his bicycle, which it had been for some considerable time. I took his details and the frame number of the bike and went outside to check on both man and machine, on the 'Q' Car's radio.

Back came the answer - Curling was known to the police, but was not currently circulated as 'wanted' for any offence - and there was no trace of the bicycle having been reported as being stolen.

I returned to the shop and gave this information to the Detective Constable. Upon receipt of this news, the apprehension which had been displayed on Curling's face vanished. His voice now rang with a confident note. He had a criminal record, it was true, he declared, but he had been staying out of trouble since his release from prison and had been going straight. Now we had come along with our vile accusations. We were not giving him the opportunity to reform with this sort of harassment, and it was clearly not good enough. He would lodge the strongest possible complaint, he said, firstly with his Probation Officer, then with his Member of Parliament and finally with the Commissioner of Police himself. Curling had, by now, worked himself into a passion and his voice grew shrill with indignation. All of us would be returned to Uniform duties and would be walking the beat for evermore, by the time he'd finished with us, he stated categorically. Our careers were finished. Any aspirations we might have had of advancement within the Metropolitan Police were to be terminated, as of that moment. We were ruined men.

Identifying me as his chief tormentor, Curling pointed a skinny, accusing finger at me and his attack then took a more personal turn. He cast so much doubt on my parentage, that I almost had a panic attack.

Curling's rantings had become so vehement that a small crowd had gathered and with measured tread, smarting with humiliation, we returned to the 'Q' Car, and drove off. I don't suppose we'd gone more than 100 yards down the road, when I received a radio call from New Scotland Yard. I was asked by the Yard's Radio operator if I had checked a bicycle frame number some 10 minutes before, because if I had, this bicycle had just been reported stolen at Chadwell Heath Police Station.

As revelations go, I suppose it was pretty-well on a par with the one experienced by Saul of Tarsus, when he made his unscheduled stop on the road to Damascus. The 'Q' Car executed a 180 degree turn and we returned the short distance to Ron's Cycle shop. 'Just leave this to me,' I said to the rest of the crew and went inside the shop. Curling was still there.

'Ron,' I said casually, to the owner, 'have you given Douglas any money?'

'Yes,' replied Ron. 'Seven quid.'

I shook my head slowly and sighed; a tacit acknowledgement to the wickedness of the world. 'Douglas,' I said. 'Give Ron back his seven quid, would you?'

Curling dropped his eyes, and trembled as he handed back the money. He now realised that any further protestations of innocence were useless. He knew, too, that any further defamations would be madness. I put my arm around his shoulders. 'Douglas,' I said. 'Please come outside with me.' We went outside. 'You and I are going to sit in the back of that car, Douglas,' I said, gently, 'and it's probably going to take us all of 15 minutes to get to Chadwell Heath Police Station. Now, before we get there, I want you to promise me faithfully that you'll remember all those other crimes that you've committed and have never been caught for, and that you'll tell me about them. Will you promise me you'll do that?'

Curling nodded dumbly. 'Oh, good,' I said.

Now, the result of unburdening his unpleasant little soul with his past misdeeds was so unsettling, that Curling was blubbing by the time we reached the Police Station. He made a full confession to a host of his grubby, petty little crimes and then took us to his home address, where, he told us, other stolen bikes would be found.

Nowadays, Dagenham has brightened up quite a bit, due mainly to many of the inhabitants being able to purchase their Council homes, but at the time of Curling's arrest, things were very different. Much of the area was very deprived and as the 'Q' Car pulled up outside Curling's house, I saw that it was the last word in degradation. In what was once called the front garden, not a blade of grass could be seen; it was simply a repository for filth. Housebricks, literally dozens of unwashed milk bottles, bits of pram, the remnants of Chinese meals, a Christmas tree, cardboard boxes and discarded nappies covered the area; it occurred to me that the Black Death had probably started in an environment very similar to this. I looked over the exterior of the house and I was not unduly surprised to see what I thought was paint peeling off the window frames and sills. I was wrong. Closer inspection revealed that any paint there had long since vanished; what I thought was peeling paint was in fact the actual wood which had cracked, split and peeled after years of inattention. A cadaverous looking dog, which might have held genetic links to the greyhound family, strolled round from the side of the house and bared its blackened teeth at us. Its duty discharged, it wandered off into the back garden and was seen no more. I pushed open the front door, which had seen so much mistreatment over the years that it was unlock-able; when the Curlings' demanded privacy, they simply blockaded the hallway. We walked into the house, where human and canine excrement vied for pride of place. What remained of the wallpaper, hung down in strips, rather like Salvador Dali's imaginative curtains which he designed for the dream sequence in Hitchcock's film, *Spellbound*. In the living room, surrounded by children of diverse ages and in varying states of undress was a woman, who was ironing the washing. She had a thin, tired face. Her belly was swollen with impending birth. 'Bin nicked, ain't I?' snivelled Curling. 'Bleedin' bikes... You tell 'em, Luv,' (sniff)...'only done it for you and the little'un's...' (sob). His implied demand for compassion and understanding fell on deaf ears, for Mrs Curling said not a word. She just calmly paused in her ironing. Exhaustion was etched into every line in her face. Looking not a day over 50, Mrs Curling was, in fact, almost 24.

Her look of calm contempt totally epitomised her thoughts. 'You amazing prat,' it said. 'What new depths of humiliation have you sunk to, now?'

And she carried on with her ironing.

As Curling went around the living room, picking up bits of dismem-bered bicycles, one of the children hugged a cycle lamp to his breast, unwilling to give it up. 'Giss that 'ere, you!' bellowed Curling, his hand raised to strike the child. 'Steady, Douglas,' I admonished him. 'You wouldn't want that to happen to you, would you?' Curling cringed, as though avoiding a blow. 'Sorry, Clint,' he whined to the child. I held my hand out. 'Give me the lamp, Clint,' I said. Young Clint gave me a look of piercing hatred, before handing over possibly the first bit of stolen property he had handled but certainly not the last.

Clint. Clinton Curling. A small boy aged four who since that day had held me accountable for being the sole reason that he ''ated the Filf.' As

I slid into bed and closed my eyes, my last thought, before I drifted off into a dreamless sleep, was that even heroes of Scotland Yard sometimes have to shoulder heavy responsibilities!

A Bloody Embarrassment

Mrs Ellie Mayhew smiled as she stepped off the No.10 bus at Woodford which had conveyed her from her shopping trip in London. She had had a lovely day, she thought, as she walked towards her sister's address. It had been wonderful seeing Jean again, after all those years, but the month in England had passed very quickly and within a few days, she would be returning to her bungalow in Port McQuarrie, New South Wales. It was such a shame that Jim, her husband, had not lived long enough to make the trip, because she just knew that Jim and her sister would have got on so well but... well, that was life. She glanced at her watch. Just coming up to 3 o'clock. She hoped Jean would have the kettle on.

These and other thoughts filled her head as Ellie entered the under-pass. After the brightness of the afternoon, the darkness of the tunnel was slightly disorientating and she knew it would take a few seconds for her sight to become adjusted to the gloom. It was just those seconds that her attacker needed to rush at her out of the shadows and grab her handbag. Ellie screamed and then, as she pulled back at her handbag, she screamed again, this time louder. As she and the hooligan pulled backwards and forwards, she dropped her shopping, screamed for a third time and lashed out at him. Suddenly, there was a man's shout from the opposite end of the underpass; with that, Ellie's attacker relinquished his hold on the handbag and ran off, up the slope of the subway.

The wireless car arrived at the same time as Ellie had started her second cup of tea. The crew obtained a very good detailed description of Ellie's assailant and promptly circulated the description to other units in the area and a search was carried out, without success. Ellie also mentioned that her attacker smelled quite strongly, something she couldn't quite put her finger on...

At 4 o'clock the following morning, Ellie suddenly awoke with a start. She had remembered that the attacker's curious odour was just like the smell which used to stink out Jim's workshop at the bottom of the garden.

It was when Jim used to make those blessed model aeroplanes - the smell was just like the glue which he used to stick the parts of the aeroplanes together...

Later that morning, I pushed the wearisome mountain of paperwork to one side of my desk, to get to the ringing telephone. The caller was Detective Sergeant Derek Kevanny from Barkingside Police Station, who explained that he had been detailed to investigate the attempted robbery on Ellie Mayhew. Derek outlined the facts of the case, as well as the excellent, detailed description of the attacker and in the course of making house to house enquiries, he had discovered that a youth, fitting this description was in the habit of hanging around that area. Since I was running the 'J' Division Crime Squad, Derek thought that this might be an ideal job for us, since I had the manpower and a nondescript vehicle to facilitate an observation on the area; and I agreed that this was an admirable idea.

My officers were uniform PCs working in plain clothes, all keen as mustard to be permanently selected for the CID and I called them in, briefed them and gave them Derek's graphic description of the attacker. 'Sarge, I know who that is,' exclaimed Reg Seaman, who was a very reliable and tenacious officer. 'It's Gary Williams. He's a glue sniffer, who's always nicking tins of glue out of Woolworths. What's more, he lives just a few streets away from the underpass.'

So, that afternoon, I decided to pay a call on Williams. There was no reply to my knock on his front door. 'Tell you what,' said Reg. 'I bet he's in the park. He's always hanging around in there.' We strolled round to the park, and as soon as we walked in, Reg exclaimed, 'There he is! He's talking to the Park Keeper.'

'Right,' I said. 'I'm going to have a word with Mr Williams. You get hold of the Park Keeper and see if he can remember seeing Williams at about three o'clock, yesterday afternoon.'

I went over and introduced myself to Williams, an unpleasant character, who did indeed stink of solvent. I quickly discovered that he had a couple of tins of glue in his pockets.

'Where'd these come from?' I asked him.

'Nicked 'em from Woolies,' muttered the spotty Mr Williams. I then mentioned the attempted bag snatch of the previous afternoon, and since he bore a very strong resemblance to the description of the attacker, I made it quite clear that I believed him to be responsible. This, he strongly denied.

'Alright, where were you yesterday afternoon at three o'clock?' I asked.

'Here, in the park,' replied Williams, defiantly. 'And if you want to know, I was with the Park Keeper. You can check!'

'He *was* with the Park Keeper, Sarge,' said Reg, who had just walked up, and had overheard Williams' comments.

'Told you so,' smirked Williams.

'Right up until three o'clock,' continued Reg, 'when he walked out of the park exit over there,' he pointed, 'which comes out right by the underpass.'

'Alright, you're under arrest,' I said to Williams, who coolly replied, 'You really think I attacked that old woman, don't you?'

'Yes,' I said. 'As a matter of fact, I do.'

'Well, fucking prove it!' he challenged.

H-m-m! I thought.

He was taken to Barkingside Police Station, where he was held on the shoplifting charge, pending enquiries to be made into the more serious matter.

It was at this time that Detective Sergeant Tony Wilson had returned from Wales, bringing with him a prisoner whom Tony had arrested for indecently assaulting a little girl. Any such assault is rightly regarded as serious but since the assault had consisted of touching the little girl's private parts over her clothing, everyone agreed that it was a matter which could have been so much worse.

The young man whose name was Cecil Prendergast (and who, I believe, was a Sunday School teacher,) had tearfully confessed his misdeeds, and Tony, who was a very sympathetic sort of fellow, had written down his confession. Cecil's parents, both decent people, had come down to the Police Station, where there had been a tearful reunion with their son. The parents were now in the charge room, talking to Tony Wilson.

'I know our son has done wrong, Sergeant Wilson,' said Mr Prendergast, 'and we know he'll have to go to prison,' (which, in fact, wasn't the case) 'but what worries us, is that so many terrible things happen to sex offenders in prison.'

Tony, who, as I say, was a very nice, understanding sort of chap, sought to allay their fears. 'Oh, I shouldn't pay too much attention to those sort of stories,' he said soothingly. 'These tales do get blown out of all proportion.'

'Well, perhaps,' said Mrs Prendergast, sounding quite unconvinced. 'But you hear so many stories, stories, too, about the police, how, when they catch a sex offender they - well, you know, rough him up - oh! I'm not suggesting that you would do anything like that, Sergeant Wilson! Our Cecil has told us that you have been the very essence of kindness. No, but you do hear, you know...'

'Madam,' said Tony, firmly. 'I can tell you, quite categorically, that nothing like that would ever happen at this Police Station. So set your mind at rest, please.'

At that moment, I walked into the charge room, en route to the cells, to see Williams. 'Ah!' cried Tony, seeing the possibility of assistance. 'Here's Sergeant Kirby, one of our most experienced officers,' he said with a flourish, rather like an extravagant magician producing a rabbit out of a hat. 'Now, Sergeant Kirby, have you ever heard of a prisoner receiving any kind of rough treatment whatsoever, at a Police Station?' he blandly inquired.

'Never,' I replied, and went into the cell area.

'There you are!' I heard Tony explaining to the doubting parents, 'and Sergeant Kirby should know! A very fair officer of the old school...'

Tony's voice drifted away as I reached Williams' cell and unlocked it. What a sight confronted me! Williams had had the Mother and Father of all nosebleeds. I assure you, I had no idea how it had occurred, but every square inch of him, south of his nose, was covered in blood. His clothes were soaked in blood, blood was in the welts of his shoes, his fingernails, his teeth and when he moved, his clothes made a creaking sound, from the rapidly congealing blood. I thought, I'd better get him to a doctor, fast.

Back in the charge room, the prisoners parents were just about to depart. 'Sergeant Wilson, we cannot thank you enough,' said Mrs Prendergast, shaking Tony's hand. 'I blame myself for listening to all those stupid stories, and I can promise you...' Her voice trailed away as I stepped into the charge room, saying, 'Get out here, you!' And out creaked Gary Williams, unable to move very quickly at all, because of all the congealed blood on his clothes and leaving a gruesome trail of bloody footprints.

Mrs Prendergast let out a piercing shriek and slumped to the floor in a dead faint. 'Merciful God!' whispered her husband. 'What's this poor devil done, to merit this sort of treatment?'

And quick as a flash, Tony Wilson winked and said, 'Oh, don't worry, Sir. He's only a shoplifter!'

As is the case with many of my stories, there's a footnote.

You see, Tony Wilson was quite right, because in the eyes of the law, Williams *was* just a shoplifter, because no matter what you and I suspect to be true, it ain't evidence, folks. I put Williams on an identification parade and waited confidently for Ellie Mayhew to make a positive identification. As she walked along the line-up, Williams quivered, like an autumn leaf in a gale. Yes, you bastard, I thought. You ought to fucking tremble. And then Ellie stopped and turned to the Uniformed Inspector in charge of the parade. 'I'm sorry, Sir,' she said, shaking her head. 'He's not here.'

I was flabbergasted. I was so certain that Williams would be picked out, because there was no doubt in my mind that he had been responsible for the attack. So what had gone wrong? Well, my pet theory is that Ellie recognised him all right, but she simply didn't want to get involved in court proceedings that would last several months. And if my supposition was correct, was it so very wrong of her to take that course of action, when all she wanted to do was to get back to her beloved Port McQuarrie? Well, I dunno. I was bloody disappointed, that's for sure.

Williams swaggered over to me. 'Alright if I go now?' he sneered. 'Well, yes, it would be if it weren't for a bit of unfinished business,' I replied. 'What?' gasped Williams. 'What unfinished business?' 'Charging you with stealing two tins of glue, the property of Woolworths,' I answered. 'Bastard!' shouted Williams. 'Oh, come, come, officer,' scoffed Williams' solicitor, who had been privy to this conversation. 'This really is a trifling matter. Wouldn't a caution suffice? I need hardly remind you that my client has been through quite a lot, you know.'

'So has Ellie Mayhew,' I replied, shortly and to the solicitor's credit, he clammed up.

The following morning, Williams appeared at the local Magistrates' Court where he pleaded not guilty to the charges of theft of the glue and, through his solicitor, elected trial by jury at Snaresbrook Crown Court. 'No objection to bail, I trust, officer?' drawled the solicitor. 'Certainly is,' I replied firmly and stepping into the witness box, I explained to the bench that I felt that there was a real fear that Williams would reoffend, if granted bail. I backed up my assertion by proving that having been granted bail in the past, he had done just that and the Bench gave him a lay-down.

Several months later, Williams came up for trial at Snaresbrook Crown Court and by now, his legal advisors realised that there was no defence to the charge and advised him to plead guilty, which he did. I noticed that during the interim period, betwixt arrest and arraignment, Williams had been deprived of his favourite pastime and was looking somewhat the worse for wear.

The prosecution outlined the facts, I gave Williams' antecedents to the Judge in which solvents and the theft of same figured prominently and a plea was made by his defence barrister for the recommendations, contained in a particularly soppy Probation Report should be endorsed. This report had only just been received and the Judge had not had an opportunity to read it, so he called for a short adjournment so that he might study the report.

Between the court rising and proceedings being reconvened, something happened. God knows how or why or who but it appeared that someone had cranked Williams up to an alarming degree. The Judge re-entered the Court, sat down, told the dock officers to put up Williams, picked up his pen and wrote the words, 'Two years Probation Order' in his desk book. With that, Williams, trembling with emotion, entered the dock. Asked if he had anything to say before sentence was passed, Williams pointed an accusing finger in my direction and loudly informed the court that I was 'Fucking dead'. Before the court had time to recover from this thunderbolt, Williams turned to the Judge and in an even louder voice, invited him to go and fuck his dead Grandmother.

Williams' grey-faced legal team tried successively to shush Williams and apologise to the Judge, who, white with fury, drew a decisive line with his pen through his original sentence and crisply informed Williams that he would go to prison for 12 months.

As Williams' shrieks grew fainter and fainter as he was dragged off to the cells, I shook my head and, as I picked up my papers, carefully avoiding the accusing looks from the defence team, I reflected that I had always thought that Williams would come to a sticky end!

The Swiss Mistake

'Man muss sich doch revanchieren,' (meaning, more or less, 'We must get our own back') is an expression that used to be used by the Germans. It was also quite appropriate in Basel, Switzerland, when I went there in 1976, to probe certain aspects of an enquiry which became known as 'The Hungarian Circle'. This was a fascinating case, which was brilliantly investigated by the late Detective Chief Superintendent (later Commander) Len Gillert, for which he received a well-deserved Queen's Police Medal. The Hungarian Circle was a gang of international con-men and forgers who, at the time of their arrest, had been active for 20 years. Their name was coined because many of them had fled from Hungary during the Communist invasion in 1956. Their forgeries included cheques, letters of credit and bankers drafts – all so brilliant that some of the genuine signatories of the documents refused to believe they were not their own. At the trial a representative from the Chase Manhattan bank stated that, had their activities remained unchecked, they had the potential to bankrupt a small European country.

My companion on this trip was the late Allan 'Charley' Cheal, then a Detective Inspector. I liked Charley very much. He was a veteran of the Flying Squad and the Regional Crime Squad and he was a very tough, shrewd investigator with a long record of successes. Charley was a very fierce disciplinarian with a hair-trigger temper who had no time whatsoever for shirkers or column-dodgers. If you were in the right, Charley would go to often ill-advised lengths to protect you from the caprices of senior officers who were determined to do you down. On several occasions, I heard officers, far senior to Charley, make a disparaging comment in his presence about an officer whom Charley had championed; the result was like a small nuclear explosion. By the same token, if you were in the wrong it was best to seek out Charley and apologise unreservedly and hope for the best; I saw the remains of some of those who didn't. But Charley treated me very well. Perhaps he saw virtues in me that others didn't; or perhaps he remembered that once, he too had been a wild, impetuous young man and made allowances for me accordingly.

It was the first time I'd been involved in an enquiry abroad - the first time, in fact, that I'd been abroad, unlike Charley who had investigated many crimes overseas. It was as the result of a large number of people being arrested in London for this international conspiracy, that officers from the Serious Crime Squad were sent all over the world to follow up their investigations. Of course, never having been anywhere before, when I was told that I was going to make protracted enquiries in Switzerland and Germany, I jumped at the chance. Who wouldn't? Well - lots of people, actually. Officers started holding out for sought-after destinations. 'No, sorry,' one of them remarked, airily. 'Can't go to Melbourne on Monday. There's this thing I must sort out in New York. Sorry.' And it was this type of retort which became commonplace, from officers who had previously never been further east than Southend.

I was once directed to escort two officers to Heathrow Airport, to ensure that they got on their plane to Saudi Arabia, when both had wished to fly off to other, more cosmopolitan destinations. The Detective Chief Inspector actually had to give them a no-nonsense order to go. Goodness, did they show off! I sat them in the back of my car, where they folded their arms, sulked all the way to the airport where, upon arrival they flounced out of the car. (In actual fact, it turned out that they had one of the better trips, investigating the circumstances in which an Arab Sheikh had been defrauded of an enormous sum of money. However, things did go a bit haywire after one of the officers made boozy, lecherous advances to the Sheikh's German mistress, and had his ardour cooled by being flung, fully clothed into the swimming pool by a brace of giant Nubian slaves.)

But to return to the relative calm of Basel, Charley and I were relaxing with a senior Swiss Detective, having a quiet beer at one of the city's many attractive pavement cafés, when I learnt what Charley, a seasoned traveller and diplomat, had known for some time - don't make stupid comments, especially when you don't know the answer, particularly when you're in a foreign country.

'What sort of wine do you drink here?' I asked the Swiss Detective. 'German, I suppose. Pity you don't grow any yourself,' I added, carelessly.

The balmy temperature dropped by about 10 degrees. Charley sighed, and closed his eyes. The Swiss Detective fixed me with a very hard stare, and then simply said, 'Komm'.

All of us went outside, got into his car and drove off, very fast into the mountains. Not a word of explanation was given, nor indeed was a single word spoken. It was clear that I had committed a gaffe of classic proportions. 'Oh, Christ!' I thought. 'What have I done, now?'

Eventually, we reached a village. We stopped outside a large church-like building, secured by two enormous church-like doors. These, the Swiss unlocked with a huge key.

Down some steps we went. I had no idea of what our fate might be. Whatever it was, Charley was clearly going to receive part of the punishment, and I remember thinking, 'I'm so sorry, Charley, I didn't mean to include you in my cock-up.'

Deeper and deeper into the blackness we went (and this was the worst part) in complete silence. My imagination was racing. 'Supposing,' I thought, 'that our host isn't Swiss at all, but German? Supposing he's part of some Neo-Nazi movement, and at this very moment, at the bottom of these steps, there's a gang of octogenarian S.S. officers waiting to plunge their bayonets into sensitive parts of my body? Oh help me God, I thought, I'll be so good in future...'

My terrified thoughts were curtailed when, as we reached the bottom of the steps, there was the sharp 'click' of a switch and light flooded into a large wine cellar. Bottles, thousands of them, were everywhere.

'This is my family's wine business,' explained the Swiss Detective. 'It has been in our family for several generations. Detective work for me is only a - how do you say it?'

'A hobby?' suggested Charley, gently.

'Genau!' exclaimed the Swiss. 'Exactly. A hobby, yes.'

Charley just looked at me, his irredeemably worthless apprentice, and sorrowfully shook his head. I was suitably chastened. Within a short while, I was suitably pissed, after our Swiss host demanded that we celebrate my new-found knowledge with a bottle or two of the family's schnapps.

The following day, I was massively bollocked by Charley. I knew I would be.

What a Gay Day!

Slang is a double-edged sword. Used correctly, it can add illumination to a sentence or wit to a story. Used incorrectly, it can subject the user to ridicule. Care must be taken not to use dated slang, slang that no-one knows the meaning of, or, as in the case of Erich Bruder, slang where it has one meaning in one language, but a completely different meaning in another...

In the mid-1970s, I was working in what was then, West Germany, with the Bundeskriminalamt (German Federal Police) and assigned to me was a very pleasant interpreter named Erich Bruder. Erich was absolutely fascinated with idiomatic language - and, in particular, with the usage of slang.

We'd been working hard all week, and on the Thursday, I said to Erich, 'Well, Erich, thank heavens tomorrow's P.O.E.T.S. day.'

P.O.E.T.S. was, of course, an acronym for 'Piss Off Early, Tomorrow's Saturday,' but Erich, quite understandably, looked completely baffled. I explained the term to him. 'Ach, so!' he cried, once realisation had set in. 'I must make a note of this!' and he pulled out a small black indexed note-book and scribbled into it. 'I love the use of slang, Herr Kirby,' he exclaimed. 'I have nearly a book full.'

'Ah, well,' I said, 'you do have to be careful with some expressions you might hear.'

Erich's face clouded over. 'This I already know, Herr Kirby,' he said, quietly. And then, he went on to tell me the following story...

Erich had previously interpreted for another Metropolitan Police officer, this one being a proper East Ender. 'You wanna fag, Eric?' had asked this officer.

'Fag? Was bedeutet das?' inquired a mystified Erich.

'Fag! You know - cigarette,' replied the officer, nonplused as to how anybody could fail to correctly interpret the Queen's English, and extending a packet of cigarettes to Erich.

'So!' exclaimed Erich, accepting a cigarette, and then, turning away, he wrote in his little black book, 'Fag = Eine Zigarette.'

That very night, Erich had the opportunity to display his new-found expertise. He had been invited to a reception at the United States Air Force Base at Wiesbaden, where, unfortunately, the usage of the term 'Fag' has, in Americanese, an entirely different meaning from its English counterpart.

Marching up to a four-star General, Erich clicked his heels together and made a small Teutonic bow. 'Herr General,' he said, giving his most engaging smile. 'You would like, perhaps, a fag?'

'God, no!' gasped the outraged General. 'I'm straight!' and he stamped off, muttering as he went, 'Goddam Nazi fruits...!'

Justice for all?

My pal Tom Bradley and I were having a quiet drink one night in war-torn Belfast, and due to the lateness of the hour, we had become quite philosophical. 'You know,' said Tom, 'it would save an awful lot of time if the criminal law recognised just two offences - one, of being 'out of order' and a second, purely indictable offence of being, 'well out of order.' It certainly makes sense to me. I'm all for a simpler world.'

A word about courts, court procedure and the once-upon-a-time dispensation of justice, before I deal with some amusing little tales of the Bailey.

During these current, troubled times, whole armies of civilians exist, ostensibly to assist police officers with court proceedings and to 'get them back on the beat,' which, as you will be aware, is a favoured saying. Like so many policy statements issued by the senior officers of the Metropolitan Police and other politicians, it is blatant bollocks.

In order to explain why, it is necessary to explain how things were.

When I joined the Metropolitan Police in the late 1960s (and, indeed, for many years afterwards) court proceedings were conducted in much the same way they had been, since time immemorial. The police did practically everything themselves. It was a system that worked well, and the following is an example, albeit a very simple one, of how it was accomplished.

A suspect would be arrested, following a crime being committed. He would be taken to the Police Station, where the Station Officer would establish that the officer had acted correctly in bringing the suspect there. Once that had been confirmed, the officer (or, in many cases, a CID officer) would question the suspect. If an admission was forthcoming, the suspect would be invited to make a written statement under caution, giving his side of the matter. The suspect would then be charged, a descriptive form would be filled in, his fingerprints would be taken and a check made at Criminal Records Office, for details of any previous convictions. He would, according to the severity of the offence, either be kept in the cells overnight, or released on bail, but in any event he would appear at the local Magistrates' Court the following morning. So far, then, so good. A total of about five forms would have been filled in, as opposed to some forty or fifty, today.

The officer who was conducting the case would normally attend the court. With a simple, straightforward case (and really, so many of them are) the defendant would plead guilty. The officer would then set out the facts to the Magistrate and (in the case of CID officers in particular) the circumstances would be presented so fairly, showing both motivation for the crime and mitigation for the prisoner, that the Magistrate would be in full possession of the facts in order to deal with the case then and there. The reason for this expertise was that firstly, the detective had attended a 10-week course of instruction at the Detective Training School, which included a sizable portion of information and advice on criminal law. Secondly, because of their years of experience and the added bonus of attending this course, the vast majority of the officers were quite capable of conducting the prosecution of their own cases at the Magistrates' Court, their skill rivalling that of many solicitors. In fact, the Aids would conduct their own cases at court against barristers, argue points of law with them, and often win.

Of course, this example of dealing with the case on the first occasion at court, could not and would not happen all the time, especially if the defendant was pleading 'Not Guilty' or if he was charged with an offence that was purely indictable (ie. one that could only be dealt with at the Crown Court) but in the majority of cases, it could. In fact, I have dealt with many cases, following an early morning arrest, where the time between initial arrest and the defendant being weighed-off at court has been no more than two hours. And then, it was back to the Police Station, where all that remained to be done was to write up the outcome in the crime book and type out the result to be sent to Criminal Records Office. It was important for that to be done as quickly as possible, obviously, so that if the same prisoner was arrested a few days later, Criminal Records would immediately be able to inform the officer dealing with the case of the prisoner's recent conviction. I always made a point, whenever possible, of typing that result the same day. Nowadays, this is done by the civilian personnel. I remember seeing one example of great sloppiness, where a result was typed-in two years after the prisoner's conviction. This, of course, was an extreme example. But I digress. What I am endeavouring to show you is that it was possible to deal with criminal cases in a fair, speedy fashion.

And often, you'd help your pals out in the CID office. If you had just one case at court and it was a straight-forward remand on bail and some-body else was appearing at court with a number of cases, you'd ask him to take your case, to allow you to get on with something else. It was a quick, simple way of justice being administered, appreciated by everybody, from Magistrate to defendant.

Then one day, a senior officer thought, 'why not have just one officer going to court all the time?' Thus, the Court Presentation Officer (CPO) was created, and so too was a little empire. It would certainly be unfair and untrue to say that all of the CPOs were sick, lame, lazy or dying but undeniably, a lot of them were. And when they copped a few more cases than they'd expected, which made it look to them as though they'd have to do an extra bit of work, they demanded a helper. Invariably, they got one. On the face of it, it was a sound idea. Just one, maybe two officers at the most, off the strength to deal with all the court work. What good sense!

It wasn't, of course. In many cases, a confused defendant would say to the CPO, 'What shall I do? Shall I plead guilty?' The CPO (who had often been recruited from the Uniform Branch) not knowing, or worse still not caring, would often reply, 'Don't ask me! See the duty solicitor!' Well, why not? It wasn't their case. Once the scent of legal aid fees had seeped into the solicitor's nostrils and the treasured green legal aid form had been filled in, the defendant would be conned into electing to go for trial by jury at the Crown Court, many months hence. On the morning of the trial (the officer on the case having spent an extraordinary amount of time amassing the evidence so that the case could be strictly proved) the defence barrister would cast an experienced eye over the committal papers, which would tell him that which the officer had known all the time - that the defendant was as guilty as sin, without a hope in hell of getting off. The prisoner would then be earnestly advised to plead guilty. So, you see, it was an enormous waste of the detectives' time and the public's money. Apart from that, the young officers (both uniform and CID) weren't attending court and gaining the experience that they should have been receiving, so that often, their first experience of giving evidence would be at a contested case at the Old Bailey, when they would be unable to withstand the usual blistering attack by the defence barrister. (At the time of the introduction of the CPOs, I was running a Divisional Crime Squad and I told the young aspirants under my charge that they would take their own jobs to court, and anyone caught going to the CPO could look forward to getting the sack!)

Three things happened in quick succession to knock the stuffing out of any possibility of anybody receiving fair justice.

Firstly the Police and Criminal Evidence Act was introduced. Basically, it meant that because every facility was given to a prisoner for legal representation, everything was monitored and as soon as a suspect was brought to the station the 'clock started ticking' and the investigating officers were under immense pressure to get everything done within a given period. And because more and more paper was being used to show how wonderfully fair the police were being, this provided more and more ammunition for the defence to attack the police in court. This was especially the case if the slightest mistake had been made in the documentation. Ludicrous situations developed. I remember going to one Police Station to be told the only place a suspect could be interviewed was the Chief Inspector's office (which, it later turned out, wasn't available) but if the prisoner was going to be detained overnight, at least he would have had the choice of two different after-shave lotions in the morning!

Ah! you cry, but think how the suspect is protected against all those miscarriages of justice! Yes, of course, every so often, there is a case of where an innocent person is wrongly convicted, but, I assure you, these cases are absolutely in the minority. Have you ever noticed in the Court of Appeal how police and forensic evidence is attacked straightaway, and if new witnesses can't be found, old ones can always be relied upon to be unsure of their previous testimony? And have you ever wondered why it is that as the long line of murderers, robbers and terrorists troop out of court, all innocents to a man, no-one is ever arrested for the crimes for which they've been so wickedly and wrongly convicted? Could it be, just possibly, that the right people were behind bars in the first place? Look at it this way. If you've been convicted for a serious offence and you've been sentenced to a lengthy term of imprisonment, what have you got to lose by screaming the place down? Nothing. It's not going to add a day to your sentence, and, chances are, someone will listen to you and, because their lives are so empty, organise an action group in support of 'The Palmers Green Two' or 'The Penge Six'. After that, it's just a question of getting the T-shirts printed and a defence invented to suit the circumstances and the occasion. Call me old Mr Cynical if you will, but often, the biggest miscarriage about those cases is the defence barrister.

Secondly, the Crown Prosecution Service (CPS) was started, whereby they took over the running of all criminal prosecutions. In years to come (unless someone comes to their senses and abolishes it) perhaps it will become a workable system, but I seriously doubt it. In the early days, certainly, it housed the most useless set of rag, tag and bobtail characters who ever attempted to become lawyers, and who would turn up at court with a huge number of cases (which were incomprehensible to them) and wonder why they were savaged by defence lawyers and roared at by Magistrates, who were incensed at their incompetence. Prosecutions were dropped out of hand, almost as fast as case papers were 'lost' and these disappearing and discontinued cases were often only surpassed by the prosecution's inability to speak coherent English. As an increasing number of guilty defendants trooped out of court, in order to help the CPS cope, an extended bail system was devised, whereby the prisoner was bailed from the Police Station to attend court several weeks hence. Feeling that they'd been 'let off', it wasn't long before they were up to mischief again.

Thirdly, in order to cope with the endess requests from the CPS for forms to be filled in, for witnesses to be warned to attend court and allegedly to act as buffer between the CPS and the police, the Crime Support Units (CSUs) were formed at local Police Stations. The failing here, was that the CSU staff were not police officers. It meant that catastrophic mistakes could be made with impunity, since the civilian staff were not subject to the Police Discipline code. Of course, there were some good, conscientious staff in these offices, but they were overshadowed by those who were sub-standard and near-illiterate. The new breed of police officers put an often misplaced faith in the staff of the CSU, thinking that on the morning of the start of an important trial, they could walk into the CSU office, pick up a neatly tied bundle of court papers and without a backward glance, go off to the Bailey, secure in the knowledge that all of the witnesses who were required for the first day's proceedings had been warned to attend and that all of the necessary papers were in place. Reality would often come to the officer with a massive jolt, usually from an irascible old Judge, who would be highly unimpressed that a full list of the defendant's convictions were not available, due to a slight oversight on Tina or Debbie's part. Oh, by the way, the original Police Order that described how one member of the civilian staff should be instructed in these duties, stated that it was anticipated that this type of work would occupy no more of their time, than 'one half-hour, per week'!

Is it any wonder that there is scant respect for law at court? Very few police officers attend the Magistrates' Court nowadays and the buildings of the inhabitants of the sprawling council estates, the gormless hangers-on, who turn up in their droves. They come complete with pushchairs, off-spring and sufficient fast-food and canned drinks to fortify them during a day's sustained giggling at the antics of the grinning local toe-rags who have actually deigned to turn up for their court appearance. Well, why not? They know little will happen to them. Their case will be dismissed through lack of evidence, chucked-out because of the inability of the CPS to get its act together, put over to another date or (and this is far more likely) committed for trial to the Crown Court at the insistence of the defence - on bail, naturally. And the people who suffer at the hands of these miscreants? Christ, I haven't even mentioned the poor bloody victims of crime...

'Officers back on the beat'? Don't make me laugh. They're so busy inside the Police Station filling in forms, I don't suppose they know where their beat is. The other night on television, a legal-aid solicitor was complaining that he wasn't being called out, because the police, so bogged-down with paperwork, weren't arresting anyone. 'Just what are the police doing about it?' he bellowed at the camera. 'That's what I should like to know!'

In a few short years, chaos now reigns where before, with a lot of hard work, no doubt about it, the detective going to court was able to keep up contact with the other detectives whilst he was waiting for his case to be called. He would chat to his prisoners and most important of all, every prisoner was treated as being a potential informant. I can tell you, as can many other detectives of my era, that just a little time spent with a prisoner, together with a few kind words resulted in some terrific pieces of information. In short, the vast majority of detectives were complete professionals. Their paperwork was as immaculate as their appearance, and every officer had his 'Old Bailey' suit, usually one in navy blue with a pinstripe. When the detective got into the witness box, the court was his stage and he was the star.

That is not the way it is now – oh, dear me, no. Those were the golden days at court and in the following stories, I shall tell you what it was like.

Look, I'm sorry about all this. I got on my high horse and sounded off a bit. I didn't really mean it.

Not much, I didn't!

Tales of the Bailey

I loved going to court. I liked the Central Criminal Court - the Bailey - best of all. I knew so many people there - lawyers, judges, police, court staff - it was more like a social gathering than anything else. And I loved the drama of the courtroom. Every year I used to sneak a quick look at the Academy Award presentations, just to see if I'd got a mention, because whenever I left the witness-box after giving my evidence, the defendants in the dock would invariably exclaim, 'Cor! What a fucking actor!'

There were other courts that I liked, as well. The old North-east London Quarter Sessions (before it became the infamous Snaresbrook Crown Court, with the highest acquittal rate anywhere) was good, and so were Knightsbridge, Maidstone and Norwich Crown Courts. Inner London Magistrates' Courts, where Stipendiary Magistrates sat, were great and some good Lay Magistrates sat at many of the outer London Magistrates' Courts. (I once outraged the sensibilities of a Senior Officer, when I asked a Magistrate, who had been invited to a CID Christmas party, to sign a search warrant. 'Just give us a quick signature, dear.')

But the Bailey remained my favourite court and, invariably, it was there that my cases were committed for trial. And some awfully funny stories came out of it...

Barry Scott was a Detective Constable, who was much admired for his acerbic wit. Personally, I didn't like him at all. I considered him to be a bombastic bully, but to be fair, Barry did have a pretty turn of phrase.

Barry had given part of his evidence in a trial at the Bailey and the court had risen for lunch; at the conclusion of which, Barry was to return to Court and complete his testimony. It was then intended to call Detective Sergeant Henry Jones to corroborate Barry's evidence. As Barry left the Court, he met Henry Jones outside, and the two of them walked off, deep in conversation, to spend the lunch hour together. This was observed by a weaseley little solicitor's runner, who scuttled back into court to convey the glad tidings to the barrister who was conducting the defence.

The imputation was clear - one officer, half-way through his evidence had met the officer who would be corroborating him. Their evidence must have been discussed. The prosecution would be tainted. The case must collapse.

At two o'clock, Barry went back into court and re-entered the witness box. The entire defence team was hugging itself with delicious anticipation.

'Officer,' said the defence Counsel. 'Is it true to say that your evidence, much of which, as you know, I have disputed on the instructions of my client, is corroborated by Detective Sergeant Henry Jones?'

'That is right,' replied Barry.

'When the court rose for luncheon,' continued the Counsel, casually, 'did you meet anyone as you left court?'

'Yes,' replied Barry, firmly.

'And was that person - by any chance,' (dramatic pause) - 'Detective Sergeant Henry Jones?' pursued the Counsel, silkily.

'It was,' replied Barry. A small, well-staged gasp came from the defence team, for the benefit of the jury.

'Did you spend the entire lunch time together?' asked the Counsel.

'We did,' replied Barry.

'Did you discuss this case with Detective Sergeant Jones?' demanded the Counsel, and this, of course, was the cruncher. If Barry said, 'No', nobody would believe him, and it was unthinkable that he would say, 'Yes'.

'Yes,' replied Barry, and a gasp, a real one this time, echoed around the court.

'What did you say to each other?' asked the astonished Counsel. Barry dropped his eyes. 'I'd rather not say,' he replied.

'Well, I'd rather you did!' snapped the red-faced Counsel.

At this point, the Judge stepped in.

'Mr. Scott,' he said quietly. 'That an officer of your experience should discuss a case with a fellow officer whilst he is half-way through his evidence, is quite wrong, as you must be fully aware. Now, would you please tell us what was said?'

'Well, m'Lud,' answered Barry, bashfully, 'I'd rather not.'

'I am not concerned with what you would or would not rather do,' snapped the Judge, getting really quite testy by now. 'I am telling you, to tell this court what was said between you and Detective Sergeant Jones during the lunch-time adjournment today!'

Barry sighed. 'Well,' he said. 'I did bump into Sergeant Jones as I was leaving the court building. 'Hello, Barry,' he said. 'How's it going?' I said, 'Fine.' Sergeant Jones said, 'What's the defence Counsel like?' I said, 'No problem. He's a right prick!'

Just a Slip of the Tongue

I associated with anyone capable of providing information about criminals and who better than some of their closest confidantes? This was how I came to be spending an evening having a drink with a solicitor and a barrister; I'd hoped for information regarding the whereabouts of a cache of firearms, deposited by one of their clients. Alas, it was a forlorn hope but during the course of this evening, I was highly amused to hear the story which follows.

Mr Justice Watkins was a very tough old Judge, who was renowned for his utter lack of humour as well as his very pro-prosecution views. His toughness stemmed from the fact that during World War II, he had been a member of the Commandos. In 5 years of warfare, the Commandos were awarded 8 Victoria Crosses, 37 Distinguished Service Orders, together with 9 Bars to the Order, 162 Military Crosses, with 13 bars to the award, 32 Distinguished Conduct Medals and 218 Military Medals. One of those Military Crosses had been awarded to Mr. Justice Watkins who, as a young Captain attached to No.3 Commando, had landed on the coast of Dieppe on the morning of 19 August 1942. Of the 460 Officers and men of that Commando who set out, only 380 reached France and during that day's determined fighting, 120 members of No.3 Commando were either killed or captured. Following the raid, among the replacements to the Commandos were 600 police officers. The commanding officer, John Durnford-Slater DSO & Bar promptly had 120 of them posted to No.3 Commando and later described them as being, 'the best single intake we ever received and every man was a potential leader; many, of course, were later commissioned and others exerted a fine influence as senior NCOs.'

These were sentiments shared by the then Captain Watkins, the more so because one of that intake was later to save his life, at no small risk to his own. Thereafter, upon his return to the bar, the solidarity that Mr Justice Watkins felt for the police was matched only by his loathing of criminals.

On this particular occasion, Mr. Justice Watkins was dealing with the very last case that he was going to hear at the Bailey, because at the conclusion of the day's proceedings, he was leaving to take up an appointment with the Northern Circuit. Philip Rollington-Smythe was a fairly junior barrister who had been briefed to pursue a Judge in

Chambers application for a felon who had little chance of being granted bail. But even though the prosecution had presented a very solid case for keeping the old crook locked up for ever more, Philip had resolved to do his very best for his client.

As the afternoon drew to a close, Philip finalised his impassioned plea to the Judge, for bail.

'And furthermore, m'Lud,' he concluded, 'I cannot agree with the sentiments of the prosecution. My client is a home-loving man, with very strong ties in the community, and if your Lordship were minded to grant bail, my client would be only too pleased to report to the local Police Station twice a day, because he doesn't give a fuck.' And with that, he sat down.

Mr Justice Watkins' eyes narrowed and his lips compressed to a thin line. He started to say something, and then, with an almost imperceptible shake of his head, he thought better of it, and said curtly, 'Application refused.'

'All stand,' intoned the usher. Within a second of the Judge leaving the court, the other barristers broke their stunned silence and rushed over. 'Phil, what on earth possessed you to say that?' gasped Jeremy Farquarson, who was appearing for the prosecution.

Philip looked puzzled. 'Say, what?' he asked.

'That your client didn't give a fuck, of course,' said Jeremy.

Philip laughed. 'I didn't say that,' he replied.

'You did! You did!' shouted everyone in court.

Philip laughed even louder. 'Of course I didn't,' he chuckled.

It wasn't until the shorthand writer was brought back into court, that realisation dawned on Philip. 'Jesus!' he shrieked. 'I didn't realise I'd said that!'

'Gosh! Are you in trouble!' said Jeremy Farquarson.

'I didn't realise,' whimpered Philip, piteously. 'What on earth can I do, Jerry?'

Farquarson thought for a minute. 'Bit tricky, this,' he admitted. 'You're lucky the old bastard didn't publicly rebuke you,' he mused, almost thinking aloud. 'But, Phil,' he added solemnly, 'you've got to do something to put it right!'

Philip thought wildly. 'Jerry!' he exclaimed, excitedly. 'It's all right! He's finished here today and he's off to the Northern Circuit.'

Farquarson shook his head sadly, as one does, before dismissing the ravings of a lunatic. 'Phil,' he said, 'it doesn't matter whether he's going to the Northern Circuit or the planet Jupiter. One day, he's going to come back and you'll have to face him again. And even, in the very unlikely event that it doesn't happen, your injudicious little remark will be the subject of comment, not only in that old bastard's darling Special Forces Club, but in every court in the land. Any Judge that you appear before, will know what you said to old Watkins. And if you don't think that your career will be in tatters because of it, you've an awful lot to learn about the Freemasonry of the Bar, old boy.'

Philip buried his face in his hands in an attempt to deflect his gaze from the black ruin that was staring him in the face. 'What can I do?' he wailed. You see, poor Philip really was a junior barrister and had a long road to tread before he could think on his feet, with the aplomb of a Flying Squad Detective Sergeant.

Jeremy Farquarson scratched his head and was deep in thought. 'All I can suggest is this,' he said, finally. 'Get yourself down to old Watkins' chambers and collar him before he leaves to catch the 5.17. Just apologise unreservedly and say it was purely a slip of the tongue. That's all you can do. Christ, it could be worse. Just think yourself lucky that the press are excluded from these applications!'

Gathering up his brief, Philip rushed from the court and headed towards the Judge's chambers, his thoughts in turmoil. Trying to frame a speech that would save his career, he gingerly tapped on the Judge's door. Hearing the gruff, 'Come!' from within, he apprehensively opened the door. There, seated behind his desk sat the terrifying figure of Mr Justice Watkins. He looked up from his papers, his grey eyes resembling discs of polished slate. Pushing aside the thought that the Judge must have looked very much like that, just prior to knifing a German sentry, Philip ran his tongue across his lips in an effort to force saliva into his arid mouth, and said, 'Excuse me, Judge, but a matter has been brought to my attention, that I feel I should address you about.' Haltingly, he continued, 'It has been pointed out to me, that just before the court rose, I made a remark to you that was as disgraceful as it was obscene. I can only apologise, Judge. I had no idea that I had said it, and all I can say is that it was a terrible lapse on my part. You could have publicly rebuked me. I am most grateful, Judge, that you did not. Once again, I apologise unreservedly. It will never happen again.' He waited, trembling.

There was silence in the room for a moment.

And then, Mr. Justice Watkins leaned forward, and looking intently at Philip over his half-moon glasses, he said, 'Thank you, Mr Rollington-Smythe. I did note what you said before the close of play, and I must confess it did cross my mind to publicly rebuke you. I decided not to,' and here, there was the slightest suggestion of a twinkle in his eye, 'because, had I done so, the way things were going, I felt that you would probably have told me not to have acted like a prick!'

The Punctured Passport

I first met Peter Connor in the early 1970s, when we were fledgling Detective Constables at Forest Gate Police Station, and after I saw him give evidence in court, I rapidly came to the conclusion that he was one of the best practitioners of that noble art that I'd ever heard. It is a view I still adhere to.

Peter and I worked together quite a lot and we notched up a good run of successes. In the years that followed, Peter worked on the Yard's C1 Murder Squad as a Detective Sergeant, at No.9 Regional Crime Squad as a Detective Inspector where he enjoyed a string of achievements, and finally retired as a Detective Chief Inspector, following a distinguished tour on the Fraud Squad. He now enjoys a prestigious position in an investigative company and our friendship has lasted for almost 30 years. Apart from possessing a terrier-like quality during his investigations, Peter could be very sharp with his words, argumentative and, on occasion, quite short-tempered with incompetent people in authority - I can't imagine why we got on so well!

We went our separate ways after serving at Forest Gate and met up again as Detective Sergeants on the Serious Crime Squad. Together, we investigated a conspiracy to improperly obtain British Passports for Hong Kong citizens. There were heavy overtones of heroin smuggling and the involvement of several of the Triad gangs. In connection with this enquiry, Peter and I travelled to Holland and we both got badly frightened when, having enjoyed a glass or two of Jong Geneva (sloe gin served in ice-cold small shot glasses), a perfectly harmless practical joke which we played on a band of militant lesbians who were leading a torchlight procession through the streets of Amsterdam to complain about men who 'mentally rape women with their eyes'. Inspired by the Jong Geneva I foolishly walked into the throng and told them I thought that their complaint was absurd. I misread their sense of humour and we had to run for our lives.

Peter (who was once convicted on trumped-up charges and sentenced to death at Newham Magistrates' Court during a raucous Christmas party by a comely, but highly intoxicated lady Magistrate) and I received notification that one of our prisoners, having unsuccessfully applied for bail at the Magistrates' Court, was now applying for bail by means of a Judge-in-Chambers application.

This sort of application is often heard in court, where everyone, with the exception of the persons directly concerned with the case is expelled from court whilst the application is made. It's quite an informal affair. Judges and barristers don't wear their wigs, but sometimes, the application is heard actually in the Judge's chambers, and, like as not, the Judge will probably be wearing a cardigan and carpet slippers. That's what happened on this occasion. Because these applications could be made at very short notice, there would often be insufficient time in which to brief Counsel for the prosecution, so the officer in charge of the case would outline the facts of the case to the judge, and then detail the objections to bail and the reasons for giving them. Now, neither Peter or I had resisted an application like this before. Thankfully, Peter volunteered to object to bail and conduct the proceedings on behalf of the prosecution.

The applicant, George Li, was represented by a barrister, who had been briefed by Li's solicitor. 'My instructions, Sergeant,' said the barrister to Peter, in front of the judge, 'are that my client knows nothing about the heroin trade, nor does he have any dealings with illicit passports. Indeed, by working long hours at his father's restaurant, as he was prior to his arrest, and which, incidentally, was his only source of income, he was only just managing to make the mortgage repayments on his modest home.'

'Your client, Sir, has not got a modest home,' replied Peter, firmly. 'In fact, your client has what might be described as an opulent home, worth in the region of ninety thousand pounds (which was a considerable sum in 1979). Far from struggling to find the mortgage repayments, I can tell you that within six months of moving into this house, he had paid for it in full.'

He had, too. Peter had certainly done his homework, which was more than could be said for George Li's solicitor. He was now sitting there, with his mouth hanging open, doing his best to avoid his barrister's furious gaze.

'Dear me, Mr Hargreaves,' said the Judge to the barrister. 'You do not, if you will permit me to say so, appear to have been adequately briefed in this matter. The application is dismissed.' And that was that.

We went outside, me, Peter, the barrister and the wretched solicitor. 'Tell me, Mr Connor,' said the barrister, thoughtfully, 'have you ever opposed a Judge-in-Chambers application before?'

'No, Sir,' replied Peter.

'Well,' said the barrister, 'if you don't mind my saying so, I thought you made an uncommonly fine job of it. Well done.' And then, turning to the solicitor, he proceeded to give him the biggest, most humiliating bollocking that I had ever heard in my life. At last, this verbal lashing came to a merciful end, the barrister turned to me and Peter, gave a slight bow, said, 'Good Morning, Gentlemen,' and walked off.

There was a bit of a silence. Actually, I felt quite sorry for the solicitor. I always think that if you're going to choke somebody off, do it behind closed doors, just the two of you. In time, that person might admit that you were right, might even come to thank you for it. Do it in public, and they'll hate you for ever, because you humiliated them in front of an audience. Mind you, the solicitor *was* a bit of a twerp for letting the cunning Mr Li bamboozle him like that.

Court Jesters

'Do you know why I love you so much?' I said one day, to my dear wife.

'Why?' said she.

'Because whenever we're dining with friends,' I explained, 'and I launch one of my jokes or stories upon a new, unsuspecting audience, you always laugh your head off when I deliver the punch-line, even though I know full-well that you've heard the same story at least a dozen times before.'

'Ah,' replied my cunning consort, 'but it's not the punch-line I'm laughing at, it's the way you tell them.'

Any wonder that I hold her in such high esteem?

Between the high estimation in which I hold my wife and the recounting of tales, this brings me rather neatly onto the subject of lawyers, who, if I were to award them any kind of status at all, would rank with the sort of admiration that I reserve for politicians in general and child molesters in particular.

Of course, there are exceptions - Mike Stuart-Moore QC, Michael Worseley QC, Dame Barbara Mills DBE, QC, Ann Curnow QC, Julian Bevan QC and a few more whose names have temporarily eluded me (all of them brilliant at both prosecuting and defending) but I wouldn't give most of the others standing room. Those of them who appeared for the prosecution, I regarded as being, at best, incompetent ditherers who, due to their ignorance and timidity were too frightened to really have a go. I'd like a quid for every time I turned up at court, to commence a fairly important trial which had taken sometimes months to prepare, only to have the prosecuting Counsel saunter up to me, fifteen minutes before the start of the case and airily remark, 'You'd better tell me about this case, officer; I haven't had a chance to read the brief.'

It was absolutely no use complaining about this; the legal system looks after its own to such an exaggerated degree that it's practically incestuous. The level of incompetence that some of them exhibited had to be seen to be believed. I remember one of the worst - his ineptitude was matched only by his colossal arrogance - who appeared for the prosecution in a very important case, where the committal proceedings alone had taken three months at the Magistrates' Court.

The case opened at the Old Bailey and after the jury had been sworn in, this Counsel got to his feet and started to outline the case to the jury. Some perplexed looks were exchanged between the police officers in Court until, after about five minutes of speech, the Detective Inspector reached over, got hold of his gown and gave it an almighty tug. The Counsel half-turned. 'What - what?' he spluttered. 'You're talking about the wrong fucking case!' hissed the infuriated officer. 'The wrong - oh, very well,' replied the Counsel, completely unperturbed by his gaffe. Putting down the set of papers to which he had been referring, he picked up a fresh set. 'May it please Your Lordship...' and he carried on with the outline of the case which the jurors were to try. It was this barrister, an officer in the same case told me, who appearing as prosecution Counsel in a murder trial, had cocked it up to such an amazing extent that a report was sent to the Attorney General regarding his conduct.

Since then the machinery of the legal system has worked so conscientiously that today, that same Counsel is now a High Court Judge. Can you imagine a police officer getting away Scot free with something like that in court? No, and neither can I.

I used to love appearing before His Honour Judge Peter Mason QC at the North-east London Quarter Sessions. He was much admired as a hard-line Judge (well, by the police, that is) and listening to him sum up was an education. To paraphrase the remarks made by a Judge who was addressing a barrister, I could have listened to his voice all night and never grown weary. But if your papers, particularly a prisoner's antecedents weren't absolutely spot on, watch out! I knew officers who were terrified of appearing before him. But as I'd say to them, if your papers aren't right, you deserve a bollocking.

And on that subject, I recall a case when a professional and very dangerous criminal was appearing at the Old Bailey on a serious charge. A conviction in front of the right Judge would have resulted in a prison sentence which would have taken him out of circulation for many years. I can only assume that Lady Luck was experiencing a spot of PMT that day because the Judge was an absolute horror; deaf, irascible and with an inclination to believe any attack made on police evidence by the defence. Peter Connor once told me that in the middle of a trial, whilst he was on the receiving end of some very fierce cross-examination, this old idiot suddenly leant forward and said, 'I'm going to ask you a question officer and I want you to consider your answer very carefully before replying!' So with a Judge like that, the defence didn't need to try very hard; however since on this occasion, the Counsel for the defence was a left-wing barrister with a loathing of police, he went to town, anyway. To complete the picture, the prosecution was represented by a barrister who was both incompetent and un-interested. It is possible that his lack of interest stemmed from the conduct and ability of the officer in charge of the case who, I have to say was certainly one of the most truly useless specimens that it has ever been my misfortune to encounter. He suffered from a complete inability to foresee the consequences of his actions. He possessed cunning, it is true, and this is an attribute that I admire amongst detectives but he used this ability to column-dodge, display laziness on a grand scale and make smart-arse remarks.

When we lost the case, amidst furious criticism of both police action and inaction from Judge and defence Counsel, this officer had the temerity to whine to me how a cruel and capricious fate had robbed us of a conviction. This is the reply I gave him and as far as I can remember, it is word for word.

'The fact that I am usually successful at court and you are not,' I said, 'is not purely due to the fact that you are a 22 carat prat, although I accept that this is a contributory factor to the problem. The main reason is because I take infinite pains to ensure that everything will run smoothly in court, that every eventuality has been anticipated and you, quite obviously, do not!'

I wish I could report that my constructive words of advice bore fruit but, alas not. I am glad to report that I was instrumental in getting him kicked off the Flying Squad. I consider it a pity that this useless individual ever bothered to join the Metropolitan Police, let alone one of its elite squads. Hard words? Well, that's up to you but consider this. I never lost sight of the fact that I was a servant of the public. It was the public who paid my wages and when when that is the case they have every right to expect loyalty from their employee and an industrious day's work in return. Thanks to this bone-idle officer's inability to get his act together on an important case (although not one that was beyond the capability of a junior officer who was prepared to insert some hard work and zeal into it) a professional criminal had walked free. Well, that's life, you might say. You might not have been of the same benign opinion if you had been the husband of the lady who had the side of her face shot off, when this particular felon was back at his old tricks of robbing building societies, some two months later.

So when Counsel who were prosecuting for me didn't come up to scratch, I felt it my duty to put them straight and you won't be surprised to hear that a lot of them didn't like it and they would have to draw very heavily on their public school pomposity. I particularly took exception when they would turn up for a Judge-in-Chambers application and not having even looked at their brief, they'd get to their feet and say, 'I'll call the officer, m'Lud.' So I would get into the witness box, outline the facts of the case, set out my objections to bail and then be subjected to an all-out attack from the defence. Now, I'm not complaining - I reckoned that I'd do a far superior job to the lazy little squirt lounging about below me - but I did object to the tax payers money being spent on someone like him, who had uttered just five words to justify his fee. On every occasion I left the witness box, I'd say, 'That's the easiest fifty quid you've ever earned, ain't it, pal?' - and I never, ever saw one who didn't blush.

So those are my sentiments on barristers for the prosecution; a mixed bunch. Some brilliant, some average and the others, a waste of space. Wait until you hear what I've got to say about defence barristers.

I used to compare defence barristers with prostitutes. Both perform a service for an agreed sum of money and many will do whatever their clients desire. Some, as I say, can be relied upon to invent a few tricks of their own. You think that's a jaundiced view? Well, again that's up to you, but should you ever be a witness to an armed robbery, you can put it to the test. Go along to court, tell the simple unvarnished truth and see the sort of reception you get from some smarmy, sneering defence barrister, who, knowing full-well that his client is as guilty as sin, has an enjoyable time belittling you, sneering at your evidence and doing his best to show that *you* are the one on trial. And if his client gets off, all well and good; it's a feather in his cap. And if not, well, that's not so bad either because if the case goes to appeal, that's another big lump out of the Legal Aid fund for them. So with the stacked deck that confronts police officers on many occasions, an incompetent barrister appearing for them, a crooked one against them and a gormless hand-picked jury ready to accept any ridiculous, concocted story, it's refreshing to hear about a case where this sort of ploy didn't work...

A team of blaggers, having made a hasty exit from a freshly robbed bank, and clutching large amounts of cash, leapt into their getaway car parked outside and roared off into the Bethnal Green Road, neatly cutting-up a Morris Minor, driven by a clergyman.

The priest, thinking that he was the victim of poor driving by a bad motorist became incensed and promptly pursued them. 'You devils!' he cried. 'You shan't escape!' The road was heavily congested and he was able to keep the bandits' car in view.

It was when the blaggers swerved into a side turning, with the priest following, and jumped out of the getaway car brandishing guns and tearing off their stocking masks and got into a second vehicle, that the priest reached the hasty conclusion that more than the Road Traffic Act might have been contravened.

Acting on a tip-off, a Flying Squad team pulled in all of the gang a couple of days later, incriminating evidence was found and the priest picked out the robbers on an identification parade.

Several months later at the Old Bailey, the priest had given his evidence in chief to the Court.

It was with a certain amount of trepidation that the defence Counsel got to his feet to cross-examine the priest. It is one thing to screech hysterically at a Flying Squad Detective Inspector that his clients had been fitted, verballed, planted, framed etc, but quite another to accuse a God-botherer of saying anything other than the unblemished truth.

'Is it - er - possible,' started the defence Counsel, 'just possible, that - and you must not, for one moment, think that I am calling your veracity into question - that you might possibly have mistakenly picked out my clients at the identification parade?'

'I fear not,' sighed the priest.

'But...' stammered the barrister, wishing earnestly that the brief for this case had been handed to his worst enemy, 'my clients are very ordinary looking fellows. Surely you can, well, to use one of your ecclesiastical terms, look into your heart, and accept that it might just be possible that you could have made a mistake?'

The priest paused and bowed his head. The barristers heart leapt, thinking that this was the breakthrough that he had been praying for. The priest raised his head and smiled, as though he had received inspirational advice from on high.

'Ah, my son,' he replied. 'I should have known them in a multitude!'

The Brothers Grim

In mentioning Mike Stuart-Moore's name, as I did in the previous story, I feel it's time to deliver a slightly more detailed introduction to that great man. The Honourable Mr. Justice Stuart Moore, Vice President of the Court of Appeal in the High Court, Hong Kong, is known as 'Stuart' to his many friends. I have a newspaper cutting from a Hong Kong newspaper, now several years old, which recounts the plight of a 21-year-old desperado from the New Territories who had been sentenced to 22 years imprisonment for armed robbery. Feeling a little hard done by, he appealed to the Court of Appeal for a reduction in sentence. In dismissing the appeal, Stuart Moore not only criticised the Trial Judge for his undue leniency but informed the stunned scallywag that the only reason that he was not substantially increasing the sentence was because the robber had come to court without being legally represented. I wrote to Stuart and suggested that the local criminal fraternity were probably eagerly looking forward to the time when the Chinese reclaimed the province, in order that they might receive some humane treatment!

But before he received this prestigious Hong Kong appointment, apart from sitting as a Recorder at the Old Bailey, Stuart was without doubt the finest prosecutor to appear for the Metropolitan Police. His clerk had to cope with an avalanche of requests for Stuart's services and he was to successfully prosecute an enormous number of cases, notably for the Flying Squad. The passion and the amount of sheer hard work that he put into every single case that he prosecuted was something that I had never encountered before and was never to meet thereafter.

Stuart had the dubious (and perhaps unique) distinction of being the co-recipient of a complaint against police. This occurred after he had successfully prosecuted a highly unpleasant armed robber who, thoroughly miffed at receiving a well-deserved 10-year imprisonment, made a long catalogue of criminal allegations against me.

Stuart was understandably excused from the accusations which alleged that the prisoner had been verballed, planted and bashed but he and I were accused of introducing a bogus witness to the court proceedings and in this and other matters, we had conspired to bring about his downfall. Now, for the life of me, I can't remember the details of this 'bogus witness' allegation; suffice it to say, this allegation was just as phoney as the rest of the accusations. However, I did think that this was a bit rich, coming from the lips of a man who, during the course of the trial, had been obliged to admit that during his cross-examination, he had deliberately committed perjury!

I first met Stuart a couple of months before I was posted to the Flying Squad, long before he had taken silk and in the case which followed, Stuart impressed me with his aggressive commitment, which culminated in me being commended by the Judge, who also mildly rebuked Stuart for his abrasive conduct towards the defence barrister! The story which follows is the build-up to this case.

During a quiet Saturday evening, a group of young men had walked into an off-licence in Woodford, Essex. As one of them discussed the merits of a bottle of Frascati with the off-licensee, the others readied themselves for what they knew was to occur. Suddenly, the off-licensee was smashed in the face by the man talking to him, who then vaulted the counter. He and the others liberally helped themselves to money from the till, and cigarettes and spirits from the shelves, and fled.

The dazed proprietor staggered to the door, to see his attackers escape in a brown Ford Escort. He wrote down what he thought to be the registration number (which, in his confused state, was incorrect) and telephoned the police. He gave as good a description as he could of his assailants, but the one thing that stuck in his memory, was that they had worn white carnations in their buttonholes.

The investigation was taken up by me and the few remaining officers, who were attached to the 'J' Division Crime Squad, after the rest had been seconded to a murder enquiry. The best clue of all was, of course, the bottle of Frascati which the attacker had handled, and which the off-licensee had sensibly put to one side and preserved. Had the Scene of Crime Officer (SOCO) who carried out the examination been less than witless, the suspect's fingerprints would have been lifted from the bottle and identified, thereby saving me an enormous amount of work. Instead, the SOCO managed with considerable style to wipe the entire bottle clean. I have often wondered since whether this was true incompetence or if it was terror at the thought of having to attend court to give evidence of his findings. My faith in SOCOs had, truth to tell, been on the wane long before that and with very few exceptions (two notably brilliant examples were Paul Millen and John Armstrong, both of whom enjoyed a distinguished tour on the Flying Squad) it has seldom resurfaced. It was to be the beginning of a long, hard slog.

Since it was fairly inescapable that the wearers of the buttonholes would have been attending a wedding, to the exclusion of any other kind of celebration, we started with the names of the participants of weddings at churches, synagogues and registry offices on the day of the robbery, within a five mile radius. These names were then checked to see if any of them triggered off any warning bells with the local Criminal Intelligence Bureaux. None did. Next, halls in the area, where receptions might have been held were inspected and their caretakers interviewed. But the outcome was exactly the same as the results achieved when we spoke to the wedding photographers in the area and scrutinised their photographs. We attended newspaper offices and went over their printed wedding photographs with magnifying glasses, in case the photographer had been summoned from outside our five-mile radius and we inquired at florists shops where the hoodlums' boutonnieres might have been prepared.

Caterers were questioned. Nothing. The five-mile radius was extended to ten miles, still with the same result. Three months had passed and having used all the traditional investigative skills, there was not even the hint of a result.

And then an unbelievable stroke of luck occurred. During a casual conversation with a local tea-leaf, the name was mentioned of an indigenous tearaway who had been the witness at a wedding. It was an unusual name, and one that started picking at my memory. I suddenly remembered him as being an up-and-coming young thief whom I had arrested 12 years previously for a warehouse-breaking. I dug a little more. None of the other wedding guests would assist me at any price. It was only after a lot more work that I unearthed an informant, and he nervously put up the names of those responsible, three of whom (including the tearaway) were brothers with a reputation for violence in the area. So frightened was the informant that I had to meet him 15 miles from the area, to pay him the reward from the Information Fund.

Matters began to fall into place, to explain my lack of success in the case. Only the names of the brides and the grooms had been checked in the Intelligence Bureaux and the reason why I had drawn a blank was because this particular couple did not possess criminal records. The group could not have been identified from wedding photographs, because none were taken. No caretaker of any of the local halls could assist, since the reception was held in a council flat. The enquiries at the florists had been a waste of time, since the carnations had been snatched from the front garden of a local house and wrapped in tin-foil. Caterers had been unable to assist because Tesco's services had been called upon, in preference to theirs. And when the booze in this squalid little gathering had started to run out, this band of heroes had swaggered out in order to replenish the stocks.

All of them were arrested and after initial denials, they admitted their part in the robbery. One of them, the owner of the getaway car, knowing that the off-licensee had seen them get into it, admitted spraying it another colour in order to avoid capture.

And this was how I first came to meet Stuart Moore, who was briefed to prosecute this case at Snaresbrook Crown Court. The public gallery was full to overflowing with the brothers' relatives, friends and hangers-on who, since the brothers were pleading not guilty to the charge of robbery, were eager to applaud points scored for the defence, groan at the police evidence and to glower at prosecution witnesses and jurors alike.

The case opened, and Stuart Moore briefly outlined the case for the prosecution for the benefit of the jury.

'It was after the defendants had been arrested, members of the jury,' he explained, 'that the police received the breakthrough that they had been seeking. The eldest of the brothers, Jimmy, called Sergeant Kirby to his cell. 'Alright, Guv'nor,' he said. 'You've got me and the boys cold. Let me have a word with them, and we'll all stick our hands up.'

'I fucking didn't!' howled a voice from the dock.

'I should get used to that, if I were you, members of the jury,' said Stuart Moore smoothly, without even looking round. 'I'm sure we shall hear a lot more outbursts like that before this trial is over!'

We did!

Snouts

'I've got a bit of info from a snout of mine,' was one of the most hackneyed phrases used in the CID. As often as not, the 'bit of info' didn't come from a snout (informant) at all. It came from an information bulletin, a collator, a Home Beat officer, perhaps another CID officer. Some of the officers who used that phrase wouldn't have known how to have dealt with a genuine snout, if one had jumped up and bit them on the knee. It was something I felt quite strongly about. If the information did originate from a genuine informant, then well and good - but if it was good information and it came from a police source, why not say so? It must have been intensely annoying for uniformed officers to give good information, in good faith to a CID officer and then be robbed of recognition because the foolish officer wanted to impress his contemporaries by untruthfully stating that he'd got a real, live underworld informant. Did they really think we respected them for it? These things have a way of embarrassingly rebounding on people like that; I've seen it happen and when it does, everybody howls with laughter - except for the absurd impostor, of course.

No, credit should be given when it's due; if a job comes off, then the officer in charge will receive recognition but the officer who put up the job in the first case should receive equal acknowledgement. Peter Wilton, that quintessential Flying Squad Detective Chief Inspector would begin his briefings by saying, 'The reason we're here, is because some very good information has been received from PC 123 Jones, a 'K' Division Dog Handler...' or 'As a result of extensive observations carried out by C11...' and, in the event of a successful conclusion to the job, this appreciation would be echoed in the SPECRIM, the teleprinter message which informed the D.A.C.'C' (Operations) of details of serious crimes.

Certainly, there could be times when it would be imprudent, sometimes downright impossible to disclose the police source of the information. For example, supposing a relative or a friend of a police officer was living with an armed robber and having grown weary of being bashed about by him, she were to discover the time and place of his next armed robbery. Having passed this information on to the police officer, who passed it on to me - well, in those circumstances, it would be foolhardy to mention the name of the police officer. At one time, if all went well, the officer would be commended for his assistance, for 'invaluable assistant in a sensitive enquiry' - impossible nowadays, of course, because the civvies who decide who gets commended for what, irrespective of what very senior police officers recommend, want everything spelled out for them; and it's my bitter experience that a secret shared is a secret no longer. However, it would certainly not preclude the police officer's friend or relative from receiving a sizable reward from the Informant's Fund at the Yard or from the Loss Adjusters or the Insurance Company, as her erstwhile partner was dragged off to spend the next 15 years, deprived of her company.

But I'm drifting away from the main character of this chapter, which is the police informant. In my early days as a detective, only the police officer knew the identity of his informant which was jealously guarded. In court, the officer would say, 'Acting on information received...' and only the most reckless barrister would ask, 'What was the source of your information, officer?' because he would be admonished by the Judge or the Magistrate for asking such a prattish question and also be smirked at by the officer.

Following the successful conclusion to a case where a snout had provided the information, the officer would submit a report through his senior officers, bearing only the pseudonym of the informant, to be considered for a reward from the Yard's Information Fund. The reward would be paid into the imprest of the officer's Police Station or Branch, he would pay the snout who would sign a receipt in his or her pseudonym and that would be that. This occasionally led to allegations that officer and snout had split the reward money between them. To counter this, a whole new system of handling informants was set up. It meant that the true identity of the informant had to be given to the D.A.C. 'C' (Operations) and that information sheets had to be submitted, giving details of the information obtained at each meeting. Further, handlers and co-handlers had to be appointed and at the conclusion of an officer's tour at a particular station, the handler had to pass the informant on to a fresh handler. Rewards had to be paid to the informant in the presence of a senior officer to deter corrupt practices. Meetings on bail had to be authorised in advance and held at nominated Police Stations and, at the conclusion of the meeting, promptly reported in the officer's Pocket Book, in the Occurrence Book of the Station within the boundaries of where the meeting had taken place, the Occurrence Book of the officer's own Station or Squad and also on a Pro-forma, to be sent to the Yard.

Accidental meetings had to be similarly reported, although these were often accompanied with nervous interrogations by supervising officers, terrified of finding themselves criticised by their own senior officers. Splendid, might say the uninitiated. A safeguard against corrupt practices. Is it? Leaving the enormous tide of additional paperwork aside, leaving aside the times when decent, hard-working CID officers trying to get the job done would overlook one of the pettifogging rules and be sent back to uniform, demoted or, more likely, dismissed from the Force by a despotic senior officer who had never carried out a days detective work in his life, let's examine the facts.

I ran informants all through my career and not one was ever compromised, nor even suspected - that's a fact. Next, with the enormous amount of paperwork generated, details of informants can (and often are) left about on desks in a CID office, usually by so-called CID officers, taking a break from uniform duties before returning on promotion. Typists leave records of meetings with informants carelessly in trays and officers from other stations, civilian staff and lay visitors wander in and out and it was not so long ago that prisoners were brought up to the CID office for interview. It is in this fashion that every man and his dog get to know about the movements, information and the identities of informants. Trials have to be frequently abandoned when the safety of an informant is compromised because the defence barristers demand to see the informant's information sheets. Sensible, productive police-work? I think not! I suppose this system of running informants stemmed from the British Army and the Security Services way of running informants. There is, however, a distinct difference. Army informants are given a four-digit number for identification and any paperwork generated goes straight into a sealed, secure unit; no unauthorised person sees it. The handlers do not go to court to give evidence. The system used for meeting informants, at a previously arranged time and place - with fall-back times and locations in case of compromise - take place in a car with a series of back-up cars with interchangeable number plates. The informant is then taken to a 'safe-house' for a full, unhurried and totally safe debriefing - or for the payment of a reward - and this procedure is so sophisticated, it beats anything the police can offer. The reason for this is two-fold; firstly they have a budget to cater for it and secondly, the handlers do nothing other than run informants. They don't have to investigate crimes, make arrests, go to court or tackle a mountain of often unnecessary paperwork.

Police informants are not regimented - they often resent being told to meet their police contact in a Police Station where there is every chance of compromise. They dislike the presence of another officer whom they don't know when the police officer that they do know and trust is talking to them. It's a wonder to me that they give any information at all - let's face it, there's a real likelihood of them being unmasked in court.

Yet, they do give information. I've already mentioned battered wives, who can certainly be an exceptionally good source of information; let's take a look at several of the other types of informants. One is the person whose sense of social justice has been affronted and who passes on a snippet of information which he's overheard - mind you, this isn't an informant as such; more the sort of 'nosy neighbour' and this is normally a 'one-off' because he's normally a straight man and therefore unlikely to be close enough to the world of criminality to provide any further useful information. A gang member, cheated of his cut of the spoils needs very careful handling - often they're not beyond planting some of the stolen gear on the other thieves, as a way of settling old scores. And for years, it's been commonplace for one drugs dealer to grass up another.

In many cases, it all amounts to the same thing - getting rid of the opposition, whether they're fellow crooks or troublesome partners. A classic case was one such informant who I ran when I was a Detective Constable; and in this and the other examples I shall mention, the names and sometimes the gender of the villain and their betrayers have been substituted. Rosie was an absolutely desperate character who possessed a low threshold of boredom. When she tired of her boyfriends (as she very quickly did) she'd phone me up and tell of their misdeeds. 'Come and pick this bastard up, Dick,' she'd say. 'He's getting on my bleedin' nerves.'

Off I'd go to her crumbling tenement block and Rosie would answer my knock at the door. 'John!' she'd call out over her shoulder. 'Old Bill's here for you!' 'What for?' would come the shouted retort. 'Well, I don't know, I'm sure,' she'd reply, giving me a saucy wink.

I charged one of these discarded suitors with obtaining drugs by means of a forged prescription. It was a very simple, straight-forward case, to which he made a full, signed confession and after charging, I released him on bail to appear the following morning at the local Magistrates' Court. This, I later discovered, was not to Rosie's liking, because she had been congratulating herself at having got rid of a tiresome lover when lo and behold, he had returned to seek overnight solace in her arms.

The following morning, I strolled into Court to find a miserable looking John, glumly waiting to have his case called.

'Morning,' I said, breezily. 'A quick guilty plea this morning, John?'

'Guilty?' he gasped. 'Not bloody likely! I'm going for trial and I'm fighting it every inch of the way!' I was amazed.

'What on earth for?' I asked.

He replied, 'Rosie said to me, "Don't you trust that bastard Kirby an inch." She said, "Give him half a chance and he'll get you seven bloody years!" '

Dear Rosie. Her treachery was not confined to her lovers!

Other types of informants? Well, the well-known one is where a criminal's been caught bang to rights and in the ordinary course of events, he can look forward to a substantial helping of porridge for his endeavours. Therefore, he's looking for a lot of help and if he can put some serious work your way, he can expect some serious support. He needs, of course, to tread carefully because it's often common knowledge that he's had his collar lifted and it's an unfortunate fact of life that when that happens, fellow criminals do tend to have reservations about consorting with them. Sometimes, the captured criminal acts as an informant participating in a crime, purely so that the main players can be arrested, for which authority has to be granted from a very senior level. Then there's the chap who provides information because he's half-way to living in a fantasy world where he's a sort of a private detective/secret agent. They do their best to persuade you to take them along with you on the job, ostensibly to point out the participants to you and invariably succeeding in ruining the whole operation and hopelessly compromising themselves and you, too. Often, the information looks quite good. Sometimes, it is. However, take it from me, this sort of informant is best treated as though he's suffering from the most contagious of anti-social diseases and avoided accordingly.

The snout motivated by greed was my favourite type of informant and I found that it was a far simpler arrangement to work with snouts on a cash-for-results basis. Gerry, one of my best informants, had previously worked as an agent for the British Army. He was reliable, with nerves of steel and he researched his quarries so meticulously that any information he gave was solid gold. In his previous employment, his brief had been to catch terrorists, but as one Judge remarked in a case of armed robbery, the actions of my parishioners had been 'one step away from terrorism' so Gerry found the thieves and gangsters of London a piece of cake. During our first excursion, not only did he provide the name and address of the target, the precise nature of his misdemeanours and the where-abouts of the loot, but Gerry decided to also advise me on the best way in which to interrogate him. This, I thought, was a bit thick, but I held my tongue and in fact, used the interview technique which Gerry had suggested. To my surprise, it worked. I mentioned this to Gerry at our next meeting. 'I knew it would,' he replied, and then went on to tell me that with regard to the next target, I should talk to him like a Dutch uncle; any mention of his sick Mother would reduce him to tears and a confes-sion - it did. Gerry and I enjoyed a fruitful relationship for years; he certainly was the richest of my informants, earning thousands of pounds per year.

I enjoyed working with informants but my word, they were a dangerous breed and I found very quickly that I had to be on my toes in my dealings with them. One of the things that I learnt was that in a police officer/informant relationship, there can only be one person in charge and that is the police officer. He doesn't wait for favours - he's in the driving seat and it's his job to inject a little resolve into his informant if it appears that he's slacking. Conversely, it's sometimes necessary to curb the impetuosity of a reckless informant. Even Gerry, good though he was, had to be held back if I could see or predict dangers unknown to him. And if an informant fell by the wayside and resorted to criminality and expected me to turn a blind eye, I didn't. I nicked them myself to demonstrate who was in charge and the funny thing was, when they came out of stir a number of them came back and started grassing, just where they'd left off. But, as I say, the road that I trod with informants was one littered with land mines and the cautionary tale that follows graphically describes the pitfalls awaiting the keen but uneducated young Copper.

I was a very new and quite ambitious detective. I had arrested Harry, a young fraudster who soon made it clear that he wished to be conscripted as an informant. Rule number one; always treat fraudsters with the greatest suspicion. Because their way of life is conning people, they're not going to stop lying when they get caught; they're going to accelerate the process. Releasing him on bail, he swore to me that he'd stick up some really worthwhile work. It was not long in coming - a villain in possession of a sawn-off shotgun; I almost swooned with pleasure. I felt sure that when this job came off, I'd have the Commander of the Flying Squad on the phone to me, his voice choking with emotion, begging me to join the Squad. Yes. That's just how green I was. Within a day or so, Harry was back on the phone, telling me that Terry, the villain of the piece was a mini-cab controller who had the sawn-off in his house – *right now*! Now, at this time, turf wars were being fought between various unscrupulous mini-cab companies and a sawn-off shotgun was considered a suitable arbitrator in these disagreements so Harry's information seemed entirely feasible.

A check on Terry revealed that he was indeed a mini-cab controller with a history of petty crime. Hoping to include a mention of serious crime within his antecedents in the near future, I obtained a search warrant under the Firearms Act from the local Magistrates' Court, and off I went. Terry opened the door of his house to me as though he'd been expecting me and viewed me with what I took to be overt dislike. I explained my reason for being there and showed him the search warrant which he read with a curled lip. I turned the house over – really turned it over, because a sawn-off is so small, it can be in the most unlikely of hiding places. I searched for hours, without success. Terry, who had said little, watched me go with that same look on his face.

Back to the nick I went, feeling thoroughly fed-up. An hour later, Harry telephoned me.

'It wasn't there, was it, Mr. Kirby?' he asked. I agreed that this was so.

'No, the bastard moved it out of the house half an hour before you got there,' he replied. 'He was tipped off - I think you've got a wrong'un in your office, Mr. Kirby!'

I looked around at the occupants of the office with suspicious eyes and privately agreed that this could indeed be a possibility.

'Don't worry,' said Harry. 'I'll do a bit more work and we'll nail this bastard.' 'Good!' I thought and thinking of the day when I could wipe that insolent look off of Terry's face, I put the phone down. But I didn't hear any more news about Terry, not from Harry, anyway. The next thing that happened, was that I received a visit from a Detective Inspector from a neighbouring station. In the presence of my own Detective Inspector, he explained that he had just nicked Harry for a little bit more than false pretences. It transpired that originally, Harry had gone to see Terry, whom he knew, and demanded money from him. When Terry refused, Harry stated that he'd got a detective in his pocket - me - and unless Terry complied with his demands, I would come round and turn him over for a sawn-off shotgun, just to show him that I was in cahoots with Harry - and in the event that no money was then forthcoming and a second visit was required, a sawn-off would be 'found' there. As this story was recounted to me, I felt my face burning with shame and embarrassment at the easy way in which I'd not only been duped but well and truly compromised. The look on Terry's face, which I'd mistaken for dislike, was contempt for what he thought was a crooked Copper. The visiting Detective Inspector was quite sympathetic. He had pulled Harry in, in order to consolidate his case which, on the face of it, was one of police corruption; to his surprise, Harry had immediately caved in and for once in his life, told the truth. I had been absolved of any criminal culpability in the case although, as my Detective Inspector acidly remarked, I still had much to learn regarding the handling of informants and life in general.

Which just goes to show you the booby traps awaiting ambitious young detectives and it taught me a much-needed lesson. I have previously mentioned that not one of my informants was ever compromised but although I had high expectations of him, Harry was no informant. He was just a cheap little con-man with big ideas who subsequently received a very severe punishment.

In addition, he was also sentenced to 18 months imprisonment.

Keep off the Grass!

Criminals often get caught by drawing attention to themselves to such an extent that they're practically begging to be arrested. Let me give you an example.

Albie Higgins was one of my parishioners when I was a Uniformed Police Constable in the late 1960s. He was also the possessor of a driving record which was so dreadful that he had managed to get himself disqualified from driving until 1997. And yet, do you know, Albie literally couldn't stop himself being arrested. On one famous occasion, he drew up in his battered Jaguar, on the opposite side of the road to where the crew of a police wireless car were sitting, writing up a report and Albie revved up the Jaguar's engine before roaring off down the road. He then stopped because, to his horror, he realised that the occupants of the police vehicle hadn't taken the slightest bit of notice of him, being thoroughly engrossed in their report writing. He therefore reversed all the way back to the police car, stopped directly opposite them and continually revved his engine and then honked his horn until the officers, who knew him well, looked up. It was at this stage that Albie accelerated sharply away and after travelling fifteen feet, deliberately stalled his car's engine, so that the police could stroll across the road and arrest him.

'Bastards!' shouted Albie, adding illogically, 'always picking on me!'

All right, so that's an extreme example, but you'd think that having pulled a job off, crooks would want to go quietly home, not wanting to draw attention to themselves. Perhaps it's just as well some of them didn't - it certainly made my job catching them that much easier!

As indeed it did, when my aiding partner and I were strolling through Romford's South Street one sunny afternoon and spotted four youths ridiculing an elderly gentleman. 'Look at those flash little bastards,' I said to my partner as the old gentleman stumped off with his walking stick, to the accompaniment of jeers and cat-calls from the youths, all of whom, I noticed, were holding carrier bags. We walked over to them.

'Hello, boys,' I said, extending my warrant card. 'What're you up to?'

'Nothing,' replied their spokesman disingenuously. 'We're just doing a bit of shopping. Want to see?' And lifting up his carrier bag, he suddenly flung the contents into the air, as did his companions and all of them fled to the four points of the compass. I was hot on the heels of the ringleader and I must have chased him for a quarter of a mile, as we dodged passing cars, buses, cyclists and pedestrians. Suddenly, he dashed into a street which I knew to be a cul-de-sac and when he, too, realised that there was no way out, he stopped, turned and squared up to me in a way that left me in no doubt that I was just about to cop a fourp'ny one. But by now, I was almost on top of him, still running flat out and as soon as I saw those fists come up, I walloped him hard, on the chin. Given the velocity at which I was travelling, the punch lifted him right off his feet and he crashed to the pavement. I took my eyes off him for two seconds, no more, as I looked around for a telephone box, when to my amazement, he suddenly bounced to his feet like a jack-in-the-box and we commenced a battle royal. My opponent, whose name was Chris Banks, later confided to me that his dream was to become a professional boxer and *that* I could well believe, as we rolled about on the pavement, scrabbling for wrestling holds and generally pummelling each other. Now, I had heard about (but never actually practised) a paralysing grip, entitled a 'sub-clavian nerve pinch' which, the instructions stated, would render one's opponent help-less. It was whilst I was endeavouring to bring the bout to a satisfactory conclusion by administering this hold, that a passer-by came along.

'Hullo, down there,' he called. 'What are you up to?'

'Phone the police,' I gasped. I was not, I fear, in the same excellent condition as my antagonist and I was getting awfully out of breath.

'Ah. Phone the police. Now, why do you want me to do that?' inquired the passer-by.

I took two hard punches in the ribs from my opponent. 'Because I'm a police officer and I want some help,' I groaned.

'I see,' said this amazing idiot. 'A police officer, eh?'

'Yes,' I croaked, copping a left hook in my ear.

'Well, now. I've only your word for that, haven't I?' asked this dolt in an infuriatingly reasonable tone.

By now, I'd avoided a head-butt from this muscular young eel and had even managed to lift myself up and land a stunning punch to his solar plexus which should have effectively ended the battle. Unfortunately, it had only the effect of producing a sharp jolt from my adversaries knee into my groin, with nauseating results.

'What?' I wheezed to this certifiable lunatic.

'I mean, have you got any form of identification, for instance?' he went on. By now, I'd given up any hope of assistance from him. In fact,

I wanted to give myself the pleasure of telling him to 'Fuck off' and the only reason that I didn't, was because I had to apply all my energy and concentration in containing the Great White Hope, with whom I was brawling.

Luckily for me, PC Fred Morris was driving past in the wireless car just then, saw my plight and came to my aid. I was exhausted. Banks, on the other hand, was hardly out of breath and still full of fight. 'Come on, then!' he kept saying.

After Fred had locked Banks up, I staggered into the CID office and collapsed in a chair. Insult was finally added to injury when I was spotted by Detective Inspector Charley Arnold. 'What's your game!' he shouted. 'You ain't going to catch many thieves while you're sitting on yer bleedin' arse all day long!'

My aiding partner hadn't managed to catch any of the rest of the team, who had been industriously engaged in a day's shoplifting, but he redeemed himself by teasing the names of Banks' accomplices from him and one by one, we captured the lot.

Banks, who was on licence to Borstal, was promptly recalled there. 'No hard feelings, Guv,' he winked and shook hands, as he went down to the cells after his court appearance.

In the months that followed, I was appointed Detective Constable and was posted to Forest Gate Police Station. One evening, I suddenly leapt out of my chair in the CID office, jumped into my car and drove to a certain address in Dagenham. My knock on the door was answered by Chris Banks' younger brother. 'Where's Chris?' I said.

'I ain't seen him,' replied the brother, but I could see in his eyes that he was not being entirely frank with me. I walked into the house and there, in the lounge was Chris Banks and another youth. 'All right, Chris, you know me,' I said. 'You're under arrest for escaping from Borstal.'

Banks flew into a rage. 'Who grassed me?' he screamed. 'I'm gonna find out and blow his legs off with a sawn-off!'

'No, you're not, Chris,' I said. 'Just calm down, because you're not going anywhere, and you...' I said to his companion, 'what's your name?'

Banks' partner's brows knitted in concentration. He was deep in thought for nearly thirty seconds. 'Smith?' he eventually offered, as though I might possibly find this acceptable. I took both of them in, since Banks' friend admitted that he, too, had gone over the wall from the Borstal establishment with Banks.

Neither of them admitted any offences whilst they were on the run, so the Borstal concerned was contacted and the two of them were detained, pending escort.

Just before he left, I had a chat with Banks in the cells. 'Do me a favour, Guv,' he said. 'Just give me the name of the bastard who set me up.'

I appeared to give the matter serious thought, and then I shook my head. 'Can't be done, Chris,' I replied.

Chris frowned and started to pace up and down. The escort was nearly due. 'It must be someone close to me,' he muttered, half-speaking to himself. 'I'd only been in the house for twenty minutes. I'd had a bite to eat, I was going to move on almost as soon as you came through that door. Who was it?'

'Who'd you think, Chris?' I asked.

'I dunno, Guv,' he replied quietly, and there was pure hatred in his young face, 'but I'll tell you this. If it's the last thing I do, I'm going to find out and when I do, I'm going to pick up a sawn-off and blow his fucking legs off!'

'Chris, you're talking wildly,' I said, soothingly. 'Just go back, finish doing your porridge and forget all this nonsense. You haven't got a sawn-off and even if you had, you wouldn't blow anyone's legs off.'

'Wouldn't I?' he replied, grimly. And with that, the escort arrived. Chris and I shook hands for the second and last time, and off he went.

I suppose that really, I could have given Chris my source of information. It's just that I'd been sitting in the CID office, when I'd picked up a copy of *Police Gazette* and had seen his photograph in there, with the fact that he was wanted for escaping from Borstal, the previous day. My arrival at his house and finding him there, had been a sheer fluke.

Still, I think it's better to keep them guessing, don't you?

A couple of years later, I was making an inquiry at Dagenham Police Station and out of curiosity, I decided to look up Mr. Banks in the collators intelligence system. The latest entry on his card revealed that following his release from Borstal, Banks had moved to an address in the Brixton area and I lost interest.

Seven more years went by and I was now a Detective Sergeant attached to the Yard's Flying Squad. I had arrested a gang of robbers who lived in a block of high-rise flats in East Ham and in so doing, I had thoroughly tuned-up many of the other inhabitants of the estate. In locking up the robbers, I was pleased to be rid of my seedy surroundings, but fate decided differently. Jimmy Dixon, a young tearaway from this estate, rapidly tired of an 18 month prison sentence and decided upon a little unofficial parole scheme of his own. With another 16 months of his exile still to run, he sawed through the bars of his cell and got clean away. Hearing that Jimmy was on his toes, I returned to the estate, tuned-up the tenants once more and promised them large quantities of misery, unless Jimmy Dixon was presented to me, gift-wrapped. Some of the occupants of this charmless estate had grown somewhat weary of lying in bed during the early morning, only to suddenly see their front door go hurtling down the passage-way, accompanied with the peremptory cry of, 'Squad!' One or two of them grudgingly stated that if they encountered any intelligence regarding Jimmy's whereabouts they would let me know, this being a small price to pay for a quiet life. And in the end, one of them did...

Sandra Parker had been the product of a joyless union, between a Lascar seaman and a worker in Manor Park's Eldorado Ice Cream factory. Without waiting for her birth - in truth, her father was not even aware of the conception - he departed for sunnier climes and never returned, leaving Sandra to be dragged up by her abandoned Mother.

As soon as her body adapted to puberty, Sandra started churning out her own brand of charmless brats. Since all of the fathers decided that marriage to Sandra or indeed maintenance of their offspring was neither necessary or desirable, Sandra grew up into a world of welfare and petty crime. To relieve the tedium of her existence, Sandra turned to alcohol and solvent abuse, which would ultimately degenerate into dependency.

But at the time of our story, Sandra had not yet toppled over the edge into final degradation. She had, it was true, the misfortune to be on bail to Snaresbrook Crown Court on a charge of causing Grievous Bodily Harm, by shoving a broken bottle into a girl's face. This had occurred when the victim - a complete stranger who, like Sandra, had been sitting on the upper deck of a bus - had had the impertinence to look at Sandra who had just withdrawn her face from a bag containing glue and was now somewhat the worse for wear. Sandra believed that she had the right to disfigure the girl, 'wot looked at me, like that,' as she explained to her despairing solicitor, who had relinquished any hope of concocting a defence for her. Since even the most immoral of Snaresbrook juries was likely to find her guilty, Sandra realised that no matter how much justification she had for her actions, substantial porridge was looming on the horizon. And so, rightly or wrongly believing that my silken words to a Judge might means the difference between incarceration and probation, Sandra agreed to keep her ear to the ground, for news of Jimmy.

On Wednesday mornings, an ominous calm used to hang over New Scotland Yard, as several hundred detectives battled their way through a week's diary. Grunts of concentration would be emitted and there would be mutterings of, 'What did we do after Court, last Thursday?' Sometimes, tempers would be ruffled when an effete senior officer would stroll through the office and tartly remark that if diaries were written up every day (as they should have been) there would be no need for this tremendous concentration of energy on Wednesday mornings which, if it could have been harnessed, would have been sufficient to light and heat Newcastle for a month. It was the consensus of opinion that this was a bit rich, firstly because the regulations stated that an officer of that rank was not required to keep a diary and secondly because that particular officer hadn't made an arrest since Christ was a carpenter.

My concentration was suddenly shattered by the ringing of the telephone on my desk. I tried to ignore it, but when one of the Flying Squad switchboard operators shouted, 'Hysterical Doris on the blower for yer, Sargie!' I picked up the telephone to hear an almost incoherent Sandra, her voice muffled with glue, babble out an address in Becontree where Jimmy Dixon was to be found, this very minute.

Slamming down the phone and picking up the green internal phone, I dialled down to Room G40, the Flying Squad drivers' rest room and gave the terse command to my driver, 'Get it up!' (This, I hasten to add, is an urgent request to bring the Squad vehicle up from the underground car-park and on to the forecourt.) Sprinting down the fourth-floor corridor and shouting for reinforcements, I gathered a car-load of Squad officers and we flew down the A13 trunk road towards East London. As the Squad car screeched to a halt and I ran towards the front door of the address which Sandra had given me and kicked it open, I could hear the sound of a window being wrenched open at the rear of the premises. As I ran into the kitchen. I was just in time to see Dixon, who was crouched on the window-sill, on the way out, suddenly topple back into my arms after Tony Freeman, having raced to the rear of the building had, with a friendly prod, encouraged this graceful display of gymnastics.

Poor Mr Dixon was terribly upset at the thought of going back to prison and, I thought, awfully upset with me, being the instrument that would send him there. In fact, he was upset with the world in general and feeling, quite rightly, that he'd been well and truly grassed up, he wanted to do some grassing of his own.

But I didn't realise this, and being hugely disinclined to hang about and be subjected to abuse from Dixon, quite apart from having other things to do, I thought I'd go and do them. Young Jimmy trumpeted so much in my absence that the Station officer at Barking Police Station telephoned the Flying Squad Office for someone to come and listen to his grassing. Since I couldn't be contacted, another officer was sent and when I found out about it later, I was quite unreasonably upset.

'You weren't about,' shrugged the other officer unsympathetically, and of course, he was quite right.

The information that Jimmy gave was pretty good. It involved a young chap who had previously lived in Dagenham, and who now lived in Brixton who had carried out a series of armed robberies. I can't bring myself to tell you his name; I don't doubt you've already guessed it.

By the way, they recovered the sawn-off shotgun from under his bed.

Wimmin!

Male police officers, particularly retired ones, often have very fixed ideas about the role of women in the Metropolitan Police. There is a school of thought that suggests that women were much better employed when their role was to take statements from victims of sexual abuse, conduct missing person enquiries and to look after kids. It is a point of view that I, in part, concur with. I do so because their expertise in these matters was unrivalled. Some officers felt that women joined the Job in order to (a) find a husband, (b) meet lesbians, (c) make the tea or (d) be the objects of sexual ridicule and harassment. Whilst I felt that (a) might have been a possible motive, (b) I felt, was confined to a minuscule minority and (c) & (d) were absolutely non-starters, these are prejudices that are slowly but surely being excised from the modern Police Force.

I mentioned agreeing in part with the Woman Police Officer's traditional role but I do think that men and women both play important parts in the Metropolitan Police. Having said that, there are jobs which should not be attempted by women, the same applying to their male counterparts.

A male officer might experience grave difficulties in obtaining urgent information from a badly frightened child, whereas a woman officer might extract that vital information within seconds, firstly because of her approach and secondly and most importantly, because she is a woman, someone the child can trust more readily than a man. Similarly, poor, brave WPC Nina MacKay died when she was the first person to crash though the door of a dwelling containing a lunatic immigrant, who had breached the bail conditions of a violent offence. She was killed by a knife thrust to her chest, because she was not wearing body armour which she felt to be uncomfortable. Was this a job that would have been more suitable for a man? Really, I think so.

The women police officers that I met throughout my career were as diverse as their male colleagues. Some were absolutely useless. Others were good, reliable, solid workers. And others still were that magic breed who were terrific; brave, talented and full of great, original ideas for solving crimes and bringing the perpetrators of those crimes to book.

There were those who considered themselves wronged; passed over for promotion, refused prime postings, being the target of sexual harassment and sometimes a combination of all three. All because they were women. They did something about it. They complained. They went to industrial tribunals. And in many cases, they were properly vindicated.

Let me make my position on this matter quite clear. If anybody in the workplace is discriminated against because they happen to be women, blacks or Asians or homosexuals, it is indefensibly wrong. Similarly, if a person is being evaluated for promotion or a posting to a specialist department, I believe they must be considered on their merits as a police officer - their experience, their proven abilities and their leadership qualities - and sex, race and sexual orientation is, in the vast majority of cases, incidental and should not be a contributory factor.

But what I thoroughly dislike is where someone - anyone - is absolutely useless at their job and they apply for a posting to a specialist department. They have been unwisely retained in the Metropolitan Police because their supervisory officers have been too frightened to risk the disapprobation of their senior officers by recommending their sacking because they happen to be female, black or gay - or sometimes an amalgamation of all three. So when they are quite properly rejected for the post, simply because they are so bloody ineffective, they scream the place down. And all of the pathetic militant groups come crawling out of the woodwork, support them to the hilt and encourage civil actions. Because, in the past, the Commissioner has felt that it would cost too much to defend such an action, he has caved in, authorised the awards of huge sums of money and has arranged for that person to be posted to the department of their desire. It has robbed officers who conduct selection boards of their credibility. It has denied the officers who should have received that posting, the chance to fulfil it. It demoralises the vast majority of decent officers. And having seen this happen time and time again, it thoroughly pisses me off.

To quote an example from my own experience: I attended a Police Firearms Course, where really first-rate training was given. I was extremely keen to pass this course and I listened attentively to the instructors and practised and practised. Before the final test-shoot, we were given a mock final. During all of the other shoots, I had scored well; out of ten shots, I would usually score ten out of ten; my lowest-ever score was eight. Now, on the mock final my average score was eight. I was a little disappointed because I wanted to qualify as a marksman but I was quite astonished when an equally astonished fellow-trainee, the late Detective Inspector Cam Burnell told me that he'd failed the mock-final. I commiserated with him, because Cam's shooting had, like mine, been consistently above par. 'Don't worry, Cam,' I said. 'It's just a spot of nerves; you'll be fine on the final shoot.' And I was right - he passed with flying colours. I failed. I simply couldn't understand it. My instructor, formally from the Special Air Service's 'G' Squadron, pointed out how my rounds had gone all over the place. I believe my average score was three out of ten. 'Don't bother to apply for any more courses,' was his final comment, adding with the sort of diplomatic skill for which the SAS is famed, 'because you obviously ain't got a clue about firearms!'

I was enormously disappointed because I'd done so well up until then but there you are; the instructor obviously knew his stuff and there was no point in arguing with him. I was officially dubbed the worst shot in the world. The second worst shot in the world was a Woman Police Officer who, some considerable time later, went on a firearms course, except that it became abundantly clear that she hadn't got a clue, right from the word go. She, too, failed - but the difference was, she complained so bitterly that she'd been discriminated against that in the end, the Firearms Section was told from very high up, to give her an authorisation to carry firearms - and that, my friends, is downright fucking *dangerous*.

Even if the militant course is not adopted, it still remains a suitable whining excuse for the unworthy. I had walked in to the front office of a certain outlying Police Station, to be confronted by a uniformed woman police officer, whom I had never seen before. Without so much as a by-your-leave, she launched into a steamy account of her recent divorce which was somehow inextricably linked with her posting to this Police Station. I was nervously considering ways in which I might make a graceful exit, my virtue still intact when, tiring of talking about herself, she asked which department I was attached to. I told her. 'Oh!' she replied, dismissively. 'The Flying Squad! I tried to get a posting to the Flying Squad - the Serious Crime Squad, as well - but because I was a woman,' she added bitterly, 'they just didn't want to know.'

'Now hang on a minute,' I exclaimed. 'You'll probably think this a minor point, but I was under the impression that to get on one of those central squads, you had to be in the CID?'

'The CID?' she gasped in horror. 'What, sit around all day long at a desk and fill in reports? Not likely! No, I wanted a bit of excitement, I wanted to get out in those fast cars and nick some criminals but because I'm a woman,' she sighed plaintively, 'I didn't stand a chance.'

What infuriates me about that sort of whining and completely unsubstantiated argument is that it denigrates anyone who has a genuine case. I cannot see how it can be considered productive to the rank and file of the Metropolitan Police who see one of the more useless of their numbers play the gender/race/sexual orientation card for all it's worth and emerge, clutching huge amounts of money and be televised with nauseatingly drippy senior officers, publicly congratulating them for their scandalous behaviour.

On the reverse side of the coin, I once saw a woman police officer, who was attached to the Flying Squad, rush in to confront a team of thoroughly dangerous young men who had just robbed a Post Office at gunpoint and had fired a shot. Unarmed herself, she disarmed the gunman and flattened him. It was one of the bravest things I had ever seen and I thought she deserved a medal. She might have received one, had the senior officer who was male, white and heterosexual not submitted a commendation report which was such utter incomprehensible gibberish that it was rejected out of hand. Apart from our unbounded admiration, she received precisely nothing; she just grinned and got on with her job. The senior officer was, of course, promoted... but it was ever thus!

The Flying Squad

I enjoyed myself all through my career - of course there were black spots, but all in all, Aiding, the Serious Crime Squad and the Divisional Crime Squads were fun. Then there were the trips - working all over England, Scotland and Northern Ireland and also in France, Germany, Holland, Switzerland, the Canary Isles and the United States of America - and they were great, too. But best of all were the times that I spent on the Flying Squad - over eight years, in all. The funny thing was, when the time came for me to go to the Squad, I couldn't have cared less whether I did or not.

This wasn't always the case. When I was an Aid, I wanted to go on to the Squad more than anything. I'd read Norman Lucas' and Bernard Scarlett's rather racy book, *The Flying Squad* and I was enchanted with the accounts of hard-faced, incorruptible Squadmen, with shoulders like oxen, rushing across the capital in fast, unmarked cars.

In 1972, I attended a board at the Yard to have my suitability assessed for permanent inclusion in the Criminal Investigation Department. The board comprised Detective Chief Superintendent Robertson from 'H' Division, Commander John Lock from the Flying Squad and Deputy Assistant Commissioner Dick Chitty. The latter was not only the chairman of the board; he was also the hatchet man.

During the course of what had become an extremely abrasive inter-view, Chitty said to me, 'If, in the event that you should be selected as a Detective Constable - and I have to tell you that in your particular case, this possibility appears to be extremely remote - where would you wish to serve?'

Now this was a stock sort of question which demanded an equally stock sort of answer. 'I would be willing to serve wherever I was posted, Sir,' I stolidly replied. This was the sort of reply which was expected because it was written into a Constable's 'Conditions of Service' that he was required to serve wherever he was ordered. However, Chitty must have grown thoroughly weary of hearing this reply because if a hopeful applicant from North London had replied in that fashion and had been told, 'Right - start at Penge on Monday!' I don't doubt he would have collapsed in a dead faint.

Chitty put a weary hand to his forehead. 'Oh, Christ,' he sighed, 'don't give me that crap. Now let me ask you again; where would you want to serve?' In fact, this was the second board that I had suffered under Chitty's ministrations and since by now, I reckoned that I'd fluffed it as badly as I had the first, I thought I might as well go for broke. 'I should very much like to serve on the Flying Squad, Sir,' I replied firmly. 'Oh,' said Chitty, his lip curling. 'Fancy yourself as a bit of a thief-taker, do you?' Now, the Division on which I was serving - 'K' Division - was so big, it was split into two and since I had topped the arrests on both sides of the Division, I felt understandably nettled at this implied slur. 'Yes, Sir.' I replied. 'As a matter of fact, I do.' Chitty sighed again, as if this was too much to bear and waved a dismissive hand in the general direction of Commander Lock. 'Oh, well,' he grunted, 'you'd better snivel round Mr. Lock!'

Saucy bugger! I thought, but John Lock, a grand gentleman, came to my aid and interjected the proceedings with some charming, inconsequential questions in order to soothe my ruffled feathers. I can only assume that the rest of the applicants fared far worse than I, because shortly afterwards I was appointed Detective Constable. The next time the Squad issue was raised was after I'd returned from a days annual leave, having been involved in a very minor way with a couple of Flying Squad cases as a new Detective Constable at Forest Gate Police Station. 'The Squad were in yesterday,' casually mentioned one of the CID personnel. 'They asked if you wanted to come up on the Squad,' and my heart hardly had time to jump at this thrilling news, because he added, 'but I told 'em, I reckoned you weren't up to it.' At this, I exploded with rage. 'Well, you want to mind your own fucking business!' I shouted. I was infuriated because I had never worked with this officer, since I made it a rule never to work with those that I considered to be lazy, drunk, incompetent or bent and therefore he was not in a position to assess me. With hindsight, he might have well been right; I might not have been up to working on the Squad at that early stage of my career. But as far as I was concerned, this was nothing more than a bit of studied spitefulness on his part - I still believe this - and I was furious.

The next time the question of the Squad came up was a couple of years later. I was now attached to the Serious Crime Squad and one day, a group of Squad officers came into the office. The Detective Inspector explained that he was looking for a useful Detective Constable for one of the East End cars. I was flattered that I should have been singled out but although I thanked the Inspector for his courtesy, I declined because firstly, I was in line for promotion to Detective Sergeant on the Serious Crime Squad and didn't want to go to the bottom of the Flying Squad heap for promotion and secondly, I was enjoying myself. It was just as well, really, because a couple of months later, that team got their collars felt for a bit of skulduggery.

Gerry Wiltshire had been my Detective Chief Inspector at Barkingside Police Station. He was greatly admired, a short, wiry man with piercing eyes behind rimless glasses who was a fine investigator and who was as hard as nails. His Detective Inspector had been Frank Rushworth, a meticulous investigator with a lot of avuncular charm and working with either of them would have been a good result. The fact that the two of them worked at the same Police Station was marvellous. The uniform Chief Superintendent was Ted Markham, a fine looking and extremely capable officer who worked very harmoniously with Gerry and Frank and in consequence, it was a very happy Station.

Gerry had been posted to the Squad and one day, he telephoned me and asked me to come up and join him. By now, I'd rather gone off the boil with regards to the Squad. I'd enjoyed my five years with the Serious Crime Squad, where I'd learnt a lot about all aspects of criminal investigation and at the time of Gerry's phone call, I was busily passing this on to the youngsters who were attached to the Divisional Crime Squad, of which I was in charge and I'm afraid I was rather casual about Gerry's offer. Eventually, I rather grudgingly accepted and my goodness, I'm glad I did. I went to work on 12 Squad, which, with 10 Squad, were the last of the two Squads of the Flying Squad ever to work at the Yard.

The Flying Squad had been formed in 1919, to provide a fluid, mobile task force, to help combat the sudden upsurge of crime, following the end of the First World War. Over the years, the Squad had earned a reputation second-to-none for shrewdness, toughness and, to many, an unorthodox approach to Policing. During those times, if you wanted to be part of the Squad (which, in 1948 became known as C8 Department at the Yard) your name went 'in the Book', so that when there was a vacancy, (and providing, of course, that you were well recommended) all being well, you'd be posted to the Squad. It could lead to abuses, of course, where an unsuitable officer could be brought up on the Squad because, for example, he was the Detective Inspector's drinking partner or because of Masonic influences. One officer had an interview with his uninformed, uniformed Chief Superintendent, who suggested that a good career move for the officer, might be to go to C8, which the Chief Superintendent thought was Criminal Records Office.

This officer, who personally thought that C8 was the Fraud Squad, eagerly accepted, inexplicably got through the net, and was somewhat bemused on his first day in the Squad office, where he was confronted by groups of large, hard-faced gentlemen, pressing, with banana-like fingers, rounds of ammunition into revolvers. He had fully expected to be surrounded by thin, studious accountants, soberly perusing columns of figures.

So what sort of men and women were successful Flying Squad officers? They were a diverse bunch, some of whom had been on the Squad previously, whilst for others it was their first time. A few were aged in their early 20s, others in their late 30s. There were Squad officers who were solidly built, whilst others possessed more modest physiques. Some had triumphed in running snouts, had used participating informants in order to frustrate the activities of dangerous criminals and had themselves been involved in undercover work. Others had made names for themselves for their interrogative techniques and their painstaking work in major investigations. There were those who excelled in the outstanding preparation of court cases. And others still, were experts in surveillance work and were masters of disguise. Many were an amalgamation of all of these attributes. If there were common characteristics which threaded through the seam of the Squadmen, it was having an absolute determination to tackle villains, coupled with a strong hint of ruthlessness. Because Squad work was so entirely different from anything any of us had done before, it would take some officers a little time to become acclimatised to the Squad ways. Others were complete naturals, and took immediately to Squad life. (I was so impressed with the confident, professional manner in which Detective Superintendent Dave Little carried out his duties on the Squad, that I once asked him how many times he'd served on the Squad before. 'Never,' he replied. 'This is my first time!')

There were some officers who were surplus to requirements and I want to be quite frank about this. Some officers were slow learners but if they had aptitude and ability and most of all, the right attitude, they could be nurtured and eventually they would become good, effective Squad officers. But there were those who hadn't a clue about Squad work, police work or indeed any kind of work. Now, in those circumstances, where those officers were like fish out of water, you would think that they would ask to be returned to ordinary duties; and to their credit, some of them did. Others, however, remained on the Squad, hangers-on to a man, just making up numbers, grabbing all of the overtime going and never contributing anything worthwhile to the Squad. I thought that they were an utter disgrace and on any enquiry that I was running, I always ensured that they were given the most demeaning jobs. I blamed the senior officers; they knew how little those wasters contributed and how much they were disliked by the workers but little, if anything, was done about them. I thought it shameful, the more so because I - all of us, in fact - knew lots of really talented, hard workers out on Division, just aching to come to the Squad and their way was blocked because of these utter wastes of space.

The vast majority of us were an enthusiastic and adventurous group and there was rivalry between the cars on each squad to get the best arrests. This was nothing as compared to the rivalry which existed between the Squads - I once surreptitiously pinned up a notice in the corner of the Squad room, which read:

IN THE EVENT OF A NUCLEAR ATTACK
PLEASE GO IMMEDIATELY TO 10 SQUAD
– THEY HAVEN'T HAD A HIT IN YEARS!

10 Squad were furious - Albert Patrick, Tommy Bradley, John Childs and Cam Burnell were but four fearsome characters out of a very tough bunch. I found it prudent to quickly disclaim all knowledge of this practical joke which, naturally I agreed, was in very poor taste.

All of us ran informants, some tried and tested, others small-fry who had been leant on, following their arrest for a no-account bit of work. They, wanting a successful conclusion at their impending court appearance, would steer us into the path of some armed robbers.

I hope I've conveyed to you what it was like to have been a member of the Flying Squad in those days. Let me give you one or two instances of the things that happened...

I didn't put all that many names in 'The Book' (that record of names and warrant numbers of potential Flying Squad recruits) but those that did, all joined the Squad. One such name was Tony Yeoman. I'd Aided with Tony for a very short period in 1970; in fact I still see him, when we run an annual race in support of my youngest son's school and he's one of those people who hasn't changed a bit over the years. Tony was a very energetic worker and I don't believe he's ever had a complaint made about his conduct; I'm convinced it was because the villains were stunned that a CID officer could be so nice! During the questioning of suspects, I would be the beastly one and Tony would be the sympathetic officer to whom the criminals longed to confess. Only on one occasion did I suggest the roles should be reversed, because I was afraid of getting typecast. The outcome was a disaster. Tony was transformed into a brooding tough, whilst I endeavoured to be a caring, sharing, compassionate do-gooder. The prisoner collapsed with a fit of the giggles at our pathetic efforts and this was laughter in which we had to join. Eventually, we had to tick the prisoner off for his misdeeds and swear him to silence regarding our risible performance. But don't get the idea that Tony wasn't tough, because nothing could be further from the truth and I'll tell you why.

Ten years went by and I was now a Detective Sergeant on the Flying Squad. I was spending the evening relaxing at a party when who should walk in but Tony; by now, a Detective Sergeant at Romford Police Station. His face was a picture of misery, since someone had unhelpfully pencilled his name in for a tour of duty on CIB2, the Police Complaints Department which Tony was eagerly anticipating as one does a dose of the clap. 'Don't worry, Tony,' I said cheerfully. 'I'll get you up on the Squad.' And I did - of course, in those days you could but this was during those golden days before the people at the very top of Scotland Yard's hierarchy let the reins irrevocably slip and permitted Personnel Department to completely run the Yard's policies. Tony was an instant success in the Flying Squad and in time, he came to run its surveillance unit, very successfully, too, and this is a propitious moment to mention Tony's toughness.

We had kept observation on a robbery team for weeks. The information was that two of the gang were going to ambush a supermarket manager when he took the takings to a night safe. Firearms had been mentioned and once the money had been seized, the robbers would run to the third member of the gang, waiting in a stolen car and escape. Other stolen cars were to be used as change-over vehicles. Therefore a large number of Squad officers and vehicles had to be utilised, not only for the surveillance and 'attack' teams but also to be used on the fall-back positions, should the robbers actually succeed and escape in the first getaway car. In addition, photographers and forensic experts were standing by so that in the event of an arrest, the robbers could be forensically examined and photographed *in situ*. It had been established roughly where the attack would take place and therefore, officers from the Yard's Technical Support Department were on hand to video the attack and, hopefully the arrest.

Now, in order to carry out a successful arrest, the attack has to be timed to a split second. Grab the robbers too quickly, before they've actually done anything and at a later stage, some silver-tongued barrister will successfully persuade a particularly dim-witted jury that his clients were only dressed in balaclavas and boiler suits whilst armed with offensive weapons on a busy High Street, because they were dress-rehearsing for a play about inner-city violence. 'After all, officer, it's not as if you actually saw them do anything, is it?' Don't laugh. It happens, I assure you. Leave it too late and somebody's going to get hurt. Which is just what happened in this case, because nobody knew who the manager was, nor what he looked like or which supermarket he managed.

The masked robbers suddenly dashed forward and broke the manager's arm with wooden staves forcing him to relinquish his hold on a carrier bag containing the day's takings – nearly £9,000. Grabbing the money, they turned and ran and it was at this moment that Tony Yeoman went into action. Still believing that the gang were in possession of firearms, Tony, who was completely unarmed, dashed forward, scooped both of them up in his arms and rammed them into a plate glass window. The huge glass plate sagged inwards and just when I thought that it was going to snap in the middle and come down on them like a guillotine blade, mercifully, it sprang out again – and I and a lot of other Squad men breathed normally again. I used to show the police video of this amazing act of courage to the recruits at Peel Centre, Hendon, when I gave the Flying Squad lecture and it never failed to raise a cheer. To tell you the truth, I felt like cheering that day, because Tony was the bravest of the brave. As a footnote, the papers on the case were so abysmally written up - 'the robbers were then arrested' the report gormlessly read, that the Squad's Acting Commander (who hadn't seen the video) dismissed the commendation of the Judge (who had seen it) and wrote, 'good... basically routine... not suitable for further commendation.' Well, the Acting Commander wasn't there that day. I was.

Julia Pearce was a terrific Detective Constable whom we wholehearted adored, who was on Detective Sergeant Peter Mellins' team. Pete was known as 'Doc' Mellins and his Squad driver, 'Dickie' Dawson explained to me that this was an abbreviation of 'Doctor Gloom' because Pete always looked as if he carried the worries of the world around on his shoulders. But they were a very successful team who achieved some excellent results, even though 'Doc' sighed and lugubriously shook his head at an unfair world whilst little Julie would explode with laughter at her blasphemous utterances.

We had ambushed a burglary team who had smashed their way in through the glass door of a warehouse and as the first suspect came creeping out through the ruined door, I grabbed hold of him. The burglar, one Alfie Fraser, gasped and tried to get back into the warehouse, dragging me with him; I, for my part, pulled at him strongly and made a couple of feet headway. Then Alfie rallied and dragged me back towards the door and it was this cretinous display of a two-man tug of war which resulted in Julie shrieking with laughter. 'Bash 'im, Dick!' she squealed until Alfie's breath and resolve ran out before mine did. The gang were rounded up and searches of the addresses of their nearest and dearest were carried out. Aggie Newman was Alfie's sweetheart and 'Doc', Julie and I went to her address which I can say with my hand on my heart was one of the most deprived (and probably depraved) dumps it has ever been my misfortune to enter.

Whilst Harold Hill still cannot be truthfully described as Havering's answer to Hampstead Garden Suburb, it is better now than it was 20 years ago. Then, with its towering tower blocks, it was, with few exceptions, the dumping ground for the flotsom and jetsom of society and Aggie Newman could accurately be described as a child of that society. Tall, paper-thin, with hair which would have made Medusa gasp with admiration and fingernails which made your eyes water, Aggie treated us to the sort of shrieking invective which was the mandatory greeting of the inhabitants of Harold Hill to visitors of authority. But anticipating such hospitality, I had decided to bring along my secret weapon, one Anthony Yeoman, known for his ability to charm the birds from the trees and who also, in a moment of weakness, had admitted that he had previously encountered Aggie. My inclusion of Tony in the raiding party proved a providential notion, because Tony stopped her in mid-screech with the most curious phrase I'd ever heard.

'Aggie,' he said, quietly. 'Stop it. You know you've got a head full of mad dog-shit.'

Aggie bowed her head. 'I know, Tone,' she replied humbly. 'I'm sorry.'

For years afterwards, I wondered about the magical properties contained in that phrase. For it was magic, no doubt about it, every bit as potent an incantation as Hey Presto! or Abracadabra! But I could never bring myself to ask Tony the meaning of it and it was an expression that I never used thereafter, fearing that if I did, the mystic power of it would be turned and used to consume me.

But after Aggie had been thus subdued, we commenced the search. As we moved around the gruesome kitchen, the linoleum making a sucking, protesting sound, as it tried to separate us from our shoes, Julia went to open the freezer. 'You don't want to do that,' said Aggie ominously. 'There's something in there.'

Julia favoured her with a sneer and opened the freezer. Julia's scream and the slamming of the freezer's door were simultaneous. 'Jesus!' shrieked Julia. 'There is something in there! It fucking moved!'

'Told you,' said Aggie, with quiet satisfaction.

Naturally, we all jeered at Julia's discomfort, me more than most, because I was still smarting from Julia's hysteria at my private tug of war earlier in the evening. 'Go on, then,' shouted Julia, furiously, 'you look, if you're all so bloody brave!'

Of course we were bloody brave; hadn't the Commissioner confirmed this, on several occasions? But our valour did not extend to re-opening that freezer door again - so we didn't.

If I tell you that the Flying Squad drivers were the best drivers in the world, you'll accuse me of being biased; but I do and I'm not. They were recruited from the Uniform branch and were all Class I drivers and they, like the Squad detectives, had to be well recommended. John 'Dickie' Dawson, decorated by the Queen with a well-deserved British Empire Medal for gallantry, after pursuing and apprehending a gunman and the late Tony Freeman and Alfie Howells are all mentioned elsewhere in this book and in between jobs, they and the other drivers would relax in the ground-floor drivers' room at the Yard, and pass the time playing

Kalooki, dissecting the detectives characters and dozing. But when the terse command, 'Get it up' was given, the scene was set for a fast memorable trip across the capital. I remember one such drive, after we'd received an urgent call to a gunman, when we tore out of the Yard and into Victoria Street, towards Parliament Square. Our side of the road, which was separated by a central reservation, was completely blocked by rush-hour traffic. With the headlights full on and the two-tones blaring, our driver, Ron Sewell, simply switched lanes and drove straight into the on-coming traffic, on the opposite side of the road, which parted like the Red Sea did for Moses.

In all of the innumerable fast drives I've had in Flying Squad cars across London, I can truthfully say that I have never had the slightest cause for concern. The drivers, whom I admired very much, were as much an integral part of the Squad, as were the detectives. It did not, of course, prevent a series of interminable working parties being formed to put the Squad under a microscope. These committees were usually headed by senior uniformed officers who had never faced an angry man in their lives and inevitably, the question asked by 13-year-old Superintendents was, 'Why do we need Flying Squad drivers? Why can't the squad drive themselves?' Normally, these pubescent cretins could be shut up by threatening them with confiscation of their teddies, but I firmly believe that if there had been no drivers, there would have been no Flying Squad for this simple reason. True professionals, such as these drivers are needed to transport armed Flying Squad officers into highly dangerous situations with the minimum of fuss and the maximum of skill and to take whatever action they think is necessary to stop escaping robbers.

A classic example of this happening was when, following an ambush on a gang of highly dangerous armed robbers, a couple of the gang made a run for it. The first of the escapees was jumped on by so many Squadmen, that he resembled pressed ham. One of the Squad drivers, Robin Mitchell - 'Mitch' - tore down the street in a nondescript van towards the second robber, who, as far as he was aware, was fully armed and ready for anything. With complete disregard for his own safety, Mitch pulled on the handbrake, leapt out of the still-moving van and putting his middle and index fingers together, assumed the crouched firearms stance. 'Hands up!' growled Mitch, 'or I'll shoot you!'

The robber started to put his hands up but alas, not quickly enough.

Mitch stepped smartly forward and tapped the robber on the forehead with his two loaded fingers. This action earned Mitch a highly-coveted Commissioner's High Commendation. It also earned the robber substantial ridicule, because believing that he had been pistol-whipped, he crashed to the pavement and with considerable co-ordination, managed to evacuate his bowels at the same time. Which substantiates my claim about part of the Squad driver's role - 'To take whatever action they think necessary to stop escaping robbers.' Mitch now lives quietly in retirement but Squad-lore has it that he still keeps his middle and index fingers oiled - just in case!

There have always been good Guv'nors on the Squad - Mick Taylor, Simon Crawshaw, Bob Harding, Bernie Hodgets, Peter Gwynn, Iain Malone and Albert Patrick were just some of them during my time - and some who were indifferent. I can remember when all of the Flying Squad hierarchy were truly excellent and that was when John 'Ginger' O'Connor was the Commander, Eddie Holbrook was the Detective Chief Superintendent and Billy Hatful and Duncan MacRae were the Detective Superintendents. And why? Simply because they'd spent all of their careers in and out of the Flying Squad. Duncan MacRae, in particular, had spent every rank, from Detective Constable upwards, on the Flying Squad. Men like these knew the Squad inside out and knew what was needed to keep the squad running smoothly in the terms of manpower, assistance, equipment and encouragement.

These were the men and women with whom I laughed, drank, followed across the pavement and into the witness box, sometimes argued and occasionally fought. And sometimes, we wept together.

The news that Johnny Fordham, the C11 Surveillance man, whom we all knew, admired and worked with had been killed, stunned us all. Many of the Squad men that I'd worked with were at the scene that night. That John had been killed, was bad enough; when the jury found it quite acceptable that an unarmed policeman could be stabbed ten times, including three knife wounds in the back and one in the head and decide that the person responsible was not guilty of murder on the grounds that he was only acting in self-defence, it became almost too much to bear.

So this is a small sample of some of the things that happened on the Flying Squad. Other Squad stories are recounted elsewhere in this book and others are still waiting to be told.

Being a member of the Flying Squad was like being part of a family.

Like any family, there were those who were loved, some were spoilt, others envied and some were so crooked they were unable to lie straight in bed and they were despised. But it was a wonderful, thrilling time to be a Squadman and I'm so glad I was part of it.

Never Talk to Strangers

I had been of the opinion, (as had the then-prosecuting authority, the Metropolitan Police Solicitors' Department) that there had been sufficient evidence in a case of conspiracy to rob employees of the Post Office to put before a jury, but as I saw Errol Washington swaggering out of Court 17 at the Old Bailey, I realised that the Trial Judge had not been of the same persuasion.

Errol, whose stocky physique resembled that of a Pit-bull terrier, had only to frown at the toughest of his fellow Afro Caribbeans, to promote terror and flight in his native Stoke Newington. As I was joined by Tony Freeman, Errol strutted up to me. Although he spoke English as well as anybody, Errol always found it necessary to communicate in an amazing patois of Rastafarian, Cockney and gibberish. In so doing, Errol thought that this provided him with immense street cred whereas the converse was true. Everyone who listened to him speaking thought he was a complete and utter prick, although this was an opinion which they prudently kept to themselves. 'Yo, mun,' he sneered. 'Mewalk, innit?' (For a fairly accurate translation, this may be interpreted as, 'Excuse me officer, but since I've been acquitted, I'll be off, now.')

'Go on, fuck off,' I said, and as I watched a small red blaze ignite in his eyes and saliva drip from his mouth (a sure sign of impending doom) I added, 'Oh, and Errol, do yourself a favour, go straight home to your Mummy and don't speak to any strange men in cars.' The fires in Errol's eyes were suddenly extinguished and he slouched off, a braggart no more.

'Blimey, Dick!' said Tony. 'I thought he was going to rip your head off!'

'Don't worry, Tone,' I replied. 'I was never in any danger. He just needed shutting up, and I'll tell you how I did it...'

This is the story that I told Tony, the story that Errol now knew that I knew.

It is not widely known, but following the Brixton riots of 1981, other predominantly black militant areas of London decided that declaring no-go areas to the police would be a splendid idea. Sandringham Road (known as 'The Front Line') is situated off Kingsland High Street, Stoke Newington, north-east London, and it is a hot-bed of villainy and drug dealing. It is also the subject of surveillance from Plain-clothes police officers, both from local and central units. Therefore, reasoned the militant young blacks of the area, if anywhere was going to be a no-go area, Sandringham Road would fit the bill admirably.

That this piece of civil insurrection failed almost from its inception, had nothing whatsoever to do with the superior strategy of the police, nor was it due to the half-hearted pleas for prudence from the community leaders. Rather, it is highly likely that God in His Heaven was feeling slightly bored and came to the conclusion that the plight confronting Stoke Newington might well be lightened by one of His little japes.

It was a sunny August morning and Errol and an equally belligerent companion were taking the air along Sandringham Road. Social Security payments were in abundance, lucrative drugs deals were on the increase and there were always Asian shopkeepers to frighten into docility for a few quid. Yes indeed, thought Errol. Life was good.

But soft! Errol choked back his rage as he spotted a Ford Granada (a vehicle much favoured by the infamous 'Sweeney') parked up by the kerb, with two white men, both in their early 30s, seated inside it.

This, thought Errol, was the stuff legends were made of. He would confront the 'Sweeney', put a much-needed flea in their ears and his social standing, already high in the neighbourhood, would increase a hundredfold. He even had a companion to act independently in the role of mediaeval minstrel, to sing tales of his daring. Was Sandringham Road a no-go area, or not? Pausing only to ignite the red spark in his eyes, Errol blustered up to the car's driver, who was sitting indolently in his seat, his window wound down, and addressed him in his near-incomprehensible gibberish. 'Hey, Guy!' he snarled. 'You da fuckin' Bill, innit?' ('I beg your pardon, but you are police officers, aren't you?')

The driver calmly regarded him. 'No, we ain't Old Bill, mate,' he replied.

Errol was enraged at the driver's nonchalance. 'Yeah, you da Bill!' he bellowed, 'an' yo fuck off before us mash ya, innit!' ('I'm sure you are police officers, and I'd be obliged if you'd leave before I become vexed.')

'Alright, mate,' replied the driver, and starting the engine, he drove off for a short distance and then, spotting a sizable gap in the parked cars, swung the car in a lazy U-turn, and drove back towards Errol and his smirking companion.

It would have been better if the Granada had roared off, thought Errol, for the purposes of the story that, he felt, would shortly be recounted to a large group of amazed admirers. But the car seemed to be fairly crawling along the road towards them, prompting Errol to think that little would go amiss if he were to roar some suitable presage of doom at its impudent occupants. The intended words froze in his throat as he saw the passenger, who was the more disgruntled of the two robbers, both of whom had been waiting patiently all morning to hit a security van, lean out of the window and point a sawn-off shotgun at him.

The '*thump!*' of Errol's body hitting the pavement, the '*bang!*' of the shotgun, as the contents therefrom barely missed him and Errol's terrified screaming were simultaneous. 'Fucking Hell!' screeched Errol. 'Get me Probation Officer! Get me Brief! Get me Mum!' And then, as an afterthought, 'Get me Community Policeman!'

Errol later found solace in the arms of a mealy-mouthed Social Worker, who tenderly bathed his fingers, which were slightly lacerated from his frenzied attempts to dig through the pavement to Australia. Errol also tried to redeem his social standing by attempting to spread tales of psychotic CID officers who were trying to maintain the status quo, but nobody really believed him. From that moment on, together with the maximum amount of publicity that I felt it my duty to impart to the area, Errol's days as a hero were numbered and, under cover of darkness, he migrated to the fresh pastures of Tottenham.

Just as I finished this tale, and Tony was still hooting with laughter, we were joined by a downcast Counsel for the prosecution. 'I'm sorry we lost that case, Mr. Kirby,' he apologised.

I was at my most gracious. 'Don't think of it as losing,' I said, putting an arm around his shoulders. 'Buy us a cup of coffee out of your exorbitant fees, and I'll tell you a story that'll cheer you up!'

A Friend at the Farm

Lucius White was a very big and a highly dangerous criminal and I had spent weeks searching for him. I had personally had dealings with him previously and I knew exactly how dangerous he was. A measure of his long and chequered criminal career was that at the tender age of 14 years for his part in a particularly brutal robbery, White had been sentenced to four years' detention. He had escaped from custody so many times that when I had arrested him and checked his details at Criminal Records Office at the Yard, an agitated clerk had requested that I physically go to his cell to establish that he was still there. A note on his file in large red letters stated that he had to be checked at extremely frequent intervals to ensure his continued detention. He was so violent that when I had questioned him, four officers were present with all of us locked in the interview room with two more officers outside - just in case.

On this occasion, White had been involved in a botched hold-up at a building society, where out of seething resentment at the young counter clerk's courage at refusing to hand over any cash, he'd discharged the sawn-off shotgun he was carrying into the counter screen, causing a sliver of glass to hit the girl near the eye.

White was well known in and around the Stoke Newington area and was feared, as well. This fear increased a hundredfold after White and the other man who had been involved in the robbery had been spotted by the crew of the local wireless car, one evening. By chance, they had a dog handler in the back, together with his charge and as the car screeched to a halt, the car crew leapt out and detained the other man. The dog handler, knowing full-well what a handful White was, simply released his dog in White's direction. White caught the dog in mid-leap, rammed it head-first into a nearby wall, and set off down the street like an express train. After that, no-one would even admit to *knowing* White, let alone having seen him.

I spent so much time around the area with my Flying Squad team, looking for White, that there are officers, even today, who swear that they served with me in the CID office at Stoke Newington. Every suspect that got pulled in, for whatever offence, got quizzed about White.

'Do you want to do yourself a bit of good? Where's White? Come on, stick him up. No-one'll know, and there'll be a safe drink in it for you.'

'No, don't know 'im, guv. Never heard of 'im.'

'You fucking liar! You got three months with him, last time you got nicked!'

'Oh, yeah, alright, I know 'im. Ain't seen 'im.'

This went on for some considerable time and after a while I got fed up and started looking around for some alternative entertainment. One day, I gave Johnny Redgrave a hand, who had got a lead on a wanted armed robber who was supposed to be living in a flat at a place named the Broadwater Farm Estate. This was several years before the disgusting murder of Police Constable Keith Blakelock and although we went there at 8 o'clock in the morning, team-handed and armed, do you know, I felt a feeling of dread about the place, even then. Premonition, I suppose.

But having bashed in the flat's front door, there was not so much an armed robber inside, as a thriving cannabis plant, together with a booklet, published in Jamaica, on how to keep the plant flourishing and a cheerful young Afro Caribbean, who was an owner to both.

Lewis Hoskins was brought into Tottenham Police Station, where his distress at being parted from his beloved cultivation was beaten hands-down by the hysterical behaviour of the local uniformed Superintendent, who had to be rubbed with ice after he'd heard that we'd dared to go on the estate without informing him beforehand, thereby frustrating any plans that he could have arranged for a jolly, consultative gathering with some of the more militant custodians of 'The Farm'.

Lewis, the proprietor of the cannabis plant, was very relaxed and chatty, so I thought I'd give him a go about the elusive Mr. White, although I certainly didn't hold out much hope. A brief chat with Lewis had established that he was very inexperienced in the ways of crime and lived miles off of White's manor.

'Seen Lucius White lately, Lewis?' I asked, casually.

Lewis screwed up his nose. 'Lucius White?' he repeated. He slowly shook his head. 'Nah. I ain't seen him - no, not for about two weeks.'

'What!' I sat bolt upright. 'Where?'

'I dunno,' he shrugged. 'Some shabeen. Why?'

'Listen, Lewis,' I said, urgently. 'I want White. If you can put the finger on him, there's going to be a nice drink in it for you.'

'Yeah?' he said, brightening up considerably, and almost forgetting the loss of his beautiful plant. 'How nice?'

'Enough to pay whatever your fine is going to be for producing that cannabis plant,' I replied, with certainty.

'O.K. Leave it to me,' said Lewis, decisively.

I began to get a little alarmed at Lewis' self-assurance. 'Er - Lewis,' I said, hesitantly. 'Look, watch yourself, son. White can be, well, a bit of a handful.'

'Fuck him,' said Lewis, scornfully. 'He don't worry me.'

And on that optimistic note, we parted. I heard nothing more, until two weeks later I was awoken from a deep sleep at 3am. 'I seen him, Mr. Kirby,' said an excited Lewis. 'I was just going into a shabeen, and White was coming out!'

'Where did he go?' I asked, shaking myself awake.

'I dunno, Mr. Kirby,' said Lewis. 'He got into a car and fucked off. If only I'd nicked a car this evening, I could have followed him for you!'

'Ah, well,' I said, disappointment seeping in, 'can't be helped, Lewis. You did your best.'

There was a pause. 'It was a red Vauxhall Velox he got into, Mr. Kirby,' said Lewis, adding carelessly, 'Did you want me to give you the number?'

Wasn't Lewis a naughty little tinker, children?

That night, I assembled a huge number of uniformed officers who were members of the Territorial Support Unit and after a detailed briefing, we split up and systematically searched the streets of 'G' and 'H' Divisions, two of the busiest Divisions in the Metropolitan Police area, looking for this distinctive car, without success. The following night, we did it all over again. As we headed for our beds after another night's fruitless searching, I reflected on the notion that White's cars were as adroit as he was at vanishing. It was as though both man and car had disappeared off the face of the earth.

The next day, I circulated the description of this car to all of the officers working these two areas. The following afternoon, the Hackney wireless car stopped at a set of traffic lights at a busy junction in Mare Street. There, across the other side of the junction, was the red Vauxhall Velox. In it, behind the wheel, was White. A quick radio call summoned urgent assistance and White, who amazingly gave up without a struggle, was arrested. He was later sentenced to ten years imprisonment.

It was clear that it was completely down to the information given by Lewis, that this very dangerous criminal had been caught. I submitted an Informants Report, outlining the intelligence given by Lewis, stressing the fearful risks that he had run and asked that he be paid a substantial reward. Whilst he had never assisted police before, I stated, it was clear that he had intimate knowledge of prominent criminals in north London, and properly rewarded, he could well be the source of further valuable information in the future.

Unfortunately for everybody concerned, this report landed in front of a very new, very inexperienced and a totally unworldly senior officer.

He stabbed a nervous finger at the penultimate paragraph in my report. 'When you say, er - 'a substantial reward',' he asked, 'exactly how much did you have in mind?'

'Two grand,' I answered, coolly.

'*Two grand!*' he shrieked. 'Jesus, you must be mad!'

'No,' I said, angrily, 'but you could be forgiven for thinking that Lewis might be. Now listen! This skinny little bastard had the balls to do what no-one else would do. His information has taken one dangerous fucker off the streets, for a long time. Now, you're the only person who can encourage Lewis, and people like Lewis, to stand up and be counted. That's what I mean, Sir, and that's why I want two grand for him.'

'I won't do it,' he stubbornly replied.

'Why not?' I snapped.

'Because - well, I can tell you, Dick,' he replied, conspiratorially. 'The other day, I asked another officer what he recommended be paid to one of his informants. He told me he thought his man deserved a grand. In fact, I wasn't too sure what a grand was (you'll keep that to yourself, won't you, Dick?) Anyway, I've never done this sort of thing before! I went and told the Commander and, and... well, he laughed at me, Dick! Well, I won't be caught like that again, I can tell you. No, Sir!'

I don't suppose he was.

The ridiculous £50 reward just covered the fine that was imposed for the production of Lewis' cannabis plant.

I never saw or heard from Lewis again.

I don't blame him one little bit.

Over the hills...

Go to practically any part of Belfast, and you'll be able to see the hills that surround the city, and very beautiful they look, too.

The IRA decided to capitalise on the practicality of the hills, rather than their aesthetic effect, when a terrorist named Sean Cargan was detained in Eire, pending extradition to the mainland, to answer charges of causing explosions with intent to endanger life.

So, up into the hills went the IRA, and persuaded a farmer, at gun-point to lend them a number of white fertiliser bags, in order that they might be arranged into giant letters. 'FREE SEAN CARGAN!' was the phosphate inspired message, stretched out across the hills, for all Belfast to see.

As a piece of clever propaganda, it was quite an imaginative piece of work. Regretfully, it was rumoured that certain members of the 3rd. Battalion of the Parachute Regiment (spoilsports to a man) had climbed the hills under cover of darkness the following evening, and had spitefully rearranged some of the sacks, so that the message that enraptured the eyes of the Ulster folk the following morning, read, 'FUCK SEAN CARGAN!'

We were all convulsed with laughter, as was the Commanding Officer of 3 Para when Sinn Fein telephoned him, in order that they might lodge a formal complaint.

Death may be the great leveller, but ridicule must run it a close second.

...and far away

Because of the difficulties experienced with the intimidation of the juries in Northern Ireland in dealing with cases of terrorism, the Diplock System was introduced, following an act of Parliament which was passed in 1973. This meant that a single Judge would sit in court, dealing with matters of law, procedure and the guilt or innocence of the accused persons. (Personally, I think it's a good system. There are no juries for the lawyers to try and bamboozle, and I've seen cases tried at Belfast Crown Court where I thought that a guilty verdict was a foregone conclusion, but the Judge, acting scrupulously fairly, decided that there wasn't quite enough evidence, and had kicked the case into touch.)

Naturally, the Judges are marked men by the terrorists, and the protection that is afforded to them, their families and their property is immense.

Their physical protection is carried out by highly trained (and extremely tough) security personnel. At least one of these armed bodyguards always travels with the Judge, in addition to an armed Royal Ulster Constabulary driver, in an armoured saloon car.

One morning, a Judge's regular driver went sick, and his place was taken by Jim Elliott, a relief driver from the Motor Transport Pool, at that time based at R.U.C. Musgrave Street station. Jim was directed to pick the Judge up at 9am.

Off went Jim to the Judge's house and parked in the front driveway a few minutes prior to 9 o'clock. Punctually at 9am, the front door opened, and a very large, well-built man walked out of the house. A broken nose and scar tissue around the eyes suggested some service in the ring. The man paused on the step, his watchful eyes flickering around the vicinity. Apparently satisfied, he walked quickly to the car moving, Jim noticed, very lightly for such a big man. The breadth of his shoulders threatened to push Jim against the driver's door as the man climbed into the front seat and grunted a greeting. For 15 minutes the large bruiser sat there in a morose silence, lost in his own brooding thoughts. At first, Jim felt uncomfortable and then, as time wore on, increasingly irritable. At last, he felt enough was enough.

'Look,' he snapped. 'When's the old fucker coming out?'

'The old fucker's sitting next to you,' replied the Judge courteously. 'Drive on!'

The Adventures of Desperate Don

That Police Constable 294 'K' Don Ellett was tough and immensely strong, was never in dispute. Almost six foot two high and, at 16 stone, solid as a block of concrete, he policed Dagenham in a no-nonsense fashion some 30 years ago. His face displayed the clear signs of past experience in the boxing ring. He would explain that since he was a big boy, none of his childhood contemporaries were suitable as contenders in the ring and therefore his opponents were always considerably older. His pugilistic skills were developed and honed after he enlisted in the army and became a physical training instructor for the Military Police. Joining the Metropolitan Police on 19 June 1950, just before his 20th birthday, he continued boxing and later, trained others for the Lafone Cup. Don's toughness was displayed impartially; a PC who showed recalcitrance towards Don, might have found himself picked up by his ankles and shaken until the loose change spilled from his pockets.

Don's beat covered an area containing the addresses and haunts of some of the worst villains in Dagenham. He ruled it with a fist of iron; not only was crime kept to a low in that area, but laughing in Don's presence was discouraged; even smiling was frowned upon. When Don spotted a motorist whose standard of driving failed to measure up to the requirements of the Road Traffic Act - a lapsed Road Fund Licence was sufficient - and who failed to comply immediately with Don's direction to stop, Don was liable to reinforce his request more vigorously. I was present at Barking Magistrates' Court to hear such a revelation.

'You struck the roof of my client's car with your fist?' gasped an outraged solicitor. 'In Heaven's name, why?'

'Wouldn't listen, would he?' replied Don laconically, and the Magistrates, well-used to Don's little quirks, nodded in agreement.

So while Don's strength was legendary, what I was not aware of at the time of the story that follows, was his extraordinary agility, seldom found in such a big man. Only the other day, I spoke to my chum and fellow pensioner, Keith Taylor, who told me that while Don was teaching him beats at Dagenham, they had had occasion to cross the busy A13 trunk road. The central reservation had a barrier running the length of it and Keith (late of 10 Para) looked around for a way in which to cross to the other side of the road. Don, who was made of sterner stuff, placed one massive hand on top of the five foot high barrier and vaulted over, feet first! Thanks, Keith, I thought, I wish I'd known, for reasons which will now become apparent...

I was a uniform PC only recently transferred to Dagenham, when I bumped into Don at the bottom of the flight of stairs in the nick, which led to the CID office and the canteen; in fact, I was just about to go to the canteen for a cuppa.

'Race you up the stairs to the canteen?' asked Don, casually. As if by magic, a small crowd gathered, amusement clearly written on their faces. Now at this point, there are two matters worth mentioning and the first is the geography of this part of Dagenham Police Station. The stairs went up to a small landing; from there, one turned left, to ascend the next flight of stairs. At the top, one turned left and immediately left again, to enter the short passageway which led to the entrance of the canteen. And the second of these considerations was the state of my physical fitness. Due to a largely mis-spent youth, I had trained in a variety of sports and although I regard myself as pretty fit nowadays, 30 years ago I weighed two stone less than I do now and I was as lean as a whippet. So the prospect of running fast up a couple of flights of stairs held no particular terrors for me. I looked at Don who smiled confidently back at me. Surely, of the two of us, I thought to myself, I must be the faster, after all, Don was 40 years old. But there was clearly something wrong; it was displayed on the grinning faces of the audience. I looked at the staircase... yes, that must be it, I thought. If Don runs up the stairs by the left-hand bannister, he'll be able to make a tighter turn when he reaches the landing - moreover, with me on his right-hand side, he'll be able to use his bulk to push me to one side when we reach the landing. Then when he gets to the top, his sheer size will stop me getting past him along the narrow passageway to the canteen. Cunning bugger! However, if I could secure the left-hand position, what with my turn of speed... I casually strolled over to the staircase, laid a proprietary left hand on the left-hand bannister and looked calmly at Don. If anything, his grin had widened. 'Ready?' said Don. 'Go!'

Up towards the landing we raced and I was little surprised that Don was almost level with me. I reached the landing and turned the corner. As I did so, I realised that Don was no longer with me. I knew he couldn't have tripped - I'd certainly have heard the smack of his weight going down - so I guessed that Don had realised that he couldn't beat me and that he'd remained on the landing and that when I got to the top, he'd make some smart remark to me, to take the sting out of him losing. Still, I dashed to the top of the stairs, turned left and left again, before tearing down the passageway to the canteen.

To my utter amazement, Don was standing in the passageway, directly in front of me. When we had reached the landing and I had turned left, Don had simply leapt straight up, caught hold of the hallway's bannister rail and pulled himself into the passageway!

It is interesting to note that prior to joining the Job, I had been a promising gymnast and such a feat was well within my capabilities but it was an option that I had not even considered. That day, Don taught me a valuable lesson in life; that when one enters a contest, the rules that govern the outcome of that contest are not the only rules and that success can be achieved in a variety of different ways.

It was something I kept in mind when, three months later, I joined the CID - it served me well for the rest of my career!

The Yellow Canary

Those of us with young children were thinking about making a move from the Squad office during the early evening of that 5th November. The surveillance team were out and about looking for a particularly unpleasant robber named Paul Jenkins but nothing seemed to be happening on that front. Jenkins, who was on the run, had previously escaped from court and had been sentenced to four years' imprisonment in his absence. He was a nasty piece of work. He had been responsible for robberies involving wealthy, elderly women who had been attacked in their own homes, tied up and stupefied with chloroform and then robbed of their most sentimental possessions. Jenkins was not acting alone and the whole set-up suggested a sophisticated criminal gang at work. Two of these robberies alone had netted the gang £30,000. An informant of Detective Sergeant John Redgrave's had pointed us in the right direction as to Jenkin's identity but finding him was proving troublesome.

I stood up and stretched; I was just about to call 'time' when there was a shout from the surveillance team on the radio. They had spotted Jenkins getting into a taxi and they were off, on his tail. We sprinted down the four flights of stairs at the Yard - the lifts were too unreliable - and jumped into the alerted and waiting Squad cars. The surveillance team were in North London, travelling north-west; keeping in radio contact, we roared off in convoy, west, towards the Cromwell Road. As the big Squad cars roared through the night, the gap between us, the surveillance team and the elusive Mr. Jenkins diminished until we were just a few hundred yards from each other. Suddenly, Jenkins realised he was being tailed and as his taxi slowed to negotiate a corner, he leapt out, crashed to the ground, staggered to his feet and ran. The surveillance team abandoned their vehicles and, just yards behind Jenkins, took up the chase. Jenkins ran into the grounds of a hospital - and vanished - right into thin air!

'Where the bloody hell is he?' gasped Detective Constable Davy Walker. 'He was right in front of me!' replied Detective Constable Julia Pearce, breathing heavily. 'He can't have got away!' But he had. Unknown to them, Jenkins was just feet away, having curled himself up into an incredibly tight ball inside a tiny shrub. Seconds later, we arrived and a systematic search of the area was carried out, without success. Tart words were exchanged between us and the surveillance team, within, I'm sorry to say, easy ear-shot of Jenkins - we, sarcastically complimenting them on their tracking ability and they, praising us on our ability to get off our arses in the first place and do some real police work.

It wasn't too long before we got a lead as to where Jenkins might be and the front door of a council flat at an address in Southwark yielded to our persuasion. 'Where's Jenkins?' I snapped to the forty-something urbanite, chicly attired in a stained vest and trousers suspended with braces over which a huge gut was draped. 'Never 'eard of 'im,' sneered my new acquaintance. A few moments of earnest conversation passed between us which saw a marked change in the flat-dwellers disposition. 'Look, Guv'nor' he said confidentially, 'that bastard Jenkins was here, but of course, I didn't crack on the Squad wanted 'im, did I?'

We parted the best of friends, me with details of a fresh address, my new chum looking mournfully at his ruin of a front door, now sadly swinging and hanging on one hinge. Twenty minutes later, the dwellers of a council flat in Bermondsey were dilatory in answering my summons - their front door, too, became detached from its fastenings and the occupants were brusquely addressed. The flat was searched, terse demands were made, answers provided and we were off again, this time to an address in Stockwell.

Three more addresses were visited in this fashion - at the last one, we appeared to be expected because as the front door of the council house in Battersea went flying down the passageway, the middle-aged coupled barely looked up from their meal. 'He ain't here,' said the husband. 'Missed 'im by 15 minutes,' added the wife. This time, we left in possession of a telephone number and I quoted it to the Squad switchboard who were instructed to discover the subscriber.

Minutes later, we were speeding to a flat in Wandsworth but as the door went in, I stopped dead in my tracks as I heard the most dreadful, terrified wailing. The occupant of the flat, Mrs Enid Roberts was an elderly widow who had been the victim of a burglary only the previous week, where entry had been effected in exactly the same way. I calmed the trembling lady, fully explained the situation to her and telephoned her son, who it turned out, was a serving police officer. He arrived 20 minutes later, and as he walked in, aghast at the sight of his mother's front door, his mother was on her third cup of tea and was having the time of her life, surrounded by the most charming bunch of chaps who made her laugh with their saucy remarks. The son's arrival coincided with that of a Squad driver, carrying the biggest bunch of flowers that Mrs Roberts had ever seen in her life and this, together with the information that the night-duty section of the local council had been stirred up and were actually on their way to discard the current door and fit a new one went a long way to Mrs Roberts and son graciously accepting my very humble explanation and apology.

We left with handshakes all round and I went downstairs and picked up the radio handset to discover what had gone wrong. The switchboard at the Yard had massively cocked-up; they had transposed two of the telephone number's digits which had resulted in Mrs Roberts erroneously being shown as the subscriber. In fact, this had happened on a previous occasion with the same operator when I was hunting an escaped convict, so I ensured that I had the correct subscriber's address before I breached all radio telephone etiquette and reviled the operator with the lexicon of the gutter. He was a much chastened man thereafter and became meticulous about his work.

At the next location, we got another address, this one in Hammersmith. It was now 1.30am and some of the team were in a mutinous mood. 'Look,' I said, 'let's just try one more and if there's nothing doing, we'll call it a day.' With grudging assent, we all drove to a large house in Hammersmith. I looked at the dirty facade with little enthusiasm - I didn't have good vibes about this one. 'I'm fed up with bashing in doors,' I said to Detective Constable Gerry Gallagher and I knocked on the front door. After a few moments, a woman looked out of the ground floor window and I was about to introduce myself when she suddenly screamed, 'Paul, it's Old Bill! Fuck off, quick!' The front door disintegrated as though it had never existed and as I ran into the house, I heard a noise from behind the closed kitchen door. This door yielded to my first kick and as I rushed in, there was Paul Jenkins in the act of making a hasty exit via the window, an unfriendly course of action from which he was dissuaded.

Now that he was nicked, Jenkins, like so many tough guys who go around beating up women and robbing them, showed his true colours - yellow, through and through. Names, places, dates, offences, registration numbers of stolen cars and their whereabouts all gushed out of him, like water from a tap. As the blueprint for a huge criminal conspiracy grew and became clearer with the role of each participant clearly set out, Jenkins, who in the past had grassed up his father and brother and had seen them sent to prison, now reached the high point of his criminal career and implicated his Mother. I had never heard of this being done before and I paid mute tribute to this unparalleled piece of slime. His gang were pulled in and all were charged with robberies and conspiracy and an enormous amount of incriminating evidence was amassed.

Months later, I received notification of the date of the trial - 'not before 12 noon' the teleprinter message read. This meant that in this particular court, a trial was just finishing, a case was up for mention or a guilty plea was being disposed of; and in this case, it was the latter. I had arrived early to ensure that all of the exhibits and papers for our trial were ready and then, I settled down to listen to the proceedings. You see, although I had heard of His Honour Judge Norton QC, I had never appeared before him and since he was going to try our case at the conclusion of this one, I wanted to get the flavour of the man.

The defendant in this case was charged with attempted murder, with inflicting Grievous Bodily Harm with intent (GBH) as an alternative. The circumstances of the case were these. The defendant was a man with a long history of violent behaviour towards women and at the time of this offence, he had just been released from prison. He had spent the evening at a Bingo Hall where he had fallen into conversation with a middle-aged divorcee. At the end of the evening's entertainment, she had accepted his invitation to escort her home and as they were walking along, he took out a sheath knife and had casually cut her throat. He then nonchalantly strolled off. There had been no robbery or sexual molestation as a motive - he had done it for the pure pleasure of cutting a defenceless woman's throat. Fortunately, this act had been witnessed by passing taxi driver, who bundled the near-unconscious woman into his cab and as he rushed her to hospital, he radioed for the police. The hospital staff managed, with considerable skill, to pump more blood into the unfortunate woman than was actually leaking out and thus saved her life. Her attacker was apprehended as he was still calmly walking along the same road. He casually handed the knife over to the police and confessed everything.

In being charged with attempted murder and GBH, the maximum penalty for both was exactly the same - Life Imprisonment. This is, of course, not a mandatory sentence, as it is for murder and there are plenty of alternatives, ranging downwards to Probation. Therefore, it would be the measure of the Judge to see how he shaped up on the sentencing.

The defendant pleaded not guilty to the count of attempted murder but guilty to the alternative of GBH. This plea was accepted by the prosecution, who outlined the facts to the Judge, just as I have given them. The officer in charge of the case gave details of the prisoner's ghastly antecedents and a whining plea in mitigation was made by the defence. As the defence barrister sat down, there was a short silence and then Judge Norton, who had been writing into his notebook, looked up. 'Stand up,' he said, crisply and the prisoner got to his feet. If what I now record is not word for word that which was said by the Judge, believe me, it's pretty close.

'You have pleaded guilty to an offence of inflicting Grievous Bodily Harm with intent, rather than contest this case and make your victim suffer the trauma of having to experience the dreadful events of that night all over again and I intend to give you credit for that,' said the Judge. 'Also,' he continued, 'by pleading guilty, you have saved this court considerable time and money and because it is important that the guilty should admit their guilt as quickly as possible, I intend to give you credit for that too, because had there been a full trial and a jury had convicted you of attempted murder, it would have been necessary for me to have imposed a very severe sentence upon you. I have listened to the eloquent plea in mitigation made by your distinguished Counsel,' (and here, Judge Norton gravely inclined his head to the smirking defence brief, who squirmed with embarrassment and who bobbed his head in acknowledgement) 'to whom I am so deeply indebted.'

'However,' (and here, there was a short but significant pause) 'having heard your history from the officer in the case, I have come to the conclusion that whilst you are at large, you represent a considerable danger to women and the sentence that I pass on you is one of Life Imprisonment. Take him down.'

Blimey! I thought. I wonder what the prisoner would have got if he'd buggered the Judge about! The court rose and for the next half-hour, I busied myself getting the exhibits, photographs, plans, statements and miscellaneous papers ready, when some of the squad witnesses strolled into court. 'What's the Judge like, Dick?' asked Detective Constable Steve Holloway. Before I could answer there was a shout of, 'All Rise!' from the Court Usher and silence fell as the Judge re-entered the court and took his seat. I turned to Steve and winked. 'Trust me!' I whispered.

Jenkins took his place in the dock, surrounded by some of London's worse scum. I should make it clear that I'm referring to his legal team - his co-accused were there as well, of course. During the next six weeks, allegations of police misconduct and impropriety flew thick and fast; Jenkin's solicitor took the stand in order to particularly defame me and when he went right over the top and made a smart but very unwise comment, Judge Norton's rebuke, which dripped with acid, made me hug myself with delight.

But eventually, Jenkins was weighed off with 12 years imprisonment and the rest of the gang received 7, 4 and 3 years imprisonment. John Redgrave, Steve Holloway and I were sprinkled with commendations but the nicest memory I have of that case sits in front of me as I write.

It is the letter which I received from Mrs. Roberts, the elderly widow whose front door we so injudiciously bashed in, charmingly thanking me for the way that we had behaved. The letter holds pride of place in my scrapbook.

The Weasel and the Spiv

'D'you know what I'd do if I were mayor of London?' asked my fellow pensioner and chum, Keith Taylor. We were propping up the corner of the bar at the Special Forces Club and I nodded; I knew full well what was coming and I raised a hand to the barman. He's a very gifted fellow who is blessed with second sight, because without a word being uttered, he unhesitatingly uncorked another bottle of Rioja and brought it over.

The blood-red nectar was decanted into our glasses while Keith revealed the extent of his mayoral ambition. 'I'd scoop up everyone who lived in Harold Hill,' he stated, 'put them into the hold of a ship, batten down the hatches, have the ship towed out to the middle of the English Channel and bloody sink it!' 'Keith,' I replied patiently, 'if you were to do that, who on earth would we have to sit on the juries at Snaresbrook?'

To anybody who has read this far and has become apoplectic with rage because his Mum lives in Harold Hill or because his wife has been summoned for jury service at Snaresbrook Crown Court, let me just say that Keith and I were talking in very general terms about the inhabitants of Harold Hill and the composition of Snaresbrook juries; well, just about. Let me explain.

In the early 1980s, which is when the tale of 'The Weasel and the Spiv' is set, Harold Hill, just north of Romford, Essex, had become a sprawling, untidy council estate. The ordinary, decent people who lived there (and many still do) had been horrified when the local government officials thought that it would be a sensible idea to fill the area with gloomy tower blocks and to insert into them the most worthless dregs of the flotsom and jetsom of society. In no time at all, the area had degenerated into a hotbed of thieving, vandalism, graffiti and drug dealing. The inhabitants of the flats - single mothers, drug abusers, thieves, alcoholics and lunatics - sought to lighten their plight by resorting to drugs, alcohol and solvents. Hot summer evenings were punctuated with the sounds of ear-splitting music from all-night parties, the screams of the despairing and the crash of unsatisfactory stolen televisions being hurled from the balconies of the flats. The headmistress of a nearby school had occasion to severely reprimand a nursery nurse who had suggested to her bullet-headed little charges that they design their own Father's Day cards. Complaints had flooded in after it was revealed that 70% of the class had no idea who their fathers were.

With the introduction of the Crown Court Act, courts of Quarter Session and Assize were abolished and in order to fill the courts in the newly erected Snaresbrook Crown Court, the catchment area was scoured for candidates with the result that whole council estates were mobilised to fill the waiting seats. Harold Hill was one such estate. They turned up in their droves for the sole purpose (so it seemed to us) of acquitting anybody who had sensibly entered a plea of Not Guilty; and if you happen to think my sentiments are a bit fierce, I can only suggest that not too many of your cases were committed for trial to Snaresbrook.

My Flying Squad team and I were generating quite enough work of our own, so I didn't really want to take the case of The Weasel and the Spiv on board in the first place. However, a Detective Sergeant doesn't have a great deal of say in the matter when a very senior officer decides that his No.1 snout has some great information so my team and I dutifully went to work. After several weeks of hard slog, we pounced on the receivers of a lorry-load of stolen toys, just as they were interesting some purchasers in this commodity, in an East End bomb site. This brought about the arrest of The Weasel. In an effort to improve his lot, he grassed up the main receiver - The Spiv - whom he was supposed to meet in a north London pub at 1 o'clock that afternoon. I appointed Detective Constable Steve Holloway to explain away the Weasel's absence and to offer his services as driver of the load. 'You'll be OK, Steve,' I said, with an assurance I did not completely feel. 'Just remember, if it comes on top in the pub, chuck a bar stool through the window and we'll get you out.'

'Thanks,' said Steve faintly, wondering what on earth he'd got himself involved in.

But despite our misgivings, Steve met the Spiv and a little later, he, several more conspirators and the lorry-load of toys were scooped in and we felt justly pleased with ourselves. The first cracks in the facade occurred when the matter was committed to Snaresbrook for trial. On the first morning, we were introduced to the very nice, extremely young, fresh-faced barrister who had received the brief to prosecute this case which, I believe was his first. Appearing for The Spiv was the heavy-weight barrister, the late Sir Lionel Thompson, who was loud, flamboyant, contemptuous and very formidable. After a nightmare trial lasting a couple of weeks, the jury failed to agree and a re-trial was ordered. The junior barrister had not done well. Worse, nobody else seemed to want the brief for the re-trial, so he was stuck with it. Whilst it had possibly been his first case and he had had the formidable Lionel against him, I felt he needed firm words of encouragement to stiffen his resolve. I took him to one side, for a quiet word. So did Steve Holloway. So, I believe did Detective Sergeant John Redgrave, who was as tough as woodpecker's lips.

If anything, the re-trial was worse.

The Spiv, a middle-aged, loud-mouthed yob, freely confessed his previous convictions for handling stolen goods and stated that as far as he was concerned, the toys were part of a job-lot, which had been honestly come by. He called his son to testify to his credibility. 'When your father was released from his last period of imprisonment for handling stolen goods, what did you have to say to him?' smoothly intoned Sir Lionel. A look of near-imbecilic pleasure crossed Spiv Junior's face. 'Can I swear?' he eagerly asked the Judge. 'Er... of course; if it's relevant,' simpered the soppy Judge and Spiv Junior replied, 'I said to me Dad, 'If I catch you touching dodgy gear again, I'll kick you right up the arse.'

This, of course, went down well with the jury who chortled helplessly. It was surpassed by the Spiv when he got into the witness box. 'I wasn't taken in by that 'olloway for a moment,' he told the jury. 'I guessed he was a cozzer. Look at 'im!' he added, pointing dramatically in Steve's direction. 'He looks like a bleedin' Greek, don't he? I wouldn't trust no bleedin' Greek, would you?' This was too much for the jury who sobbed with uncontrollable laughter.

Detective Constable Gerry Gallagher was next to be vilified. Genial Gerry was a formidable heavyweight from Ulster who had come to the

Flying Squad after recovering from being stabbed in south London and he had figured prominently in several of my cases. A wonderful character and a fine detective who had recently been commended by the Commissioner for his part in tackling a dangerous armed gang, Gerry was being pilloried in the witness box concerning his alleged ill-treatment of one of the prisoners. Gerry waited until the whole catalogue of his misdeeds had been laid before the jury, before he sorrowfully shook his head. 'I can't understand why your client is saying this,' he said, sadly. 'I thought we got on so well together!'

The Spiv's venom spilled over onto Sir Lionel Thompson, whom he accused of not doing enough to procure his freedom. 'The way you're going about things, I'll be going down for something I ain't done!' he bellowed and a short adjournment was hastily called. The Spiv's howls could be heard from the cell passageway, much to our delight at hearing the pompous Lionel being savaged.

As the hearing resumed, the Judge leaned forward. 'Sir Lionel,' he asked, anxiously, 'am I to understand that your client wishes to dispense with your services?' 'If, indeed that is the case,' replied Lionel wearily, 'nobody, I assure you, will be more relieved than me!'

I had arrested a van driver in connection with this case, who had made a complete confession, contained in a signed statement. As was usual, the declaration at the conclusion of the confession, beginning, 'I have read the above statement and I have been told, etc.' had been written in his own hand. True, there were spelling mistakes but the declaration was quite readable.

'That Kirby, 'e told me what to write and how to spell it, too,' he told the jury. 'See, I can't read and write. Never 'ave been able to. That Kirby, 'e made it all up.'

Since he had named just about everybody involved in the case, together with their respective roles in the conspiracy, he did need to claw back a bit of credibility, so attacking me was the best answer. After some general cross-examination, our barrister turned his attention to the prisoner's profession.

'Do you make deliveries in your van to the immediate area in which you work, or do you go further afield?' he asked.

'Me? No, I go all over the place,' replied the van driver.

'Where?' probed the barrister. 'Birmingham? Manchester?'

'Further than that,' boasted the driver. 'I've been up to Scotland, loads of times.'

'Indeed?' said the barrister. 'And how do you arrive at your destination?'

'Wot?' vacantly asked the prisoner.

'You see, since you have told the court that you cannot read, it follows that you are unable to read a map,' explained the Counsel patiently. 'And consequently, it would be useless looking at the road signs, because you cannot read them, either. That being so, I shall ask you again, how do you manage to arrive at your destination?'

This was a little unexpected and the driver was deep in thought for a full minute. 'Well?' prompted our barrister. 'What happens is this,' replied the luckless driver, slowly. 'My boss points me in the right direction and then I, er... ask people the way.'

'Really?' said the barrister, raising his eyebrows incredulously as he turned to the jury to judge their reaction. He might have saved himself the trouble. Not only did the jury acquit the van driver, they acquitted The Weasel, The Spiv and everybody else.

Well, that was that. Our barrister was almost in tears at having failed so spectacularly to secure a conviction so early in his career. Before he could smash his water glass and do irreparable harm to his wrists, I commiserated with him and told him that he had slightly redeemed himself in our eyes with his imaginative cross-examination of the venal van driver. Had the jury been less iniquitous than the defendants, I explained, a conviction would have been ours.

A year or so later, I bumped into an old acquaintance. 'What happened to that job of yours, the one with the lorry-load of toys?' he asked. 'Oh, that,' I replied. 'It went to a re-trial and got chucked. Typical bloody Snaresbrook jury.' He nodded. 'I'm not surprised,' he replied. 'I know someone who was on the jury. Your brief opened the case and when he was halfway through, they broke for lunch. Some mouthy yob on the jury made himself the spokesman in the canteen and said to the rest of the jurors, 'I've heard enough - that lot's getting a not guilty!' Well, that's Snaresbrook for you!' I laughed, but I wasn't particularly surprised; a charge of Handling Stolen Goods was anathema to any self-respecting Snaresbrook jury.

It was much funnier when I met Detective Sergeant Tony Yeoman for lunch, several years after I had retired. He mentioned that he'd been in Court quite recently and had bumped into the barrister who had forlornly prosecuted The Weasel and the Spiv. When he learnt that Tony had been attached to the Flying Squad, he asked him who he had worked with and my name was one of several that Tony mentioned. 'Sergeant Kirby?' exclaimed the barrister. 'I remember him well!' and added confidentially, 'he used to think I was a wanker - he told me so!' Feeling he had exposed a little too much of his deficiencies, he quickly added, 'but he did mention that I had improved!'

Tony

Crete is one of my favourite places and its people amongst the best in the world. I love the people because they are brave, chivalrous and passionate and they love their friends (the English) and openly loathe and despise their traditional enemies (the Germans and Italians).

Crete is the fifth largest island in the Mediterranean, measuring 160 miles by thirty. Originally, the inhabitants, the Minoans, were great traders who brought enormous prosperity to the island and who, some 2,500 years before the birth of Christ, sailed as far north as Scandinavia to promote commerce. They skilfully managed to skirt past England, because at that time, our contribution to the cultural revolution was to nakedly jump up and down, smacking ourselves on the arse, uttering shrill cries and painting ourselves with woad. In 1500 BC, Dorian invaders, from what used to be called Yugoslavia, overran the island and the peaceful Minoans who were certainly ill-equipped to deal with this sort of aggression, were completely subjugated. Since then, Crete has been the target for invaders and it has always valiantly fought back, sometimes against insurmountable odds - little wonder that Mothers still name their sons Eleftherios - freedom.

In 1941, the German army attacked Crete and the population suffered the most dreadful deprivations at the hands of the invaders. The allied forces struck back - the New Zealand Division in particular fought valiantly - and Britain's SOE (Special Operations Executive) infiltrated secret agents to help arm and supply the *andartes* or resistance.

So answer me this. If you were a member of the nation whose soldiers had terrorised an entire population, who had shot the men out of hand and who, having set whole villages ablaze then threw the women and children into the flames, would this be a place where you'd want to spend your summer hols? No, and neither would I, but guess which nation does? Honestly, my wife and I have witnessed middle-aged German tourists being bodily thrown out of shops and on several occasions - I swear this is true - German youngsters hire open-topped Jeeps, drive through the towns with the front seat passenger standing up, head high, gripping the windshield as though he was in a bloody Panzer. They must be as bonkers as conkers - some of those old shepherds can still aim a mean rifle.

My wife and I were once staying in an apartment in Tavronitis, on the north-west coast which was where some of the most savage war-time fighting took place. Even today, the pock-marked bullet holes can still been seen in the bridge spanning the river Tavronitis. On the first morning of our holiday, I trotted down to the village to buy some bread for breakfast. I was dressed in my habitual holiday gear - shorts and because the ground is so stony, boots - so with my cropped hair, I suppose I did have a slightly Teutonic appearance. I strolled into the village bakers and there, behind the counter was a walnut with arms and legs. This was the proprietor who regarded me with considerable distaste. 'Greetings,' I said in my careful Greek. 'May I have a small loaf, please?' I was rewarded with a look of pure venom. 'It's not ready,' he growled. 'You'll have to wait 20 minutes.' What astonished me was not his surliness but the fact that he had spoken to me in German. 'That's fine,' I replied in the same language. 'But why are you speaking to me in German? I'm English.' At this, he gave a snort of derision and giving me what I imagine was the Cretan equivalent of, 'Sez you!' he disappeared into the bakery.

It was of little consequence and I soon forgot about it and my wife and I spent a lazy day wandering around the large town of Chania, returning late in the afternoon for a swim and a meal. The following morning, I had just stepped out of the shower when I was frozen to the marrow as my wife let out a piercing scream. She had just opened the front door of our apartment, to discover that during the night, someone had decapitated a ram and had deposited its head on our doorstep. Its sightless eyes stared glassily at us and its mouth was twisted into a sort of ghastly leer. Blood was everywhere. Flinging on some clothes, I rushed outside roaring for the apartment's manager. Pointing to the gruesome remains outside my front door, I demanded an explanation. I had, of course, dropped any pretence at attempting this conversation in Greek and my voice was so loud, with my conversation peppered with such blasphemy that other occupants of the apartments were by now hurriedly removing their children from earshot. A small deputation from the village had assembled and although they were unable to comprehend a single word that I was shouting, nevertheless they were intensely interested. It was later explained to me that they felt that when this story was translated to them, it might make a useful mantinada - a fifteen-syllable rhyming couplet, which is sung solo with the last line being repeated by the entire company, who shout 'Ela! Ela! Ela!' after it. The manager weakly suggested that this unfortunate incident might well have been a practical joke. By now, I had put two and two together and was fairly certain of the culprit's identity. However, I kept my own counsel on this and suggested that whilst I appreciated a joke as much as anybody, if there was any recurrence, I would make it my business to discover the identity of the prankster and put his sense of humour to the test by tearing his ears off and sticking them where the sun don't shine. This was duly translated to the ever growing crowd who murmured their assent to such a proposed course of action before they drifted away. One elderly crone crossed herself, rolled her eyes and I heard her exclaim, 'Panayia Mou!' (All Holy Virgin!) An old-timer, wearing vraka breeches, tucked into knee-high boots saluted and grunted something which sounded complimentary and some of the younger men grinned and waved. After that, things went swimmingly. We were invited to a christening, where the baby's parents simply took over a taverna for an entire evening and the best of food and drink were served. Toast after toast was drunk with fiery tsikoudia, each salute more extravagant than the last. Glowing with good cheer, I was about to propose my own lavish toast in what I now firmly believed to be my fluent Greek, when a volley of exuberant revolver shots had me diving under the table. Thankfully, the rest of the congregation were roaring out the last line of a very popular mantinada and therefore missed my craven display. So everybody enjoyed themselves, because the whole village turned out - all that is, except the baker. Apparently, somebody had spread a completely malicious rumour throughout the village to the effect that during the war, he had been a German collaborator who had personally delivered freshly baked bread to the German aerodrome at Malame. I certainly never saw him again; and neither, I believe, did anybody else.

At the end of our fortnight we returned home and within 15 minutes of entering the house, the telephone began to ring.

Now, hang on a minute, I hear you say. This talk about Crete may all be very interesting (or not, as the case may be) but what on earth has it got to do with the Metropolitan Police? Well, the short answer is, nothing. I thought you'd like a break from police stories. But the reason I mentioned it, was because the name of the person on the other end of the ringing telephone was Tony Freeman. He's mentioned elsewhere in this book but I'm going to introduce him rather more fully, firstly because I want to and secondly because it's high time that I discharged an obligation in respect of him. This second consideration I shall deal with at the conclusion of this story.

Tony was my Flying Squad driver and he and his wife and family were good friends to me and my family. My youngest son, Robert, absolutely adored him. My wife picked up the phone and for the next quarter of an hour, she dwelt in graphic detail on my misfortunes with the baker and the ram's head. As I walked in and out of the lounge, I could hear Tony's shouts of laughter from the other end of the phone. Eventually, I managed to prise the phone away from my wife and frostily told Tony not to extract so much pleasure out of others calamities. We laughed and chatted for a bit and then, almost casually, Tony mentioned that he had cancer of the stomach and that shortly he would be dying from it. I felt stunned - as though I'd received a very hefty one-two. It couldn't be true, not the indestructible giant who was like an elder brother to me. I said something - I can't remember what, something almost certainly gormless, such as, 'Are you sure?' and put the phone down. I still thought I'd misheard Tony; yes, misheard him, that was the answer, but what was it he'd said, in that case? Slowly, I realised that I hadn't misheard him and as my stomach knotted and grew cold, I called my family into the lounge to impart the dreadful news...

I first met Tony when I was posted to Forest Gate Police Station in 1973, having been appointed Detective Constable. Tony had joined the Met on 16 October 1962, a week after the present Commissioner, Sir John Stevens QPM, LL B, had joined and I should think that the two of them were the tallest candidates in the school. His erect, imposing deportment carried more than just a suggestion of his National Service days as a Royal Military policeman and with his easy Irish charm, it was difficult not to like Tony. He drove the West Ham/Forest Gate Wireless car with great skill and was constantly in demand for the 'Q' Car; when I was choosing my crew for 'Kilo one-one' the only reason why Tony didn't drive me, was because he was 'strapping' for the Flying Squad at the time, a posting which would become permanent in 1979.

Our ways parted and then, one day in the late 70s, Peter Connor and I went up to the Yard to extract large sums of money from C1's imprest to fund an enquiry which the Commander would certainly later describe as being 'extravagant'. As we entered the Yard and made our way across the ground floor towards the lifts in the Victoria Block, my mind was working overtime on just how to obtain a great deal of that valuable commodity when a tall, vaguely familiar figure stepped out of Room G.40 and warmly greeted Peter and me. After a few minutes conversation, we resumed our walk to the lift. 'Who was that?' I muttered to Peter, my mind still full of facts and figures. 'So much for the famous Kirby memory!' laughed Peter. 'That was Tony Freeman, of course - you remember, from the Gate.' 'Oh, yes,' I said, nodding absently. 'Nice bloke,' I added and forgot about him for a few more years.

My first posting to the Flying Squad was in 1981 and I was given a vehicle, a driver and two Detective Constables. The vehicle was a London Taxi, fine for surveillance work but largely useless for getting from 'A' to 'B' in a hurry. The driver was right at the end of his service and had little interest in the job. He insisted on garaging the cab at the Yard every night and returning home by train, home being Hertfordshire. Useless, once again for late-night jobs or for getting called out for a piece of work in the middle of the night. One of the Detective Constables was a good worker, the other was... unreliable. We had an exchange of views about it and he, the cab and the driver were out.

Tony Freeman who had been at a loose end after being the driver of a Detective Chief Inspector who had now left, jumped at the chance of a bit of action and he and his sleek Rover 2600 and later Detective Sergeant Johnny Redgrave and Detective Constable Steve Holloway were co-opted on to the team and Central 923 was up and running. The Rover, by the way, was the only Squad car at that time to have a multi-channel set which could be tuned-in to any police radio frequency in the country and therefore, during the Pope's visit to Britain, this car was swiped off us by Special Branch so that they could parade His Holiness about in it. The Rover became irreverently known as the 'Popemobile' and Tony, a lapsed Catholic, basked in its reflected glory. In return, we were given an Austin Princess, a very grand car and in the mistaken belief that the car contained high-ranking officers we were given so many salutes as we swept importantly into Police Stations that it quite turned our heads. On one particular occasion, one Police Constable at Cannon Row Police Station was so overcome at our impressive arrival that in flinging up his salute, he completely overdid it and overbalancing, he slowly and majestically toppled over backwards.

It was a wonderful couple of years. Information, upon which we were totally reliant, poured in and we had success after success. Often, late at night, I would get a whisper of information and I'd telephone Tony, who lived a couple of miles down the road from me. 'Tony,' I'd say. 'If Edna lets you, can you come out to play?' 'Oh, yes, please Sargie!' Tony would cry and another adventure would commence. I suppose I could be accused of looking back on those halcyon days through rose-tinted spectacles and to a certain degree, it would be true; it's easy to forget the jobs that didn't come off, the times that one would have appreciated a bit of backing from the senior officers and didn't get it but I still don't think that I have ever had so much fun, packed into a couple of years. Don't think that my use of the expression 'fun' implies frivolity, either; it was hard work, no doubt about it, but it was never onerous; it can't be when you're getting so much enjoyment out of a job.

To this day, Steve Holloway still laughs when he remembers the time that we'd locked up a team of robbers and the wife of one of the suspects had telephoned the office, demanding news of her incarcerated husband. The noise in the background, which I took to be the television, was absolutely deafening and the robber's wife and I were having to shout to make ourselves understood. 'Look, just turn that shit off, will you?' I snapped, irritably. 'That's not shit!' exclaimed the outraged lady. 'That's my children!'

Or the meticulously planned ambush of Junior Stevens, a large black and much-wanted armed robber which came to fruition at Dalston Junction when his car was suddenly overtaken by a bit of superb driving by Squad driver, Alfie Howells who forced him to stop, whilst Tony hemmed his car in from behind, leaving Stevens completely boxed in. I raced across to Stevens' car, reached in through the open driver's window and dragged him out. He was so big, I kept on pulling and pulling and he kept coming out of the car, bit by bit, rather like slightly stiff toothpaste. 'I'm going to call you 'Jack' from now on,' laughed Tony afterwards.

'Why's that, after Jack Regan?' (the fictional tough-guy Detective

Inspector, featured in the television series, *The Sweeney*) I asked, my face flushing with pleasure at the very thought of such an accolade.

'After a Jack Russell, actually,' replied Tony. 'The way that you scuttled out of the car with your little legs flying, I thought you were going to bite his ankles rather than nick him!'

Stevens was committed for trial at the Old Bailey and incredibly was granted bail and promptly absconded. I received a tip-off from a very reliable informant and we sat up on an address in Hornsey, north London. After hours of waiting, Junior Stevens turned up with his girl-friend in a car and once again, one Squad car blocked his way, another cut off his retreat and again, I jumped out of the car, grabbed hold of him through the open window and started to drag him out. 'Oh, Junior!' wailed his girl-friend. 'It's orl right, bitch,' replied Stevens, with commendable coolness. 'Thuh Kirby, 'im always arrest me like this!'

Stories like these were told and re-told with liberal embellishments late at night over a glass in the Squad office, and also at the Baroc. This was how we referred to the Barocco Bar, situated in the West End of London - an Italian family-run establishment where the most delicious food was served at reasonable prices. Inevitably, the entire team would order veal and spaghetti with double bolognaise sauce, a house delicacy. And yet, I think the reason why these soirées were so enjoyable was because they were entirely spontaneous. For example, the whole of 12 Squad might assemble for an early morning search on the other side of London. By the time we had finished, carried out all of the necessary documentation and returned to the Yard and checked for messages to see if any work was imminent it would be almost lunchtime. All of a sudden, someone would say, 'What about a Baroc?' Within minutes, the Squad room would be deserted and several car-loads of heavy, hungry young men would descend into the heart of London's theatreland. Because the Baroc didn't possess a liquor licence, it would be necessary to nip into a nearby off-licence to procure a sufficiency of lubrication and then we would march to the Baroc which, for the next couple of hours at least would become our superior incident room. As plates of steaming, succulent food were served, the telephone would ring incessantly from the Squad office, passing messages and offering information, operations would be planned, previous operations would be discussed and dissected and, as I've mentioned Squad stories would be told, those stories would be topped with others and the place would echo with laughter.

Sometimes, officers would disappear, only to return later with top-rate information or a search warrant or both and the forthcoming job would be eagerly discussed.

In order to achieve this desirable state of affairs, it was necessary for the premises to be cleared out of its existing customers. These, in the main, were male dancers from the nearby theatres who would buy a cup of coffee and make it last for hours. A look of relief would appear in the faces of the management when we turned up, because we were solid, paying customers. In fact, I think the dancers experienced a feeling of sensual enjoyment when hard-faced thugs in leather bomber jackets leaned menacingly over their tables, uttering the deadly words, 'bout time you fucked off, ain't it?' because they used to gasp and squeal with mock-histrionics, 'Well, really! Anyway, we wouldn't stay now if you begged us! Come on, girls!' And out they'd swish, leaving us roaring with coarse laughter.

The years have rolled by since then and both Outrage! and the Lesbian and Gay Police Association will be relieved to hear this particular Flying Squad practice has long since ceased. Only the other day, I was en route to the Groucho Club for lunch when I felt in imminent need for a little nostalgia and I re-routed my journey for a glimpse at the old place. The Baroc was no more. Instead, a notice invited the injudicious traveller to tarry with the 'big, busty birds' who possibly inhabited the dark interior of the premises and my nostrils twitched in vain for the smell of *Salsa di Carne*. No, as I adroitly stepped aside to avoid entanglement with a furiously pedalling messenger, I recognised the folly of going back. Never do it, chums; you're doomed to disappointment.

My fall from grace from the Squad is documented elsewhere in this book but after my two years in the wilderness, I was back on the Squad again. During that time, Tony and I had stayed in touch and we constantly visited each other's homes and now we slotted back into the routine of working together again. In the years that followed, we investigated scores of armed robberies and arrested a lot of the people responsible for them. Tony was always ready to give good, common sense advice for which I was immensely grateful and any successes I achieved were as a result of our partnership.

During 1989, I was once again temporarily promoted to Detective Inspector when I was Staff Officer to that grand Flying Squad Commander John 'Ginger' O'Connor. In one of my duller moments at the

Yard, I idly flipped through the Divisional records of the Squad officers and when I came to Tony's entry, I noted that he had never been commended. Now, for such a hard-working, skilful and resolute officer, this surprised me and I resolved to do something about it. I decided that on the next opportunity when Tony carried out some stirling work, I would put him up for a Commendation. But as I was later to write in my letter of condolence to Edna, Tony's widow, 'events overtook me.' We never worked together again. I was seconded for duties in Northern Ireland, then came the holiday to Crete and that was followed by Tony's telephone call.

I was called back from Ulster to attend his funeral which was well attended with over 300 mourners. Bill Wells, his friend and fellow Squad driver who visited him daily until the end, spoke movingly of Tony's work as a Squad man.

So I never did get Tony that commendation and, as I say, I have a duty undischarged. The best I can do is give my own recognition to the man who was my friend.

COMMENDATION TO POLICE CONSTABLE 259'CO' ANTHONY FREEMAN
For courage, devotion to duty, matchless skill in the driving of motor vehicles, enormous common sense and for being such an integral part of the Flying Squad family.

...and in conclusion

Well, there it is. I should mention that where I have referred to informants, I have taken liberties left, right and centre in disguising their names, sexes and racial origins, for obvious reasons.

Many police officers are correctly mentioned by name. Those who are not, are John, the overweight arresting officer, mentioned in the introduction; the incomparable and incompetent Detective Chief Inspector John Hacker; Harry, the prodding Detective Constable; Barry Scott and Henry Jones, the Old Bailey conspirators; the inebriate Detective Constable Trevor Bayliss; Detective Sergeant Steve Williams, who reached rock-bottom; the licentious Detective Constable Peter Newall; the irritable Royal Ulster Constabulary Constable, Jim Elliott; the venal Detective Sergeant Joe 'The Duke' Collins; Detective Constable Jim West, the distributor of out-of-season Christmas presents and Terry Johnson, the apprehensive and embryonic Detective Sergeant.

With regard to the judiciary, the names of Mr. Jones, Mr. Rollins, Mrs. Travis-Jones, Mr. Hargreaves, Philip Rollington-Smythe, Mr. Justice Watkins, Jeremy Farquarson, His Honour Judge Norton and His Honour Judge Michael Stone QC, are all fictitious.

And dealing lastly with the criminals (in direct opposition to those who insist on putting them first) with the exceptions of Francis Davidson 'Mad Frankie' Fraser, David Ralph Martin, Donald McKay, Walter 'Angel Face' Probyn, the brothers Messina, Dixon, Tibbs, Richardson and Kray, all of the other names are as flawed as their owners.

GLOSSARY

I hesitate to include a glossary, but I do so because many of the terms that I have used in the book are now defunct, and I should hate to have the thought that some of my younger readers might have cause to scratch their heads in wonderment.

Approved School The now-abolished system of dealing with recalcitrant young offenders for up to 3 years detention, in order to stop their youthful criminality developing into maturity; regretfully, often the reverse was true.

Arraigned To stand one's trial, previously at a court of Quarter Sessions or Assize, and now at Crown Court.

At it Committing crime.

Bang to rights To be caught red-handed.

Bent Corrupt. Also, homosexual but normally seldom used in that context.

Big stick, waving the Issuing an unequivocal directive.

Bitch Afro-Caribbean expression meaning Lady.

Blagger A robber, especially the armed variety. Very high in the criminal pecking order.

Bollocksed Thwarted, neutralised.

Bonkers as Conkers Immeasurably foolish.

Borstal Borstal Training was a term of incarceration awarded to young offenders, aged from between 15 - 21 years, for periods of between 6 months to 2 years in the often forlorn hope that they would receive reformative training.

Carpet 3 months' imprisonment

Chucked To be found not guilty at Court.

Citizen's arrest A common-law power, enabling ordinary citizens to detain criminals who are committing a serious offence. It is encouraged by the Crown Prosecution Service who often charge the citizen, rather than the criminal since this is an easy way of keeping up their conviction rate.

Come on top, to Where circumstances suddenly change, to one's detriment.

Commission Rogatoire A formal written request, usually issued by the Director of Public Prosecutions to foreign Magistrates, asking that British police officers be permitted to conduct criminal investigations in their country, with their assistance.

Cosh Typical blunt instrument for bashing people over the head.

Coshed-up To be on the receiving end of a cosh.

Cozzer East End slang for a police officer.

Crack on To comprehend.

Crank-up To bring someone into a state of irritability.

Doris A dismissive term for a woman.

Fartful A minimal amount of intelligence.

Filf (or Filth) Horrid slang for detective.

Fitted A whining excuse, often heard in court, that a guilty person has had evidence manufactured by an unscrupulous detective.

Flogging Corporal punishment, which consisted of violent criminals being beaten with a cat-o'-nine-tails, in prison. Regretfully abolished under the provisions of the Criminal Justice Act 1948.

Framed Where a disgruntled criminal has been found guilty, despite having pleaded his innocence and has made a number of damaging allegations in respect of the detectives' probity. (See also *Fitted*, *Verballed* and *Planted*)

Good'un A well respected person.

Grass (Grassing, Grassed) To be an informant, to inform and to be informed against. See also *Snout*).

Lie straight in bed (Inability to) corrupt.

Lay-down A remand in custody.

Long-firm fraud A well-known phrase in police and criminal circles. It is where credit is obtained from a wholesaler from whom goods are ordered and then promptly paid for. This process is repeated and the wholesaler's confidence is gained. Then comes the sting: an enormous order is placed, sold on very quickly, whereupon the fraudsters disappear into thin air.

Manor An area, in which a police officer works and a thief steals.

Nice drink A generous ex-gratia payment (see also *Safe drink*).

Non-descript van A plain, unmarked police vehicle used for observation purposes. It is identified for what it is by any criminal, possessing even a modicum of experience or intelligence.

PACE Police and Criminal Evidence Act. *See p108*

Pension An unofficial (and usually quite unlawful) gratuity.

Pimping The act of living off the immoral earnings of a prostitute. It may also be used to describe a person who, whilst he may not be a Pimp *per se* is none the less thought of as being a disagreeable person of low morals.

Planted A desperate last-ditch ploy used by unimaginative barristers that incriminating evidence found in possession of their clients was deliberately put there by the detective.

Plod A rude term for a uniformed police officer.

Police Gazette A confidential police publication, containing photographs and giving details of persons circulated as being wanted for offences, especially prison escapees.

Police Orders A much lamented police publication, which succinctly informed police officers of commendations, promotions, transfers, punishments, new legislation and other essential information. Now replaced with a series of separate publications, containing gibberish.

Pond life The lowest form of human existence. This is a favourite expression used by the British Army in Northern Ireland, when describing terrorists.

Porridge A term of imprisonment.

Prefabricated Building Prefab Homes that were erected on a purely temporary basis, following the destructive bombing during the Second World War. A few still exist and often look more attractive than the more permanent sprawling council estates.

Safe drink An ex-gratia payment (see also *Nice drink*)

Sargie Informal and a rather affectionate way of addressing a Detective Sergeant.

Screwed To break into premises. Also, to have performed a sexual act and in addition, to have received a disservice.

Shabeen An illegal drinking club.

Snout Informant (See also *Grass*, *Grassing* and *Grassed*)

Squad! Usually, the first introductory word heard by violent criminals when Flying Squad officers effect an arrest or an entry to premises.

Strapper A strapper is a Divisional Class I driver who may stand in for a temporarily-unavailable Flying Squad driver. Strappers filled the shoes of drivers (sometimes on a fairly permanent basis) who, through death or dishonour, had left the Squad.

Sweeney Rhyming slang, viz. Sweeney Todd = Flying Squad.

Tea-leaf Rhyming slang, Thief.

Tearaway An adolescent hoodlum, who aspires to be a gangster.

Tec Diminutive of 'Detective'.

Toe-rag Rhyming slang for 'Slag' - a mean, no-account class of criminal. Slag is also used to describe ladies who associate with them.

Toes, on one's Escaping justice, especially a prison escapee.

Trumpet To bellow or complain.

Verballed A dreary excuse used in court, that untrue statements have been attributed to a criminal by a less than ethical detective.

Wall, gone over the To escape from a place of lawful incarceration.

Weighed-off Sentenced at court.

Wireless Car Also known as an Area Car. A fast, marked police vehicle, driven by uniformed police officers. In the late 1960s, this was usually a 3.4 litre 'S'-type Jaguar. This type of vehicle would now be referred to as a 'Fast Response Vehicle'.

Wrong'un (to do someone a) a disservice or injustice. It also serves to describe a person of questionable morals and at one time was used by the criminal fraternity to describe one of their number, who was thought to be a grass.

AGAINST ALL ODDS

the remarkable adventures of PC Jim Beard

Jim Beard wanted action when he signed up for the Metropolitan Police Force – and he got it. Here is his own story of the extraordinary events that crossed his path as he protected the public of central London. Jim narrowly misses becoming another victim of the mass murderer Dennis Neilson when he was invited back for a night cap. He leaps into the river Thames to try to save three tiny children from drowning. Wearing only his swimming trunks he arrests 'dippers' in Hyde Park; he solves the mystery of the amorous Swedish au pair; and he describes his colourful encounters with the politicians, royals, actresses, villains and heroes who make up the 'manor' he polices.

Injured several times on duty, broken but not bowed, this is a fascinating and moving true story.

£7.99 paperback

Available from
Merlin Unwin Books, 7 Corve Street, Ludlow SY8 1DB.
Orderline: 01584 877456